WHO KILLED THE CONSTITUTION?

WHO KILLED THE CONSTITUTION?

The Federal Government vs. American Liberty
from World War I to Barack Obama

Thomas E. Woods Jr. and **Kevin R. C. Gutzman**

THREE RIVERS PRESS

NEW YORK

Published in the United States by Three Rivers Press, an imprint of the
Crown Publishing Group, a division of Random House, Inc., New York.
www.crownpublishing.com

Three Rivers Press and the Tugboat design are registered trademarks of
Random House, Inc.

Originally published in hardcover in slightly different form in the United States by
Crown Forum, an imprint of the Crown Publishing Group, a division of Random
House, Inc., New York, in 2008.

Library of Congress Cataloging-in-Publication Data

Woods, Thomas E.
Who killed the Constitution? : the federal government vs. American liberty from
World War I to Barack Obama / Thomas E. Woods Jr. and Kevin R. C. Gutzman.
p. cm.
Includes bibliographical references and index.
1. Constitutional history—United States.   2. Executive power—
United States—History.   3. Legislative power—United States—History.
4. Political questions and judicial power—United States—History.
1. Gutzman, Kevin Raeder, 1963–   II. Title.
KF4541.W66.2008
342.7302'9—dc22   2008007055

ISBN 978-0-307-40576-0

Printed in the United States of America

Design by Lauren Dong

10 9 8 7 6 5 4 3 2

First Paperback Edition

To Heather, for making it all possible
—T.W.

To my mom, Linda Y. Gutzman, and my dad, Chuck Gutzman
With love
—K.G.

Contents

WHO KILLED THE CONSTITUTION?

Introduction

The Constitution Is Dead

MANY AMERICANS WORRY that the Constitution is dying. Leading the chorus are those critics, mostly on the Right, in whom the first initiatives of the Obama administration have awakened a concern dormant for eight years. Their arguments recall those made only yesterday by others, mostly from the Left, deploring the George W. Bush administration's supposedly unprecedented attacks on the Constitution.

We have bad news for both sets of critics: the Constitution is *already* dead. It died a long time ago.

To be sure, every politician claims to admire the Constitution, and government officials must swear to uphold it. When they get the oath wrong, they may even take it again. But what does their fidelity to the Constitution really amount to in practice?

Nothing.

Even those who bewail our present constitutional crisis miss the much larger story. The assaults on the Constitution are not the work of one branch of government, or of one party, and they did not emerge overnight. *Every* branch of the federal government has trampled on the Constitution, almost without interruption, for close to a century. The crisis we face today is the culmination of decades of offenses against the Constitution by Democrats and Republicans, justices, presidents, and congresses alike, all of whom have essentially rejected the idea that the Constitution possesses a fixed meaning limiting the power of the U.S. government.

That idea was not a minor aspect of the Constitution; it was the *very purpose* of the Constitution.

The Dirty Dozen

Nowadays, the Constitution is no obstacle to any conceivable federal program. Would you like to have the federal government take over the delivery of health care? No constitutional issue comes to mind. Do you think the Department of the Treasury should pump three trillion dollars into failed banks without taking a single vote in Congress? No problem. Would you like federal agencies promiscuously to mine everyone's e-mail and telephone calls? Why not? As few as ninety years ago, advocates of such novel federal initiatives would have understood that they must be preceded by constitutional amendments Not today. To most politicians (including judges) of both parties, all that matters in evaluating a federal initiative is whether it seems likely to raise the GDP, help resolve a social epidemic, or contribute to national security. If they consider it desirable, they do it. The change in administrations in January 2009 has brought no change we can believe in on this score whatsoever.

Instead of constitutionality, federal officials rely on their noble intentions. Yet noble intentions can never be the basis for judging whether the federal government is taking proper constitutional action. In fact, as this book will show, the government has often deformed our Constitution and insidiously subverted the rule of law with precisely those actions that Americans have been taught to celebrate. The received wisdom is that seemingly unconstitutional actions in pursuit of laudable goals were heroic, and that they have brought tacit amendment in a constitution that otherwise would have become outmoded.

The received wisdom on America's recent constitutional history is, unfortunately, almost entirely wrong. That is why we need a sweeping reassessment that lays bare exactly who killed the Constitution.

In this book we chronicle a dozen of the worst examples of the federal government's defiance of the Constitution—twelve actions from the past century that, taken together, dealt the death blow to the Constitution. This "dirty dozen" does not represent the federal government's only constitutional assaults, but the accounts here illustrate exactly how congressmen, presidents, and judges have flouted the Constitution.

Some of the cases we chronicle are well known and the subject of heated debate, while others, no less important, are practically unknown, overlooked in conventional histories. Some of our choices will, on the surface, be familiar to readers, but the constitutional problems they raise will be surprising because standard treatments ignore them. Some of these assaults on the Constitution involve the various branches of the federal government working together, contrary to simplistic accounts that pin the blame on individual actors. And some have long gone unchallenged simply because it is considered taboo even to question certain acts of bygone federal officials.

For example, a couple of the cases we document involve the highly charged subject of race. People who draw conclusions in that area like the ones we have drawn in this book can be assured of smears and character assassination, regardless of how strong their constitutional arguments are. Since the reigning assumption is that the Constitution does not really matter, the intentions of anyone advancing such arguments are simply assumed to be bad, and their reasoning is therefore ignored. Likewise, those critical of the Bush administration's constitutional theories will be accused of "aiding the terrorists," despite the constitutional merits. Rational discussion of what the Constitution actually says is unusual in such an environment—and that's just the way the government likes it. Every significant appeal to the Constitution, supposedly the fundamental law of the land, is a thought crime of one kind or another. But if we are truly to confront a government that has gone off the constitutional rails, we must not shy away from calling attention to abuses, regardless of whom it offends.

Why the Constitution Matters

Why, some may wonder, should we care about the Constitution? Libertarians, for instance, might legitimately ask: Isn't "liberty" all that matters, Constitution or no? Our answer is that while government misdeeds may work in favor of liberty in the short run, there can be no enduring freedom where government is not bound by a constitution. "In questions of power, then," Thomas Jefferson warned, "let no more be heard of confidence in man, but bind him down from mischief by the chains of the Constitution.[1]

Otherwise, Jefferson feared, government would become arbitrary. He had seen even his good friend and fellow revolutionary John Adams yield to the authoritarian impulse. He would trust no one in power ever again. Jefferson knew that Rome's republic fell when its rulers began to ignore its constitution, and he worried that the same fate would befall America. He feared a lawless empire bestriding the world, a government contemptuous even of its citizens' just claims, a basically republican system degenerating into tyranny.

His fears were well founded.

The U.S. Constitution has proven inadequate to the task of preventing federal officials from behaving arbitrarily. Now that the restraining elements of the Constitution have been abandoned—now that the government has, to borrow Jefferson's metaphor, broken free of its chains—what is left to tether federal officials? Only voters. The plain truth is that today we are governed by little more than simple prudence—government officials' sense of what they can get away with. This startling statement will seem to be a statement of the obvious by the end of this book.

1

Congress Shall Make No Law
(Unless It Really Wants To):
Woodrow Wilson and Freedom of Speech

To all appearances, Maryland's Edwin Seidewitz led a successful and contented life. He served as mayor of Annapolis from 1899 until 1901. He later became a successful florist in Baltimore, and served as president of the local Rotary Club.

Then he made a mistake.

Not long after the U.S. government entered World War I in April 1917, Seidewitz met some Germans at a hotel bar. They were officers of German ships that had been unable to leave Baltimore harbor since the outbreak of European hostilities in 1914. They were commiserating about friends and family they longed to see, and about their concern that they would be interned as enemy aliens in the United States until war's end.

Seidewitz felt sorry for the men and sat down for some beer with them. Then, as a gesture of sympathy, he kissed one of them on the forehead. And there was his mistake.

As soon as word got around town that Seidewitz had "kissed a German," his business dried up. He was thrown out of the Rotary Club without being given a chance to defend himself. This once prosperous and respected man found himself completely ruined, practically overnight.

Perhaps the return of peace might have reversed Seidewitz's string of misfortunes. We shall never know. On August 24, 1918, Edwin Seidewitz shot himself in the head.[1]

That was the kind of cultural climate in which the Espionage Act of 1917 and the Sedition Act of 1918 were passed. With these restrictive acts, all three branches of the federal government colluded against the Constitution in order to clamp down on Americans' freedom to dissent from government policy.

Intimidation and Suppression

World War I was not the first time in American history that the federal government tried to muzzle its citizens. The year 1798 saw the passage of the Alien and Sedition Acts, which were said to be necessary in light of the Quasi War with France. Thomas Jefferson and James Madison didn't buy it: for them, these were obviously partisan measures designed to intimidate and suppress the opposition party (namely, theirs). Peel back all the patriotic rationales and that's what the legislation amounted to, as far as Jefferson and Madison were concerned.

Then there were the constitutional problems: Jefferson argued that the Sedition Act violated both the First Amendment (in its restrictions on speech) and the Tenth Amendment (since the states never delegated to the federal government any power to criminalize speech, such power remained with the states). When Jefferson took office as president in 1801, not only did he release from jail all those who had been imprisoned under the act, but he also tracked down those who had paid fines for violating it, and repaid them with interest. (Supreme Court justice Oliver Wendell Holmes would later cite Jefferson's action as an admission by the federal government that the Sedition Act had been wrong.) The Sedition Act of 1798 expired in 1801, and for more than a century afterward the federal government had no anti-sedition law on the books.

That changed with the Espionage Act of 1917 and the Sedition Act of 1918.

"Curses" and "Bludgeons"

Although organized polling did not begin until the late 1930s, anecdotal evidence suggests that when the Great War broke out, the American people did not want their country getting involved in the senseless carnage across the Atlantic. Even the worst outrage Germany perpetrated against the United States—the 1915 sinking of the *Lusitania*, the famous British ocean liner, killing some 128 Americans on board—provoked very few calls for American intervention in the war. By the time President Woodrow Wilson's reelection campaign made it to the Midwest in 1916, the slogan "He kept us out of war!" had become firmly attached to his candidacy. Then, after the United States declared war, Joseph Tumulty, President Wilson's private secretary, expressed concern because "the people's 'righteous wrath' seems not to have been aroused."[2] Senator Robert La Follette of Wisconsin argued in an antiwar speech before Congress in 1917 that the perceived need to pass restrictive legislation in the first place proved that the general public did not support U.S. entry into the war. In fact, in order to carry on the war successfully, the U.S. government considered it necessary to criminalize opposition sentiment, conscript millions of men into the army, and launch a propaganda campaign on behalf of the war that was unique in American history.

With the United States finally in the war, the Wilson administration launched various efforts to promote the U.S. government's view of the conflict. The key figure in this important undertaking was George Creel, the Missouri journalist and longtime Wilson partisan. Creel headed the Committee on Public Information (CPI), which Wilson established by executive order in 1917, and used every available instrument of communication to carry out this propaganda mission.

It worked. Throughout American culture Germans began to be portrayed as subhuman savages. Journalists, the entertainment industry, and even professional historians succumbed to the most juvenile stereotyping and jingoism. Symphony orchestras refused to perform works by German composers. Sauerkraut became "liberty cabbage." German shepherds were now "Alsatians." Other effects were more serious: Germans found themselves driven from their jobs, frightened into changing their names, and even, in rare cases, beaten or killed. In Iowa and South Dakota the German language was altogether forbidden in public—with the exception (in South Dakota) of funerals, for which people could be issued special permits. Texas banned teaching the German language.[3]

Volunteer enforcement organizations were founded, boasting such names as the Sedition Slammers, the Terrible Threateners, and the Boy Spies of America. The *Literary Digest* called upon its readers to be on the lookout for sedition and to "clip and send to us any editorial utterances they encounter which seem to them seditious or treasonable."[4] State and local councils of defense, outgrowths of a national Council of Defense that Congress had created to coordinate the war effort, turned much of their attention to getting public opinion in line. In Missouri, some of the local councils of defense used "Red, White, and Blue Cards" to intimidate people into silence. According to the records of the Missouri state council:

> The person to whom the first warning card is sent, generally takes it as a warning that they are being watched and immediately becomes very careful in their expressions. It has been found necessary in only a few cases to send a blue card to anyone and the red card has never been sent. The red card is simply a statement from the Council of Defense that the recipient will be reported immediately to the United States Secret Service.[5]

Oh.

The stories that come down to us from that period sound like fiction. A movie about the American War for Independence called *The Spirit of '76*, which portrayed the British in an unflattering light, got its makers in trouble with the law: since the United States was now allied with Britain, such images could promote discontent in the American armed forces and interfere with recruitment. They received a prison sentence of ten years.[6] A Christian minister in Vermont was sentenced to fifteen years for writing a pamphlet, which he distributed to five people, arguing that Christ had been a pacifist and that Christians should not participate in war. A mob broke into a school in Marysville, Nebraska, looking for any material about Germany or written in the German language, and burned all of it, including German-language Bibles. A man was arrested under the Minnesota Espionage Act for saying, in reference to women who knitted socks intended for soldiers, "No soldier ever sees these socks." Michigan's Clarence Nesbitt, who purchased $1,500 in Liberty bonds, was tarred and feathered by a group of men who thought he should have purchased $3,000 worth instead.[7]

Nesbitt's fate was not unique. Walter Ferguson, an Oklahoma farmer, vainly protested that he had purchased all the bonds he could afford. Local war enthusiasts didn't believe him and proceeded to make his life miserable. "It would require a book to tell of the devilish ways in which he was hounded afterward," Ferguson's wife later recalled. "Merchants refused to sell him groceries, women cut his wife dead in church, neighbors set fire to his barn."[8]

So many more such cases could be cited that the rest of this book could easily be filled with them.

President Wilson had supposedly seen it all coming, and deeply regretted this ugly deformation of the old America. He is alleged to have said, "Once lead this people into war, and they'll forget there ever was such a thing as tolerance. To fight you must be brutal and ruthless, and the spirit of ruthless brutality will enter into the very fiber of our national life, infecting Congress, the courts, the police-man on the beat, the man in the street." Conformity, the president went on, would become the only virtue, and any man who refused to conform would pay the penalty.

For a long time scholars thoughtlessly accepted these words as Wilson's own. That could be because, as one of them says, Wilson "bears the onus of moral responsibility for demanding intervention. How much less onerous this is, however, when Wilson's suffering and sagacity receive emphasis. . . . Wilson seems so human, and his plight so tragic, when his 'mental agony,' 'turmoil,' 'horror of war,' and 'anguish' are stressed."[9] But historians now doubt that Wilson ever made those remarks.[10] Wilson never had a particularly stellar record as a civil libertarian, and the evidence that this aspect of war especially troubled him is essentially nil.

Even before any restrictive legislation was passed, the government was already pressuring people not to express certain opinions, even certain facts. George Creel called on the press to refrain from publishing any speculation relating to a possible peace, or regarding any issues that divided the Allies. Newspaper editors generally heeded his request, contacting Creel's office to inquire about questionable cases. Creel was said to have told a State Department official that he wanted "nothing whatever published in regard to cable or mail censorship . . . The less said about any sort of censorship the better. . . . It is desirable that no one should know just where the censorship is working."[11]

Teachers and professors, many of whom had spoken out against war before its outbreak in 1914, either adopted the party line upon their government's entry into the conflict or allowed themselves to be intimidated into silence. Those who spoke out were often punished. And "speaking out" did not necessarily mean denouncing their government or its war effort. Professors were dismissed from their jobs for questioning the true extent of German atrocities in Belgium or even for suggesting that the various peoples involved in the war all had good and bad qualities. When Columbia University dismissed two professors—one for his ties to pacifist groups and another for his public opposition to a variety of war measures—some members of the faculty issued protests. Charles Beard resigned. "If we have to suppress everything we don't like to hear," Beard charged, "this country is resting on a pretty wobbly basis. . . . I was among the first to urge a declaration of war by the United States, and I believe that we should now press forward with all our might to a just conclusion. But thousands of my countrymen do not share this view. Their opinions cannot be changed by curses or bludgeons. Arguments addressed to their reason and understanding are our best hope."[12]

Such incidents ran from the chilling to the absurd. Professor Willis Mason West was a member of the Committee on Public Information, and yet even he was not above suspicion. Montana public schools were ordered to stop using a history textbook West had written because he was declared to have been insufficiently hostile in his treatment of the Teutonic tribes prior to A.D. 812.[13]

"The Greatest Danger"

It was precisely this climate that the Espionage Act and the Sedition Act had either created or aggravated. The first of them was passed in June 1917. Section 3, the relevant part of the legislation, instructs:

> Whoever, when the United States is at war, shall willfully make or convey false reports or false statements with intent to interfere with the operation or success of the military or naval forces of the United States or to promote the success of its enemies and whoever when the United States is at war, shall willfully cause or attempt to cause insubordination, disloyalty, mutiny, refusal of duty, in the military or naval forces of the United States, or shall willfully obstruct the recruiting or enlistment

service of the United States, to the injury of the service or of the United States, shall be punished by a fine of not more than $10,000 or imprisonment for not more than twenty years, or both.

The Espionage Act also gave the postmaster general the discretionary authority to remove from the mails any material that he believed would hamper the war effort.

When Congress passed the legislation, its members did not understand themselves to be approving an open-ended power to prohibit a wide range of expression. Criticism of the war as such was not being criminalized. In fact, the version of the bill that Congress approved was more lenient than the original proposal, which among other things would have authorized censorship of the press. But this caveat does not exonerate Congress, since it should have been obvious that a zealous executive could simply interpret the legislation's key phrases so as to allow the kind of censorship and control that President Wilson had been disappointed to see missing from the final version of the legislation. What, exactly, would constitute an "attempt to cause insubordination"? What kind of activities would be viewed as tending to "obstruct the recruiting or enlistment service of the United States"? Would a speech or article against the war qualify as doing either of these things? It would surely be difficult in practice to keep such phrases from reaching an ever-wider range of activities, particularly in the hands of a crusading president.

The Sedition Act, passed the following year, was an amendment to the Espionage Act that authorized precisely the press censorship that Congress left out of the first piece of legislation, and criminalized still more activities. It imposed potentially heavy fines and lengthy prison terms on anyone who should "willfully utter, print, write, or publish any disloyal, profane, scurrilous, or abusive language about the form of government of the United States, or the military or naval forces of the United States, or the flag." It also gave the postmaster general even broader authority to intercept and return mail. (Since the Sedition Act was passed so close to the end of the war, the vast majority of convictions occurred under the earlier, unamended Espionage Act of 1917.) One of the arguments in favor of the Sedition Act was that if the federal government punished war critics more severely and effectively, enraged mobs would consider it less urgent to take the law into their own hands—and there would thus be fewer lynchings and other acts of summary justice.

Senator Joseph France of Maryland tried without success to insert an amendment into the act to the effect that "nothing in this act shall be construed as limiting the liberty or impairing the right of any individual to publish or speak what is true, with good motives, and for justifiable ends." Assistant Attorney General John Lord O'Brian strongly opposed the amendment on the grounds that it would make prosecuting people more difficult. It would be especially challenging to prosecute clergy who favored pacifism, since their appeals to the Bible would make it hard to show bad motive. And that would not do, since according to O'Brian the "greatest danger to the country, internally, to-day is the use of different sorts of seditious propaganda, particularly the false pacifist propaganda."[14]

The Courts Step In

Opponents of the Espionage and Sedition Acts had vainly warned that "judges and jurors cannot reliably distinguish between 'good' and 'evil' intent in a wartime atmosphere of fear, suspicion, and patriotic fervor." Determining subjective intent is never an easy matter, but defendants are far less likely to receive the benefit of the doubt from jurors and judges when they hold minority views that the majority (including, by and large, the jurors and judges themselves) holds in contempt. Professor, lawyer, and civil libertarian

Zechariah Chafee warned that freedom of speech is of particular importance "in times of popular panic and indignation" and that "it is precisely in those times that the protection of the jury proves illusory."[15]

The federal courts tended to interpret the Espionage Act (both before and after its amendment by the Sedition Act) very broadly, in line with the wishes of the executive branch, such that it wound up criminalizing more behavior than Congress appears to have intended. A few judges tried to be more lenient. For instance, George Bourquin, a federal district judge in Montana, ruled in the 1918 case of Ves Hall, a man who on several occasions had made remarks in public places that attracted the attention of the authorities. Specifically, Hall was accused of violating the Espionage Act for expressing the hope that Germany would "whip" the United States and claiming that the war was being waged for the benefit of "Wall Street millionaires." Judge Bourquin explained that in order for an action to qualify in a legal sense as an "attempt" to do something, it had to meet two essential criteria: it had to be intended to commit a specific crime but to have failed in its execution, and it had to be "of sufficient magnitude and proximity" to the accomplishment of its goal that it would have had a reasonable expectation of succeeding. Hall made his comments in a town of sixty people, sixty miles from the nearest railway and hundreds of miles from any soldier. That did not seem to Judge Bourquin to constitute an "attempt" in any real sense, and he could find no proof that these scattered remarks proved any intent to interfere with the military.[16] So he acquitted Hall.

Faced with a statute such as the Espionage Act, Judge Bourquin had recourse to important common-law principles. Although rarely acknowledged in Espionage Act prosecutions, for an act to amount to an "attempt" under the common law it had to "come dangerously near to success," be "sufficiently near completion to be of public concern," or be "very near to the accomplishment of the act." Few judges brought such sobriety to these cases.[17]

Shaffer v. United States, a case that reached the U.S. Court of Appeals, is a good example of how the judiciary typically interpreted the Espionage Act. The defendant's crime involved shipping copies of a book called *The Finished Mystery* through the mail. Among the sentiments in that book that were said to violate the Espionage Act was this: "If you say it is a war of defense against wanton and intolerable aggression, I must reply that . . . it has yet to be proved that Germany has any intention or desire of attacking us. The war itself is wrong. Its prosecution will be a crime. There is not a question raised, an issue involved, a cause at stake, which is worth the life of one blue-jacket on the sea or one khaki-coat in the trenches." The Court of Appeals upheld the defendant's conviction on the grounds that although "disapproval of the war and the advocacy of peace are not crimes under the Espionage Act," the "natural and probable tendency and effect of the words" was to undermine support for the war. The courts had recourse to this "bad tendency" test throughout the war, and it became the touchstone of countless dubious convictions.[18]

It wasn't until 1919—in other words, well after the war had ended—that the sedition legislation was subjected to the scrutiny of the Supreme Court. Three historic cases were heard that year: *Schenck v. United States*, *Abrams v. United States*, and *Debs v. United States*.

Schenck involved the general secretary of the Socialist Party in Philadelphia. Charles T. Schenck, along with others in the party, printed up some fifteen thousand anti-conscription leaflets with the intent of mailing them to men who were being conscripted into the army. (They got the men's names from the newspapers, where lists of men who had passed their physical examinations for the draft board could be found.) The leaflet, which began "LONG LIVE THE CONSTITUTION," denounced conscription as unconstitutional, a position that Daniel Webster had advanced on the floor of Congress toward the end of the War of 1812. It described a conscripted man as "little better than a convict," as he "is deprived of his liberty and of his right to think and act as a free man." And it called upon people to overturn the conscription law through the normal channels of government: "Join the Socialist Party in its campaign for the repeal of the Conscription Act. Write to your congressman and tell him you want the law repealed. Do not submit to intimidation. You have a right to demand the repeal of any law. Exercise your rights of free speech, peaceful assemblage and petitioning the government for a redress of grievances." The leaflet went on to urge, "If you do not assert and support your rights, you are helping to 'deny or disparage rights' which it is the solemn duty of all citizens and residents of the United States to retain." (The words "deny or disparage rights" are based on the Ninth Amendment: "The enumeration in the Constitution, of certain rights, shall not be construed to deny or disparage others retained by the people.")[19]

Only a portion of the fifteen thousand leaflets were actually mailed, and anecdotal evidence suggests that relatively few people actually received them. The envelopes and the handwriting on them were distinctive enough that they could be identified with a reasonable degree of certainty, and the postal inspector impounded 610 of them when he realized what they were. When the prosecution called to the stand eleven men to whom the leaflets had been sent, eight testified that they had never received them. Seven of those eight saw the leaflet for the first time while on the witness stand; the other had been handed an envelope containing one when he saw the U.S. attorney several months earlier, though he had not opened it. The men testified that the leaflet would not have persuaded them to evade the draft. Of the three who did receive the leaflet, all of them testified that they simply reported it to the authorities.[20]

Justice Oliver Wendell Holmes delivered the opinion of the Court, which found the defendants guilty of violating the Espionage Act. "The question in every case," Holmes explained, "is whether the words used are used in such circumstances and are of such a nature as to create a clear and present danger that they will bring about the substantive evils that Congress has a right to prevent. It is a question of proximity and degree. When a nation is at war many things that might be said in time of peace are such a hindrance to its effort that their utterance will not be endured so long as men fight and that no Court could regard them as protected by any constitutional right."[21]

The problems in the Court's decision are legion, but consider just a few. Justice Holmes's "clear and present danger" standard, which sounds rather strict, is apparently malleable enough to bring about the criminalization of a wide variety of speech and action, for nothing in the trial showed that the leaflet in question posed a "clear and present danger" of producing any kind of "evils." The leaflet urged people to petition the government to overturn a law that they, not to mention American statesmen from the past, believed to be unconstitutional—*this* is a "clear and present danger" to the republic? We also read in *Schenck* that the First Amendment does not actually mean what it certainly appears to mean, and that the absolute prohibition on congressional abridgment of the freedom of speech is not so absolute after all. It depends on the circumstances— and the Supreme Court will of course be right there to tell us what those circumstances are and when they exist.

Furthermore, it was in *Schenck* that Justice Holmes advanced his famous argument about falsely shouting "fire" and creating a panic in a crowded theater. Historian Richard Polenberg describes the "shouting fire in a crowded theater" line as "the most brilliantly persuasive expression that ever came from Holmes's pen."[22] No one, Holmes said, would deny that the man who does such a thing deserves the punishment of the law. He concluded on the basis of this example that free speech could not be an absolute or inalienable right, but it could be curtailed in the interest of the common good— as in his view it had been in the Espionage Act.

Justice Holmes's analogy to shouts of "fire" in crowded theaters, although superficially plausible, is completely invalid. Justice Hugo Black understood this point. Writing more than four decades later, he gently rebuked Justice Holmes for his famous statement: "That is a wonderful aphorism about shouting 'fire' in a crowded theater. But you do not have to shout 'fire' to get arrested. If a person creates a disorder in a theater, they would get him there not because of what he hollered but because he hollered. They would get him not because of any views he had but because they thought he did not have any views that they wanted to hear there."[23]

What we have here, in other words, is a property rights issue, not a freedom-of-speech issue. When you patronize a theater you agree to terms by which the theater owner allows you onto his property; surely those terms include the understanding that you may not interrupt the performance and disturb your fellow theatergoers. "We have a system of property," Justice Black explained, and that means "a man does not have a right to do anything he wants anywhere he wants to do it." If you buy a theater ticket, you are not thereby entitled to give a speech there. Likewise, although you have every right to deliver a speech against the Supreme Court, you do not have the right to do so in Justice Black's home.[24]

As a simple matter of property rights, restrictions on shouting "fire" in a crowded theater do not involve the suppression of free speech at all. Yet it was on this flawed basis—we suppress shouts of "fire" in crowded theaters, so we can also suppress antiwar publication—that Justice Holmes justified federal criminalization of unflattering comments about the U.S. government.

Still another problem with Justice Holmes's reasoning has been observed: even supposing that someone may be justly restrained from falsely shouting "fire" in a crowded theater because of the riot and commotion that would thereby ensue, what about someone who *accurately* shouts "fire" in a crowded theater? Commotion will ensue as in the first case, but doesn't the alert regarding the fire outweigh this concern? In other words, is it not possible that the truth that a statement conveys might be sufficiently valuable to compensate for any commotion it may cause?

A week later, Justice Holmes gave the opinion of the Court in the case of *Debs v. United States*. Perennial Socialist presidential candidate Eugene V. Debs had delivered a provocative speech in which he claimed, among other things, that the capitalists were responsible for the war fever, and that as usual the common man had never had a chance to express his own preference for peace or war. For that offense Debs had been sentenced to ten years in prison. Holmes upheld Debs's sentence.

Requests to free Debs that made their way to President Wilson's desk were denied. It was Wilson's Republican successor, Warren G. Harding, who finally freed the incarcerated folk hero. (Debs was in prison during the 1920 elections but still received one million votes; a campaign button featured the candidate's face, around which were written the words "For President: Convict No. 9653.") Harding, who is reviled by historians—unlike Wilson, the unassuming Harding wasn't a "great president"—remarked that the poor souls who had been locked away for speeches they'd given or articles they'd published never meant any harm. As for Debs, Harding said, "I want him to eat his Christmas dinner with his wife."[25]

United States v. Abrams, which was heard nine months later, was one of the relatively few cases in which the defendants were accused of violating the Sedition Act of 1918 rather than the unamended Espionage Act of 1917. The defendants were a small group of Russian radicals—"anarchists," most of them called themselves, along with one socialist—who objected to Wilson's military intervention in Russia. They composed some leaflets consisting of predictable boilerplate to the effect that the capitalists of the West were seeking to choke the Bolshevik Revolution in its infancy, and they demanded that all such intervention cease. The leaflets were not pro-German, and in fact one of them observed, "We hate and despise German militarism more than do your hypocritical tyrants."[26] A lower court had sentenced all five to prison time: three received twenty years, another one fifteen, and another three.

Once again, defendants accused of offenses such as this were subject to the "bad tendency" test, and as usual, they failed. According to the Court, the purpose of the Russian radicals was in fact to obstruct the successful prosecution of the American war effort against Germany. Their intent was to turn people against the American government in time of war, and so their punishment was upheld. A famous study of civil liberties during World War I finds the significance of this case in "an increasing tendency . . . to look, not so much for overt acts, but for the bent of the defendant's thinking. Men's minds were explored more fully to try to ferret out unpatriotic thoughts and words."[27] That should speak for itself.

By the time the *Abrams* case reached the Court, Holmes's views had evolved from what they had been in *Schenck*. Historians note that Holmes had been in correspondence with a number of prominent figures who championed free speech, and believe he had been persuaded by much of their argument. In Holmes's *Abrams* dissent there is a distinct shift in emphasis: the "clear and present danger" test changes from an instrument for restricting speech into one for protecting it, at least most of the time.[28] In this case, said Holmes, twenty-year sentences "have been imposed for the publishing of two leaflets that I believe the defendants had as much right to publish as the Government has to publish the Constitution of the United States now vainly invoked by them." He concluded, "I think that we should be eternally vigilant against attempts to check the expression of opinions that we loathe and believe to be fraught with death, unless they so imminently threaten immediate interference with the lawful and pressing purposes of the law that an immediate check is required to save the country."[29] This was at least an improvement over the "bad tendency" test. Justice Louis Brandeis joined Justice Holmes in his dissent. The seven justices who constituted the majority, of course, did not.

The Forgotten Constitution

"Congress shall make no law . . . abridging the freedom of speech," says the First Amendment. The enumerated powers of Congress, given in Article I, Section 8, do not include a power to suppress any kind of speech under any circumstances. According to Thomas Jefferson, if any governmental body might possess a power to interfere with free speech, it was the states.[30] Whether the states would be wise or warranted in exercising such a power is of course a separate matter, but that is all the Constitution has to say about the subject.

As usual, though, government officials did what they wanted to do.

2

Another "Great President" versus
the Constitution:
Harry Truman Seizes the Steel Mills

A T THE END of 1951, American steelworkers indicated their intention to go on strike. That seems unremarkable enough, until we recall that in doing so they set in motion a series of events that tell us much about presidential ambition, the Supreme Court, and the Constitution.

The owners of the nation's steel mills had refused to negotiate any wage increase until they received assurances from the federal government's Office of Price Stabilization—yes, there really was such a thing in 1951—that they would be permitted to increase steel prices adequately at the same time. They also responded to labor's demand for a wage increase by noting that (1) steelworkers were among the highest-paid industrial workers in America (true), (2) their compensation package had consistently stayed ahead of the rise in the cost of living (true), and (3) any wage increase would be inflationary (false—no wage increase causes inflation in the sense intended here of a rise in prices; if more money goes to workers in the form of increased wages, less money is available for other sectors, thereby offsetting any overall upward trend in prices).[1]

On March 20, 1952, the Wage Stabilization Board—yes, that also existed—announced a plan it considered fair. The steel companies disapproved of the plan, however, and the situation reverted to where it had been at the end of the previous year, with the two sides dead-locked and a strike looming. Unless the deadlock could somehow be broken, the steel strike was set to commence on April 4.

Convinced that a work stoppage in the nation's steel mills would imperil the war effort in Korea, President Harry Truman decided to act. He ordered his secretary of commerce, Charles Sawyer, to seize and operate the steel mills for the federal government. Truman ex-plained his actions before a national radio and television audience on April 8, justifying the seizure through an appeal to "the Constitution and laws of the United States" and his powers "as President of the United States and Commander in Chief of the armed forces."[2]

The response was swift and almost certainly came as a surprise to Truman. The business community, naturally, was appalled. *Business Week* warned that if tyranny were to come to America, it would take the form not of a single seizure of power but "imperceptibly . . . in small steps, one reinforcing the other." Truman's steel seizure was one such small step, according to the magazine. Writing in *Nation's Business*, Felix Morley compared Truman's "inherent power" with the "divine right" of Charles I, noting that the distinction between the two was "more apparent than real." Unsurprisingly, steel executives were especially irate. Inland Steel president Clarence B. Randall told the press, "I had always supposed that the old phrase that comes down through Anglo-Saxon history, 'due process of law,' meant some-thing other than an appearance on television."[3]

For the most part, the nation's editorial pages were equally hostile. According to the *Washington Post*, Truman's seizure would "probably go down in history as one of the most high-handed acts committed by an American President." The *New York Times* said Truman had created "a new regime of government by executive decree."[4]

And even if supporters of the president's action tended to be on the Left, Socialist Norman Thomas condemned the federal govern-ment's constitutional claims, as did the American Civil Liberties Union.[5]

Some editorialists tried to warn those on the Left that there was nothing to guarantee their domination of the country's governing class, and that they should not mindlessly support the growth of government power under the comforting delusion that that power would never be exercised in a way they might dislike. The "sword has two edges," cautioned the *Pittsburgh Press*. "Mr. Truman can use it today in behalf of labor. Some future president, with Mr. Truman's precedent to guide him, can use it against labor. If industry can be blackjacked into paying higher wages, labor also can be blackjacked into taking a cut." The *Nation* urged that "a just settlement of a labor dispute" could not justify the "arbitrary exercise of executive power."[6]

A President's Prerogatives?

Just one of the problems with the president's account was that there was no "law of the United States" that gave the president statutory authority to seize private property in general or the steel mills in particular. In fact, the president did have several legal options at his disposal for dealing with the threatened strike, but he chose not to act upon any of them. None of these alternatives is especially attractive, and while each is legal in the sense of having been authorized by Congress, they all amount to an extraordinary grant of power to the president. Had Truman followed one of these courses, he would have satisfied some of his critics, for whom the only relevant question was whether the seizure of private property was done with congressional authorization.

One came from the Taft-Hartley Act, which empowered the president, in cases when he believed a strike would be dangerous to the nation's health or safety, to impose a cooling-off period for up to eighty days in which workers would be enjoined from striking and negotiation could take place. This was one congressionally authorized alternative to outright seizure.

Another source of authority came from the Defense Production

Act of 1950, which allowed the president to seize property whenever he believed "that the use of any equipment, supplies, or component parts thereof, or materials or facilities necessary for the manufacture, servicing, or operation of such equipment, supplies, or component parts, is needed for the national defense." This statute represented an explicit extension of the federal government's eminent domain powers, which were limited in this case, as in others, by the requirement that the property owner be paid just compensation.[7]

Still another possibility was Section 18 of the Selective Service Act of 1948. That section stipulated that the president could order from any manufacturer that produced goods needed by the military or the Atomic Energy Commission, once the contents of the order had been approved by Congress. If a manufacturer failed to fulfill the order by the president's deadline, the president could have that manufacturer's property seized and operated for the purpose of producing the goods needed by the government. As in the Defense Production Act, just compensation to the owner was required. Thus if Truman placed an order for steel and the steel was not delivered, he was arguably authorized under this statute to take over the steel mills.

Truman had followed none of these statutes. The federal government all but conceded the lack of statutory authority behind the president's act of seizure in federal court the very next day when Assistant Attorney General Holmes Baldridge based the seizure not on a particular statute but on "the inherent executive powers of the president."[8] Baldridge was in court in the first place because the steel companies, within half an hour of Truman's seizure speech, had urged a federal judge to issue a temporary restraining order and perhaps even an injunction in order to prevent the federal government's seizure from taking place. Federal district judge Walter Bastian replied that the government's side of the matter would first have to be heard.

When the steel companies' motion was transferred to Judge David A. Pine, an unusually memorable confrontation ensued between this federal judge and the assistant attorney general regarding the powers of the president. Their exchange, in part, went like this:

JUDGE PINE: So you contend that the Executive has unlimited power in time of an emergency?

BALDRIDGE: He has the power to take such action as is necessary to meet the emergency.

PINE: If the emergency is great, it is unlimited, is it?

BALDRIDGE: I suppose if you carry it to its logical conclusion, that is true. But I do want to point out that there are two limitations on the Executive power. One is the ballot box and the other is impeachment.[9]

Earlier in the proceeding, this exchange had ensued:

PINE: If the President directs [Commerce Secretary] Mr. Sawyer to take you into custody, right now, and have you executed in the morning you say there is no power by which the Court may intervene even by habeas corpus?

BALDRIDGE: If there are statutes protecting me I would have a remedy.

PINE: What statute would protect you?

BALDRIDGE: I do not recall any at the moment.[10]

Baldridge, said Judge Pine, was setting forth an extraordinarily broad view of the president's powers in an emergency. Did Baldridge hold further that "the Executive determines the emergencies and the Courts cannot even review whether it is an emergency"?

"That is correct," Baldridge answered.[11]

Baldridge went on to claim that while the legislature was bound by the enumerated powers delegated to it in Article I, Section 8, the executive branch was not so bound. Judge Pine, trying to be sure he was understanding Baldridge correctly, asked him: "So, when the sovereign people adopted the Constitution, it enumerated the powers set up in the Constitution but limited the powers of the Congress and limited the powers of the judiciary, but it did not limit the powers of the Executive. Is that what you say?"

"That is the way we read Article II of the Constitution," said Baldridge.[12]

The press had a field day with Assistant Attorney General Baldridge. (This was back when sweeping claims of executive power were considered cause for concern.) Newspapers across the country declared that the Justice Department believed the president's powers were unlimited.[13]

Historians have not been kind to Baldridge, either. According to Bernard Schwartz, a historian of the Supreme Court, in defense of the seizure "the Government advanced arguments that had not been heard in an English-speaking court since the time of Charles I."[14] Constitutional scholar David Gray Adler has compared Baldridge's claims of presidential prerogative to the claims made in the 1642 ship money case in England, in which the king claimed to possess an unchallengeable right to carry out whatever action he believed was necessary for the country's welfare.[15] ("The president has the power to keep the country from going to hell" is how Truman put it to his staff.)[16]

Justice William Rehnquist, writing about the case in 1986, noted that although Baldridge's argument was perhaps not as "bizarre" as it may have appeared, such provocative claims should have been avoided in such a high-profile case. "While it may have been a plausible or at least an interesting legal argument in the abstract, it was not the sort of argument which should have been used by the government in a case on which there was as much public attention focused as on this one."[17] The government is evidently better off keeping such arguments to itself. That Baldridge had blurted out such a thing was immediately recognized as a terrible blunder. "The government quickly sensed that it had made a mistake in making these arguments and within days Holmes Baldridge had issued a statement saying in a thinly veiled way that he had not meant what he said."[18]

Most unkind of all to Holmes Baldridge was Judge Pine himself, whose finding against the government and its claim of inherent, unreviewable presidential powers was relentless and withering. In the course of showing "the utter and complete lack of authoritative support" for the government's position, Judge Pine declared:

> The non-existence of this "inherent" power in the President has been recognized by eminent writers, and I cite in this connection the unequivocal language of the late Chief Justice [William Howard] Taft in his treatise entitled *Our Chief Magistrate and His Powers* (1916) wherein he says: "The true view of the Executive function is, as I conceive it, that the President can exercise no power which cannot be fairly and reasonably traced to some specific grant of power or justly implied and included within such express grant as proper and necessary to its exercise. Such specific grant must be either in the Federal Constitution or in an Act of Congress passed in pursuance thereof. There is no undefined residuum of power which he can exercise because it seems to him to be in the public interest, and there is nothing in the *Neagle* case and its definition of a law of the United States, or in other precedents, warranting such an inference. The grants of executive power are necessarily in general terms in order not to embarrass the Executive within the field of action plainly marked for him, but his jurisdiction must be justified and vindicated by affirmative constitutional or statutory provision, or it does not exist."[19]

(Pine's decision made little headway with the president, who told his staff that he had read Judge Pine's opinion—"read it, read it, and read it"—and could not figure out why he had been found to be in the wrong.)[20]

"Degenerating into Despotism"

Judge Pine's decision went a long way toward turning public opinion against the president. But Truman's own comments, scattered throughout various press conferences held over the course of the ensuing days and weeks, did not help matters. One was especially memorable: when asked on April 17 whether in his view his inherent power to seize private property extended to the possible seizure of American newspapers and radio stations, the president replied: "Under similar circumstances the President of the United States has to act for whatever is for the best of the country. That's the answer to your question." The *New York Times* reported the next day, "The president refused to elaborate. But White House sources said the president's point was that he had power in an emergency to take over 'any portion of the business community acting to jeopardize all the people.'"[21]

In the wake of the seizure and of the president's remarks to the press, Congressman George Bender, Ohio Republican, went so far as to call for Truman's impeachment. "I do not believe that our people can tolerate the formation of a presidential precedent which would permit any occupant of the White House to exercise his untrammeled discretion to take over the industry, communications system or other forms of private enterprise in the name of 'emergency.'"[22] Senator Robert A. Taft likewise declared that the president's action justified impeachment.

Impeachment never came, of course, but the president at least recognized that he had hit a nerve with his comments about his power to take over the American media. The following week Truman denounced all the "hooey" in the press about the seizure of the press and the radio stations. He assured everyone that "the thought of seizing press and radio has never occurred to me." He said he had "difficulty imagining" the government running those industries.[23]

The president's position alienated even those who otherwise

favored an executive with expansive emergency powers. Lucius Wilmerding, writing in the *Political Science Quarterly* and himself sympathetic to the presidential exercise of emergency powers, came out strongly against Truman. Wilmerding cited evidence that early American statesmen had conceived of moments when it might be necessary for the president to take extralegal action. These statesmen, however, supported this position not because they believed the president possessed plenary authority to act in an emergency, or that the Constitution envisioned a presidency with vast, unenumerated "inherent" powers. In fact, the consensus was that if the president ever claimed that he had stepped beyond his constitutional and statutory limits out of sheer necessity in a case of dire emergency, he would have to justify himself in front of Congress after the fact.[24]

If Truman had followed this example, he would have "gone immediately to Congress, confessed his illegal act, and thrown himself upon the justice of his country and the rectitude of his motives." That would not have been easy. Among other things, he would have had to prove that his illegal action, at a time when Congress was in session, was absolutely necessary, and that the action he took was the same course Congress itself would have pursued had it been able to act swiftly enough.[25] Truman did no such thing, of course, pointing instead to inherent powers that he claimed resided in the president.

Such an appeal to congressional clemency would not have comported with Truman's understanding of executive power and its scope, which owed much to Theodore Roosevelt. Ken Hechler, special assistant to Truman, recalled in 2002 that the steel seizure was an excellent example of Truman's philosophy of the presidency in action. He subscribed to the two major philosophical planks that have informed the activist presidency since being decisively and self-consciously introduced by Roosevelt in the early twentieth century. First, the president was the unique representative of the American people. According to Hechler, Truman once took him aside and said, "The president of the United States is the only public official elected by all the people in all 48 states, and he is the chief lobbyist for the people."[26] Second, as Chief Justice Rehnquist put it, Truman believed (with Roosevelt) that "the president's power was absolute unless some provision of the Constitution expressly denied authority to him."[27] It can hardly come as a surprise that such a president would put so much emphasis on his inherent powers at the expense of the authority of Congress.

Wilmerding concluded:

> If the President be conceded a sort of chancery power to suspend or dispense with laws, or with the execution of laws, or to make laws for the time being, on suggestions of equity or expediency, for the safety of the people, then the acts of Congress are uncertain and positive law is brought under the discretion, that is the pleasure, of the President. . . . For if the President is the judge of the necessity, his power is unlimited; he may apply his discretion to any instance whatever; and, since "men by habit make irregular stretches of power without discerning the consequences and extent of them," one small wrong must lead to a greater one, and in the end force must become the measure of law, discretion must degenerate into despotism.[28]

The Landmark Decision That Wasn't

By May the steel seizure had made its way to the Supreme Court, in the form of *Youngstown Sheet & Tube Co. v. Sawyer* (1952). Gone from the government's argument were the extreme claims of executive power that Holmes Baldridge had offered before Judge Pine. The government instead spoke of past precedent involving presidential seizure of private property, argued that a fair reading of the powers granted to the president in the Constitution made the seizure lawful, and made somewhat more mainstream if still highly debatable claims about the president's inherent power to act in emergencies (which he himself identified and designated).

At a press conference held after the conclusion of oral argument and in anticipation of the Court's decision, Truman was asked if he would prefer that Congress enact a broad statute authorizing him to seize property, or whether it would be better to go to Congress for authorization in each specific case. Truman replied, "The President *has* the power, and they can't take it away from him." He elaborated: "Nobody can take it away from the President, because he is the Chief Executive of the Nation, and he has to be in a position to see that the welfare of the people is met." When reporters asked Truman what exactly the Court was deciding on if the president's inherent seizure power could not be taken away, the president replied that he could not comment on the matter before the Court.[29]

On June 2, 1952, in a 6–3 decision the Supreme Court overturned the president's seizure of the steel mills. Justice Hugo Black, writing for the majority, held that the president possessed only those powers expressly given to him either in the Constitution itself or by Congress. Black considered the three constitutional clauses most frequently cited by supporters of a powerful executive: the Commander in Chief Clause ("The President shall be Commander in Chief of the Army and Navy of the United States"), the "Take Care" Clause ("he shall take Care that the Laws be faithfully executed"), and the Vesting Clause ("The executive Power shall be vested in a President of the United States of America"). None of these clauses could bear the weight that the government's case imposed on them, Black concluded. He also found no congressional statute authorizing presidential seizure of the steel mills. To the government's claim that the president had previously seized property during labor disputes without express congressional authorization, Black replied that such incidents do not deprive Congress of its lawmaking power. Black's argument for the Court boiled down to this: the president's task was to enforce the law, not to legislate, and Truman's seizure of the steel mills in the absence of any legal authorization amounted to a legislative act.

That each of the four concurring justices wrote a separate opinion strongly suggests that the decision was less decisive than commentators normally concede: a majority agreed that the steel seizure had to be overturned, to be sure, but they differed on exactly why. Justice William O. Douglas held, with Justice Black, that Truman had unconstitutionally engaged in legislation in defiance of the traditional tasks entrusted to the executive. But Justices Harold Burton, Felix Frankfurter, and Robert H. Jackson offered a considerably less sweeping rationale for their rejection of Truman's action. A majority of justices in *Youngstown* did not deny that the president possessed implied or residual powers that enabled him to take various actions without congressional authorization.[30]

Justice Frankfurter disagreed with Justice Black's contention that past examples of executive seizure could not in and of themselves alter the constitutional equilibrium between the executive and legislative branches. According to Frankfurter, long experience of executive activism can become a "gloss" on the executive power vested in the president in Article II, Section 1, and it is unreasonably inflexible to emphasize the constitutional text to the exclusion of the testimony of experience. Frankfurter went on to say that the examples of presidential seizure the government had cited in this case were insufficient "in number, scope, duration or contemporaneous legal justification" to qualify as such a gloss, but he did not reject the principle that the Constitution could be altered by long-standing practice rather than by formal amendment.[31]

The seizure examples were especially embarrassing for Justice Jackson. During his tenure as U.S. attorney general from 1940 to 1941, Jackson had argued for the legality of Franklin Roosevelt's seizure of the North American Aviation plant, a precedent that the government was now citing on behalf of its argument for the seizure of the steel mills. He now had to claim that he had simply been engaging in the standard overreaching in which all attorneys general indulge. "I claimed everything, of course, like every other Attorney General does," Justice Jackson admitted. "It was a custom that did not leave the Department of Justice when I did."[32] Jackson's admission recalls H. L. Mencken's satirical rewrite of the Constitution in the wake of Franklin Roosevelt's New Deal regime. Of the attorney general, Mencken's mock Constitution instructed: "It shall be his duty to provide legal opinions certifying to the constitutionality of all measures undertaken by the President."[33]

The Court did not give a definitive answer, in this much-touted decision, regarding the president's alleged "inherent" or emergency powers. "The issue before us can be met, and therefore should be met, without attempting to define the President's powers comprehensively," wrote Justice Frankfurter. What the majority, which was itself divided on the rationale for striking down the steel seizure, managed to agree upon was simply that Truman had failed to abide by any of the several legal ways he could have dealt with the steel strike, all of which had been duly approved by Congress. Moreover, the majority noted, Congress had expressly rejected the idea of inserting a seizure power into the Taft-Hartley Act.

Thus for several of the justices who found against Truman, the issue at hand was not whether the president possessed implied powers that allowed him to take action in the complete *absence* of congressional authorization—the more interesting question and the one that plagues us to this day. Rather, the question was whether a president's action could be upheld when Congress had laid out a much different course from the one he had chosen—a far narrower question.[34] Justices Burton and Tom C. Clark, in fact, were willing to entertain the possibility that the Court might uphold even some presidential actions that occurred in the face of outright congressional opposition. And this is not to mention the dissenting justices, who were prepared to concede a variety of implied powers to the president and spoke explicitly of a presidential "power of seizure."

Justice Jackson's opinion has often been credited with setting out a useful framework for evaluating presidents' use of executive power. According to him, the president's authority to perform a given action varies in proportion to the following factors:

1. When the President acts pursuant to an express or implied authorization of Congress, his authority is at its maximum, for it includes all that he possesses in his own right plus all that Congress can delegate. . . .

2. When the President acts in absence of either a congressional grant or denial of authority, he can only rely upon his own independent powers, but there is a zone of twilight in which he and Congress may have concurrent authority, or in which its distribution is uncertain. . . .

3. When the President takes measures incompatible with the expressed or implied will of Congress, his power is at its lowest ebb, for then he can rely only upon his own constitutional powers minus any constitutional powers of Congress over the matter.[35]

Jackson finds that the steel seizure falls into the third of these categories, the one in which the president is on the weakest ground.

This breakdown is not as useful to those who would limit presidential power as it might at first seem. For one thing, in the second possibility, how helpful is the vague phrase "a zone of twilight"? In the first and third cases, how exactly can one determine when the authorization of Congress has been "implied"? Justice Jackson provides no guidance for resolving this matter.[36] President George W. Bush seriously argued that his warrantless wiretapping program, which became public in late 2005, had been implicitly authorized by Congress in its resolution authorizing the use of force against the perpetrators of the September 11 attacks. There seems to be little mischief for which a president could not contrive some labored excuse under this guideline.

In general, then, the Court's ruling achieved little of significance. It struck down little of the federal government's open-ended claim to emergency powers and left the central issue of the extent of executive power fundamentally unresolved.[37] "The language in the concurrences," writes law professor Patricia Bellia, "is sufficiently open-ended to support a number of different outcomes in any given case," and "provides no specific guidance as to how courts should decide any concrete dispute."[38] As another scholar put it, quoting Justice Owen J. Roberts in *Smith v. Allwright*, the *Youngstown* ruling belongs "in the same class as a restricted railroad ticket, good for this day and train only."[39]

The Youngstown Legacy

Despite the relative insignificance of the *Youngstown* decision, legal commentators have typically spoken with breathless excitement about the case's importance.

Justice William Rehnquist hypothesized in 1986 that public opinion had had much to do with the Court's decision. The overwhelmingly negative coverage that Assistant Attorney General Holmes Baldridge's appearance before Judge Pine had drawn, and the alarm that had been raised about the former's capacious view of executive power, had swung public opinion against the seizure.[40] However scaled back the government's claims were by the time the seizure case reached the Supreme Court, Rehnquist doubts that "the government's arguments in the district court could have been erased from anyone's mind." Had public outrage not been excited, in other words, the Court probably would not have rendered even the timid decision it handed down, and *Youngstown* instead would have been business as usual, as a Court packed with FDR and Truman appointees rubber-stamped yet another unconstitutional federal act. But the Court can sometimes find itself unable to act in complete isolation from public opinion, textbook platitudes about the Court's pure, undisturbed exercise of ratiocination notwithstanding.[41]

The Supreme Court had dealt with the subject of emergency powers far more clearly in the past than it did in *Youngstown*. In

1934 the Supreme Court heard *Home Building and Loan Association v. Blaisdell* (known as the Minnesota Moratorium Case), which involved a state statute that, in the name of economic "emergency," imposed a moratorium on mortgage foreclosures. The Court upheld the statute as a legitimate emergency measure. Chief Justice Charles Evans Hughes explained, on one hand, that emergency "does not create power" and "does not increase granted power or remove or diminish the restrictions imposed upon power granted or reserved." On the other hand, recalling a point advanced in the 1917 case of *Wilson v. New*, Hughes noted, "While emergency does not create power, emergency may furnish the occasion for the exercise of power"—whatever that means.[42]

Chief Justice Hughes instructed his countrymen that the Contracts Clause of the Constitution and its prohibition on government interference with contracts should not be thought of as "absolute" or read with "literal exactness." When the Constitution said that no state "shall pass any law . . . impairing the obligation of contracts," you see, it really meant that the "economic interests of the State may justify the exercise of its continuing and dominant protective power *notwithstanding interference with contracts*."[43] There's your Constitution.

The minority argued that the government possessed no emergency powers that could justify departure from the general principles set forth in the Constitution. For them, the important precedent was *Ex parte Milligan* (1866), which declared: "The Constitution of the United States is a law for rulers and people, equally in war and in peace, and covers with the shield of its protection all classes of men, at all times, and under all circumstances. No doctrine, involving more pernicious consequences, was ever invented by the wit of man than that any of its provisions can be suspended during any of the great exigencies of government. Such a doctrine leads directly to anarchy or despotism."

Without such a principle, said dissenting justice George Sutherland, the Constitution "would cease to be the 'supreme law of the land,' binding equally upon governments and governed at all times and under all circumstances, and become a mere collection of political maxims to be adhered to or disregarded according to the prevailing sentiment or the legislative and judicial opinion in respect of the supposed necessities of the hour . . . If the provisions of the Constitution be not upheld when they pinch as well as when they comfort, they may as well be abandoned."[44]

Sutherland was joined in his dissent by justices Willis Van Devanter, Pierce Butler, and James Clark McReynolds, all conservatives.

By the time of *Youngstown*, this line of argument was scarcely to be found. Rather than expressly affirming the finding in *Ex parte Milligan* or revisiting the important dissent in the Minnesota Moratorium Case, the justices had little to say about emergency powers in themselves, other than to suggest that they existed to one degree or another. No one suggested that it might be dangerous or undesirable to grant the federal government, in whatever branch, the power to seize property during emergencies—especially since the federal government itself claims the exclusive authority to define and declare the existence of an emergency. Political economist Robert Higgs concludes, "The Constitution was read in this case, as in many others, not as a bulwark against governmental oppression of private citizens but rather as the institutional setting within which high officials in the different branches of government conduct their internecine struggles for supremacy."[45] In other words, the Constitution was treated not as a document intended to limit government power but as an instrument that merely apportions government power among the various branches. For the Court and later commentators, *Youngstown* was an interesting separation-of-powers case, instead of being an interesting seizure-of-property case.

Why, then, *is* the case significant? For one thing, we learn that a supposedly landmark case left the central point of contention open and suggested only the most vague, easily evaded principles for judging executive behavior. Furthermore, there can be little doubt that even the most exaggerated claims for presidential authority that the government made over the course of the steel seizure incident are precisely what influential thinkers and government officials in fact believe today. The commentary surrounding the case, from Holmes Baldridge and the president himself through subsequent observers, reveals that the philosophy of an activist executive possessing inherent powers that override congressional prerogative is not a recent development at all but has been an integral part of the thinking of most of the presidents our historians teach us to admire. Demonizing only one president, as the Left has by and large done in recent years, is far too timid. So many others merit the same treatment.

3

The Third Rail of American Jurisprudence:
Brown v. Board of Education

A S POLITICIANS HAVE long understood, it's easy to stand on constitutional principle when a law, a court ruling, or a presidential action is unpopular. But what happens when a popular, even resoundingly acclaimed decision is at issue? Responsible citizens are not supposed to raise questions about any such government action—it was wonderful, and that's that.

But the simple fact is that just because a government decision seems beneficial or "right" doesn't mean it's *constitutional*. Indeed, this is a key assumption underlying the entire federal system that the U.S. Constitution established. Good intentions, even positive policy outcomes, do not ensure proper government action. In the long run, good policy outcomes can undermine the rule of law if they are adopted contrary to the actual meaning of the Constitution.

This brings us to the U.S. Supreme Court's landmark 1954 decision in the case of *Brown v. Board of Education of Topeka, Kansas*. In forbidding segregation of schools on the basis of race in *Brown* and in a tandem case, *Bolling v. Sharpe*, the Court made its most significant (and celebrated) rulings of the twentieth century. While the decisions actually had limited effects on the subject at hand—namely, racial assignment of students—they earned the Court an unprecedented level of prestige.

Today, virtually no one dares criticize the Supreme Court's behavior in *Brown v. Board of Education* (although the decision was highly controversial at the time). In fact, law professors now skip past constitutional questions about *Brown* and instead, as one prize-winning historian of these decisions put it, decide why the decision was right and weigh its impact on American race relations.[1] The same goes for historians and lawyers who hope to become federal judges. Support of *Brown*, or at least silence on the question, is essentially required of anyone who wants to become a law professor, history professor, or federal appointee.[2]

This hands-off approach to *Brown*—this focus on the policy outcome rather than whether there was justification for it—avoids addressing a fundamental flaw in the Court's decision: *it wasn't constitutional*. While few today have the temerity to point out problems in the *Brown* ruling, the Framers and ratifiers of the Fourteenth Amendment certainly would have recognized that the decision ran counter to what they intended to accomplish through that amendment.

The reality is that the *Brown* Court demonstrated a breathtaking lack of concern, even disdain, for the structure of the federal system and for the principle of republicanism. The justices were aware that the Court's fifty-eight-year-old decision in *Plessy v. Ferguson* had been correct in declaring that racial segregation did not violate the Equal Protection Clause of the Fourteenth Amendment, which was *not* intended to outlaw racial segregation. Rather than a legal decision, then, *Brown* was the justices' statement of a policy preference: they simply disapproved of racial segregation and would not enforce this policy they found so distasteful.

Uncomfortable as some people may be blasting open a supposedly closed question such as *Brown v. Board of Education*, doing so gets at the very heart of the constitutional crisis we face today. To make exceptions for government actions that seem "right" but aren't consistent with the Constitution is to make arbitrary, and quite dangerous, distinctions. Doing so breaks "the chains of the Constitution" that, in Jefferson's memorable phrase, are needed to "bind down" politicians. Once we allow the government to go outside the bounds of the Constitution, we have created a precedent for other extraconstitutional actions later.

Alas, the government's next move might not seem so "right" or desirable.

What the Fourteenth Amendment Really Meant

Since the justification of any constitutional decision must originate in the Constitution's historical background, it is important to understand the background of the Fourteenth Amendment before we can evaluate *Brown*. Racially segregated schools had existed in the United States virtually from the moment that blacks began to receive formal education here. Even Boston, Massachusetts, long recognized as the least anti-black of American jurisdictions, segregated its schools by race in the nineteenth century. Before the Civil War a few isolated reformers, such as future senator Charles Sumner, argued that segregation of Boston schools was impermissible, but their views gained no traction.

In those days, of course, the situation for blacks was far worse in other parts of the country, as the great majority of blacks were slaves, and many states banned any kind of formal instruction of blacks, slave or free. That situation changed drastically with the Union victory in the Civil War and the adoption of the Thirteenth Amendment. Reconstruction governments in the South followed charitable institutions there and elsewhere in endeavoring to impart basic literacy to blacks. Primary and secondary schools, and even colleges, committed to educating African Americans began to dot the landscape. Virtually all of these schools remained segregated, however.

Beyond the historical background on segregated schooling, there is the constitutional background. The *Brown* ruling centered on the Fourteenth Amendment, which was adopted in the aftermath of the Civil War.

In the elections of 1866, the first round of congressional elections since the subjugation of the former Confederate states, the southern electorate voted in a host of Confederate and antebellum southern officials, among them the former vice president of the Confederacy, Alexander Stephens. Republicans in control of both houses of Congress, recognizing the danger that Democratic victories in the South posed to Republican plans for remaking southern society—and to hopes of long-term Republican domination of Congress—refused to seat them.

More or less simultaneously, the legislatures of many southern states adopted Black Codes—suites of laws designed to ensure the continued social subordination of blacks and to leave control of black labor power in the hands of white landowners. In the immortal words of Pete Townshend, "Meet the new boss, same as the old boss."

In response to these developments, the Republican majority in Congress attempted to guarantee the basic rights of blacks, such as the right to own land and the right to make and enforce contracts for labor. It did so by passing the Civil Rights Act of 1866. President Andrew Johnson, a southern Democrat devoted to Jacksonian constitutional views, vetoed the act, correctly noting that through this legislation Congress had assumed control over matters the federal Constitution reserved to the states. The Republican Congress overrode the veto.

This did not resolve the matter entirely, however. The Republicans recognized that the Supreme Court's 1857 decision in *Dred Scott v. Sandford* had permanently blocked blacks from obtaining U.S. citizenship. Blacks still might be mistreated or denied the franchise by the southern states. There was a political consideration, too: perversely, the emancipation of the slaves stood to make the southern-leaning Democratic Party even more powerful than before. Under the Constitution's Three-fifths Clause, slaves had counted less than freedmen would in congressional (and thus also in Electoral College) apportionment. The fact that blacks now were free meant that they counted as one person each for purposes of congressional apportionment. So if southern whites disfranchised freedmen while also obtaining augmented representation for them, there would be more white southern representation in Congress than there had been before the war. Ex-Confederates, then, might cement the permanent ascendancy of the Democratic Party. And as soon as Democrats regained their accustomed majority status in Congress, Republicans recognized, they might well repeal the 1866 Civil Rights Act.

Facing these lingering problems, the Republicans pushed through the Fourteenth Amendment. There was, as the Supreme Court noted in its first pass at applying the Fourteenth Amendment,[3] no mystery about the meaning of the amendment's provisions: they were to ensure that recently freed slaves had the basic rights of citizens.[4] The amendment's first section annulled the *Dred Scott* decision by declaring that anyone born in the United States was a citizen of the United States and of the state in which he resided. It also forbade states from abridging certain basic rights of U.S. citizens (the Privileges and Immunities Clause), required state judiciaries to give everyone the benefit of traditional procedures before punishing them (the Due Process Clause), and required state executives to protect all alike (the Equal Protection Clause). Section 2 of the amendment penalized states if they denied blacks the suffrage.[5] As the esteemed constitutional scholar Raoul Berger documented, the Fourteenth Amendment's Framers in Congress regarded its first section as "identical" to the Civil Rights Act.[6]

The Court first considered the meaning of the Fourteenth Amendment in the *Slaughter-House Cases* (1873). There, the Court made short work of the Privileges and Immunities Clause, which it said guaranteed only rights such as the right to travel to the federal capital, the right to the federal government's assistance to citizens traveling outside the country, and the right to use the federal waterways. The Court also said that the white butchers who had initiated the suits consolidated in *Slaughter-House* did not have a claim under the Equal Protection Clause. In fact, the Court added, it could not conceive of any situation in which a nonblack might make a valid claim under that clause, as everyone knew that it had been added to the Constitution to protect black Americans against the former master class.

Richard Kluger, author of the most influential book on *Brown*, notes that the Civil Rights Act of 1866, which the Fourteenth Amendment's first section was intended to constitutionalize, was amended to remove a general ban on discrimination. He adds that at the time the Fourteenth Amendment was proposed, twenty-four of the thirty-seven states segregated their schools, which makes it hard to believe that the state legislatures would have overlooked school segregation in discussing an amendment intended to abolish that practice. Besides, Congress segregated schools in the District of Columbia from 1864 on, and it did not address this issue in the Civil Rights Act of 1875. Finally, Kluger asks, "Could it be reasonably claimed that segregation had been outlawed by the Fourteenth when the yet more basic emblem of citizenship—the ballot—had been withheld from the Negro under that amendment?"[7]

The Court's most significant segregation precedent before 1954, *Plessy v. Ferguson* (1896), held that segregation did not violate the Equal Protection Clause of the Constitution.[8] The *Plessy* majority offered very little by way of analysis of the understanding of the Fourteenth Amendment's ratifiers beyond saying, "The object of the amendment was undoubtedly to enforce the absolute equality of the two races before the law, but, in the nature of things, it could not have been intended to abolish distinctions based upon color, or to enforce social, as distinguished from political, equality, or a commingling of the two races upon terms unsatisfactory to either. Laws permitting, and even requiring, their separation, in places where they are liable to be brought into contact, do not necessarily imply the inferiority of either race to the other, and have been generally, if not universally, recognized as within the competency of the state legislatures in the exercise of their police power. The most common instance of this is connected with the establishment of separate schools for white and colored children, which have been held to be a valid exercise of the legislative power even by courts of states where the political rights of the colored race have been longest and most earnestly enforced." As Raoul Berger showed, this was consistent with the ratifiers' understanding.

Because They Could

The U.S. Supreme Court first heard cases involving segregation of primary and secondary schools in the 1952–53 term. (The Court would hear rearguments the following term and decide the cases in 1954.) At the time, seventeen states and the District of Columbia still segregated their schools.[9]

As they came before the Court, the plaintiffs in *Brown v. Board of Education* and *Bolling v. Sharpe* needed a way to explain (or explain away) the historical record on segregation and the Fourteenth Amendment. The NAACP Legal Defense and Education Fund, representing the plaintiffs, consulted several well-known historians concerning the Fourteenth Amendment. One, Henry Steele Commager, responded that Congress did not "intend that [the Fourteenth Amendment] should be used to end segregation in schools" and advised the NAACP not to argue about the original understanding of the amendment.[10]

Similar conclusions were reached inside the Supreme Court. Justice Felix Frankfurter charged his law clerk, Alexander Bickel, with the task of investigating the Congress that had drafted the Fourteenth Amendment to determine its intentions regarding school segregation. Bickel, who would later become a prominent constitutional law professor at Yale Law School, reported to Justice Frankfurter that "it is impossible to conclude that the 39th Congress intended that segregation be abolished; impossible also to conclude that they foresaw it might be, under the language they were adopting."[11]

Note the language: *it was impossible to come to* certain conclusions. Here Bickel's report indicates that Frankfurter viewed the *Brown* litigation from an advocate's point of view and had assigned Bickel not the judge's task of finding what the historical record of the events in question said but the advocate's task of finding what it might be *said* to say.[12]

While the record could not be read in the way Frankfurter had hoped it could, the clerk added, the language of the Fourteenth Amendment itself could be said to be too vague to answer the question at issue—whether segregation of schools was unconstitutional—one way or the other.[13] Once the uncertainty of the Fourteenth Amendment's meaning had been asserted, Frankfurter might more plausibly argue that it should be read to mandate the policy outcome he preferred: a Supreme Court ban on school segregation. Frankfurter, one should note, was then and is now typically characterized as a proponent of "judicial restraint," the idea that judges should allow the democratic process to determine the outcome of policy disputes. Arguing for "judicial restraint" had served his policy preferences well in the 1930s, when conservative activists controlled the federal judiciary and felt free to make policy from the bench. By the 1950s, however, the Revolution of 1937 had left liberals in charge of the Supreme Court, so Frankfurter no longer needed to wear that mask. He now could reconcile himself to the idea of a nakedly political court, and he could be a nakedly political justice.

Frankfurter was not alone on the Court, of course. The chief justice, former California governor Earl Warren, joined Frankfurter in favoring the policy outcome of a ban on school segregation. Unlike Frankfurter, Warren would never hide his devotion to twisting legal provisions and legislative history in favor of his preferred outcomes. He lobbied his colleagues vigorously in the days before the Court's *Brown* and *Bolling* decisions were announced—in a way that recalls the behavior of Chief Justice Roger B. Taney and President James Buchanan in the run-up to *Dred Scott v. Sandford*.[14]

Warren's colleagues needed convincing that this was the right thing to do. When the matter of school segregation was first argued before the Court, the justices had divided nearly evenly.[15] But Chief Justice Fred Vinson's death had provided an opportunity for a new majority. As Vinson's replacement, Warren worked tirelessly to convince his colleagues that they not only should vote to ban school segregation but also should do so unanimously, since it was bound to be a superlatively controversial decision. Such intense lobbying was necessary because the Court's precedents said that school segregation was consistent with the Fourteenth Amendment's intended meaning and thus was constitutional.

Frankfurter was not the only justice who understood this. Pressed on the matter, Justice Robert Jackson circulated a memorandum among his colleagues explaining why he would file a separate opinion concurring in the judgment but rejecting the majority's reasoning: "I simply cannot find, in surveying all the usual sources of law, anything which warrants me in saying that [the Court's decision invalidating school segregation] is required by the original purpose and intent of the Fourteenth or Fifth Amendment." The Court must squarely concede, he insisted, that it was simply "declaring new law for a new day."[16]

There it was: the Court set itself above the Constitution. It would amend it at will. How could one account for this breathtaking arrogation of authority, the Court's assumption of a power that the Constitution, in Article V, had left to the states? As Frankfurter explained in a private memorandum, the original understanding was not alone binding, but "the effect of changes in men's feelings for what is right and just is equally relevant in determining whether a discrimination denies the equal protection of the laws."[17]

How did Frankfurter propose to identify "changes in men's feelings for what is right and just"? He could not have meant for such changes to be identified democratically, because what he intended was for the unelected members of the U.S. Supreme Court to invalidate a plethora of state and local laws enacted by elected state and local legislators. No, he would identify such changes in "men's feelings" by polling justices of the Supreme Court. The Court, then, would serve as America's supreme legislative body, its nine-lawyer membership as a kind of super-Senate.

Why would the justices feel entitled to behave in this way? Because they wanted to, and because they could.

Making a "Judicial Decision out of a Political Conclusion"

While the Supreme Court's ruling in *Brown v. Board of Education* is hailed as a landmark in American history, the fact is that the opinion Chief Justice Warren wrote for the Court contains flawed (even non-existent) legal reasoning and non sequiturs.

Warren had given a foretaste of his thinking on the case the first time he participated in the Court's *Brown* deliberations. "[M]y instincts and feelings," he said then, "lead me to say that, in these cases we should abolish the practice of segregation in the public schools— but in a tolerant way." Here on full display was Warren's practice of, as Justice Abe Fortas put it, placing "human values" first in judging. Fortas noted that "opposition based on the hemstitching and embroidery of the law appeared petty in terms of Warren's basic value approach."[18] In Warren's hands, then, the separation of powers among the branches of the federal government, the division of powers between the federal government and the state governments, and the right of the people alone to amend the Constitution through the Article V processes were "petty." Law, in short, had to yield before moral claims. The justices' oath to uphold the Constitution was as naught before a "basic value approach." If Justice Jackson thought it would be difficult "to make a judicial decision out of a political conclusion," Warren recognized no such distinction.[19]

The *New York Times* headline the day after the decision captured the Court's approach in *Brown*: "A Sociological Decision: Court Founded Its Segregation Ruling on Hearts and Minds Rather than Laws."[20] In other words, *Brown* was not a legal or constitutional decision, but an anti-legal, anti-constitutional one. It was a legislative act, an instance of judicial arrogation of the powers of the Congress and the states to amend the Constitution.

Warren kicked off his and the Court's *Brown* opinion by noting that the question raised by the four cases consolidated here was whether it was constitutional under the Equal Protection Clause to segregate students by race. He said that the Court, after hearing arguments in this matter in 1952, had requested reargument in regard to certain matters in 1954. Warren said that this extensive consideration of the historical record had not answered the question of whether banning segregation in public schools had been among Congress's intentions in drafting the Fourteenth Amendment. That is to say, the chief justice adopted a position compatible with the view law clerk Alexander Bickel had outlined in his report to Justice Frankfurter.

To explain the supposed lack of clarity in the historical record, Warren claimed that there was no public schooling in many areas when the Fourteenth Amendment was adopted, and that in many places where there was public schooling, it was confined to a handful of months per year in ungraded environments and with a rudimentary curriculum. "As a result," he concluded, "it is not surprising that there should be so little in the history of the Fourteenth Amendment relating to its intended effect on public education."

This argument was entirely untrue, however. The reason that the sponsors of the Fourteenth Amendment had not described its intended effect on education was that they did not intend for it to *have* any effect on education. The purpose of the Fourteenth Amendment's first section was to constitutionalize the Civil Rights Act of 1866, which did not extend to blacks' protection of a right to unsegregated education. Indeed, it would have been shocking if Congress, composed of members from a North thoroughly antagonistic to blacks, had done so.

But ultimately, Warren insisted, the Court of 1954 could not be bound by the understanding of people who had lived in 1868, so it must evaluate the situation in light of the role that public education had come to play in American society. "In approaching this problem," he instructed, "we cannot turn the clock back to 1868 when the Amendment was adopted, or even to 1896 when *Plessy v. Ferguson* was written. We must consider public education in the light of its full development and its presence in American life throughout the Nation. Only in this way can it be determined if segregation in public schools deprives these plaintiffs of the equal protection of the laws."[21] Warren's embrace of such a vague standard was the telltale sign that he intended to make "new law for a new day."

Next came a non sequitur paragraph in which Warren lectured on the significance of public education in 1950s America. Public education, according to the chief justice, was "perhaps the most important function of state and local governments." Not police protection. Not fire protection. Not enforcement of contracts. Not punishment of criminals. Public education.

And what effect did segregation of children otherwise given equal facilities have on minority children? "Whatever may have been the extent of psychological knowledge at the time of *Plessy v. Ferguson*," Warren intoned, a finding that segregation in itself depressed black students' ability to learn was "amply supported by modern authority."

What "modern authority" did Warren have in mind? He referred in footnote 11 of his decision to the doll studies of psychologist Kenneth Clark. Clark had asked black students from segregated backgrounds whether they preferred black or white dolls, and the majority of them had selected the white ones. This, according to Clark, demonstrated that segregation hurt blacks' self-image. Yet studies along the same lines using students from nonsegregated backgrounds showed blacks *more* likely to choose the white doll over the black. The sum of the doll studies, then, was that segregation made black students *less* likely to prefer white dolls.

Never mind: Warren needed merely to justify a legislative outcome that he had a predilection to reach, not actually to inquire into the effects of segregated schooling. If he had not had Kenneth

Clark's doll studies at hand, he easily might have based *Brown* on some alternative foundation.

Having ruled that public school segregation violated the Equal Protection Clause, Warren told the contending attorneys to return for arguments concerning the relief to be granted in the case. After all, *Brown* was intended not merely to resolve a dispute involving four school districts in different states but also to spark a revolution in education systems throughout much of the country. The majority therefore put off granting relief to the children who had "won" in *Brown* until at least the following Court term.

Bald-Faced Judicial Imperialism

After disposing of school segregation in the states, the Supreme Court turned immediately to the question of segregated schools in the District of Columbia. The purported basis of the *Brown* decision, the Equal Protection Clause of the Fourteenth Amendment, affected only policies of state (including local) governments, not those of the federal district, which was subject to congressional jurisdiction. Therefore, the Court felt the need to decide that issue separately in *Bolling v. Sharpe* (1954)—or really, it had to devise a different constitutional rationalization for its desired policy outcome.

If *Brown* was a dizzying display of judicial imperialism, *Bolling* was even more unjustified by the actual text of the Constitution, as explained to the people at the time of its ratification. According to Chief Justice Warren in *Bolling*, it was inconceivable that the District of Columbia should continue to have segregated schools after such schools had ceased to be permissible in the states. Besides that, according to Warren, "discrimination may be so unjustifiable as to be violative of due process." Therefore, the Due Process Clause of the Fifth Amendment banned segregation in the District.

Yes, that is what he said: the Fifth Amendment—which was drafted chiefly by James Madison (a substantial slaveholder who never did anything to undermine slavery), referred to the states by a Congress composed largely of slaveholders, and ratified by a number of states firmly devoted to the ongoing enslavement of virtually every person of African descent within their borders—banned the provision of free public school to black people on a segregated basis because school segregation is so unjustifiable as to violate due process.

Infallible?

One Supreme Court justice commented in the twentieth century, "We are not final because we are infallible, but we are infallible only because we are final."[22] His point is valid, in relation both to the flawed thinking that can pervade Supreme Court decisions and to the fact that there is no one to appeal to beyond the Court. So when it came to the Court's decisions in *Brown* and *Bolling*, it seemed at first as if people would simply accept the final authority of the Court. As then-governor Herman Talmadge of Georgia explained in his memoirs many years later, the southern political elite had seen the outcome in *Brown* coming for years and was not even slightly surprised by it.

But sometimes the Court isn't the final authority. Rather than comply with *Brown*, many states and localities actively resisted desegregation for many years. One state declared a formal policy called Massive Resistance. In time, this defiance, joined to the justices' frustration with the limited effects even of good-faith compliance, led the court to shift its mandates for compliance and to impose a far more radical response to the problem than had been contemplated by the *Brown* court.

4

Discriminating to End . . . Discrimination: The Forced Busing Fiascoes

T HE U.S. SUPREME Court's decision in *Brown v. Board of Education* set off a round of constitutional revision by the federal courts, and especially by the Supreme Court, that continues to this day.

In the immediate aftermath, the Court instructed the parties to return the next year for new arguments concerning remedies to the situation. It then ruled in *Brown II* (1955) that segregation of state schools must be brought to an end "with all deliberate speed."[1]

Many segregated jurisdictions adopted a number of devices, including freedom-of-choice plans, to replace segregation in school assignment. In passing the Civil Rights Act of 1964, Congress adopted a policy that "desegregation" was "the assignment of students to public schools and within such schools without regard to their race, color, religion, or national origin" and added the redundant statement that " 'desegregation' shall not mean the assignment of students to public schools in order to overcome racial imbalance."[2]

The Supreme Court, however, disagreed. Rather than accept the outcome of the great sea change in American racial attitudes that occurred in the mid-twentieth century by accepting race-blind school assignment, the Court decided that race must continue to count.

The Court clung fiercely to its new outcome-based policy—one that was obviously unconstitutional—in a series of decisions over the course of many years. This stubborn stance proved to be a disaster for Americans. It led, ultimately, to federal judges' ordering students to be shipped two hours round-trip every day in order to establish a racial balance in the schools that only the judiciary could decide was satisfactory.

This judicial policy making violated traditional American notions of republicanism—the idea that governmental decisions ought to be made by elected officials. And those hurt most of all by judges' relentless efforts at social engineering were the ones who were supposed to be helped in the first place.

Court-Ordered Race Discrimination

By the 1960s, as Congress was passing the Civil Rights Act, the Supreme Court began dealing with the fallout from its 1954 ruling in *Brown v. Board of Education*. In 1968, it took up the issue of freedom-of-choice plans. The case of *Green v. County School Board of New Kent County* involved a freedom-of-choice program that a Virginia county had instituted.[3] Though the county government was not segregating schools on the basis of race and was honoring the Civil Rights Act's stipulation that jurisdictions not assign students to public schools "in order to overcome racial imbalance," the Court decided that this was not good enough. In a sign of things to come, the justices said that freedom of choice must give way to integration—that is, proportional racial mixing. The only way to achieve this Court-imposed goal would be actually to discriminate among students by race. Integration was not desegregation but an alternative to it; it was not nondiscrimination but discrimination for a "benign" purpose.[4]

In 1971, the Supreme Court turned its focus to a different plan meant to achieve integration. North Carolina had instituted a school assignment plan featuring mainly geographic zoning and incorporating a free transfer provision.[5] In other words, in compliance with *Brown*, North Carolina had completely abandoned segregation, ceasing to assign students on the basis of their race and instead assigning them on the basis of residence. If a particular student's parents did not want him to attend the school to which his address led him to be assigned, they could ask that he be reassigned to a different school.

A federal district court had approved the school assignment plan in 1965. But in the wake of the Supreme Court's *Green* decision, the district court ordered the school board in North Carolina's largest city, Charlotte, to come up with a replacement plan. As Chief Justice Warren E. Burger would write in his opinion for the Supreme Court in *Swann v. Charlotte-Mecklenburg Board of Education* (1971), the school assignment plan was inadequate because it "fell short of achieving the unitary school system that those cases [*Green* and its companions] require."[6]

In response to the district court, the Charlotte board proposed a way to ensure that nine of the ten high schools had student bodies that were 17 to 36 percent black, and that the tenth would be 2 percent black. In Burger's description, "The proposed attendance zones for the high schools were typically shaped like wedges of a pie, extending outward from the center of the city to the suburban and rural areas of the county in order to afford residents of the center city area access to outlying schools."

Finding the school board's plan unacceptable, the district court appointed an "expert," Dr. John A. Finger, to devise a new desegregation plan. Finger essentially adopted this part of the board's proposal, except that he provided for more blacks to be bused to the nearly all-white tenth high school. For the earliest grades, he went much further, redrawing attendance zones, grouping suburban and inner-city schools, busing black first- through fourth-graders from the city to the suburban schools, and busing white fifth- and sixth-graders to the city schools. Finger grouped a total of nine inner-city schools with twenty-four suburban schools. In short, the district court had ordered that integration be implemented, and the chief mechanism it insisted on for accomplishing this was forced busing of students.

Note what this meant: among the losers in this scenario would be nonblack students who were bused to what were presumed to be inferior schools. The reason they were to bear this burden was their race. None of the affected children was a wrongdoer even under the innovative understanding of the Equal Protection Clause adopted by the majority in the line of cases culminating in *Green*.

But the Supreme Court disregarded this fundamental problem plaguing the busing scheme that the district court had ordered. Led by Chief Justice Burger, the Court found forced busing to be an acceptable remedy to the supposed problem of racial imbalance in student bodies.

In Burger's view, "segregated education" existed in Charlotte because the schools in the system were racially identifiable. Indeed, throughout his description of the facts in the *Swann* opinion, Burger used the terms "Negro" and "white" to describe the schools, even though legally all of them were open to enrollment by either major race. For Burger, as for the Court in *Green*, there was no difference between a racially identifiable school from which the law excluded a particular race and a racially identifiable school whose student body was drawn mainly from the racially identifiable neighborhoods surrounding it. What mattered, that is, was not the system in place but the racial balance that resulted, even though the Civil Rights Act specifically forbade assigning students on the basis of race to achieve a certain racial balance.

According to Burger, *Brown* stood for the principle that since separate educational facilities were inherently unequal, racial identifiability of schools could not be allowed to exist. Yet, he said, in the fifteen years since the Court's second *Brown* decision, the Supreme Court and inferior federal courts had encountered unexpected difficulties "in implementation of the basic constitutional requirement that the State not discriminate between public school children on the basis of their race."

Burger could not conceivably have meant what he said here. After all, busing white children from suburbs into the city and black children from the city into the suburbs *was* "discriminat[ion] between public school children on the basis of their race." The students who were bused were bused because of their race. If they had been of the other race, they would not have been subjected to this undesirable treatment. That is the essence of discrimination—at least, in non–Supreme Court English.

Burger claimed that dilatory tactics undertaken in bad faith accounted for the fact that the *Brown* mandate had not been fulfilled. This assertion was simply incorrect. The Court still faced such difficulty in 1971 because in 1968 it had created a completely new requirement: rather than simply barring states from segregating students in public schools, it now required them to integrate public schools. States had not been resisting a requirement to integrate in the years between *Brown* and *Green*, because there was no such requirement.

The Court's abruptly changing requirements were just part of an embarrassing record of reversals. With *Swann*, the Court was endorsing forced busing of students as a way to solve the segregation problem, even though during *Brown v. Board of Education*, the NAACP's attorneys had argued that even nine minutes' daily busing harmed black pupils enormously. Similarly, the Supreme Court was now requiring state and local governments to direct the mixing of races in schools, despite the fact that the chief litigator for the NAACP Legal Defense and Education Fund during *Brown* had said that the Constitution required not integration but merely an end to segregation.[7]

That NAACP litigator was none other than Thurgood Marshall, who by the time of *Swann* was a member of the U.S. Supreme Court majority in favor of integration and forced busing.

"To Remedy Past Wrongs"

As the Supreme Court shifted its requirements and positions, it offered vague standards for compliance. In *Green*, the Court said, "The burden on a school board today is to come forward with a plan that promises realistically to work . . . now . . . until it is clear that state-imposed segregation has been completely removed." By "to work," the Court meant "to result in integration"—that is, "to eliminate racial identifiability of schools in the jurisdiction in question." This novel standard left the district court in *Swann* free to mandate extensive busing of students, which surprised Carolinians.

The Court's confusion in this area permeated Burger's opinion in *Swann*. The chief justice repeatedly quoted *Green*'s statement that a formerly segregated system must be converted "to a unitary system in which racial discrimination would be eliminated root and branch." How was this to be achieved? According to Burger, the federal courts were free to craft "equitable remedies," and their discretion in shaping such remedies was very broad.

In order to understand what Burger was saying here, one must have an idea what an "equitable remedy" is. At the time of the North American colonies' settlement, England distinguished between courts of "equity" and common-law courts.[8] An everyday matter for which a plaintiff sought money damages could be heard in a common-law court, but if he wanted a resolution of an ongoing injury and/or one for which money damages could not be an adequate remedy, he might ask for relief from a court of equity.

What kind of ongoing injury might a court of equity resolve, and how? Say, for example, that two farmers own adjacent farms with a stream running through them. The upstream farmer dams the stream, which significantly reduces the flow of water to the downstream farm. The farmer downstream, whose access to water has been impaired by his neighbor, has a legal claim, but money damages will not solve the problem, because the injury is ongoing. He needs a court to order his neighbor to remove the dam. An equity court can solve his problem.

Traditionally, courts of equity had discretion to grant far-reaching remedies to injured parties. In America, almost every state has eliminated the distinction between common-law and equity courts. The federal system makes no distinction between courts of equity and common-law courts, but allows federal district courts to grant equitable or legal relief as seems appropriate. In Burger's *Swann* decision, the chief justice said that the district court in North Carolina had wide-ranging powers to grant relief, "for breadth and flexibility are inherent in equitable remedies."

Of course, one element of traditional English, and thus of American, law was that only the malefactor found responsible for the plaintiff's injury would be punished. One reason the Boston Port Act of 1774 so offended moderate patriots such as John Adams, for example, is that it punished not just the offenders— participants in the Boston Tea Party—but other residents of Boston and New England, as well. In crafting equitable "remedies" for school segregation, federal courts necessarily would run afoul of the traditional idea that courts should target the guilty and not inflict their punishments on a broad class of people—such as, say, children of the same race as the guilty. The problem was that once schools had been segregated, the people who had been harmed by segregation could not be brought back into second grade, seventh grade, or tenth grade and given an unsegregated education, nor could the beneficiaries of past segregation be made to surrender the benefits of that system.

Leave aside the fact that prior to *Brown*, the Court had said that segregation was legal and prior to *Green*, it had not required integration—in other words, leave aside the fact that at the time the student assignment process in Charlotte-Mecklenburg was devised, it complied fully with the Supreme Court's latest requirements. Even if that were not true and the plans being "corrected" in *Swann* had been unconstitutional, forced busing of students on a racial basis punished not those who supposedly had committed the violation, but completely innocent children. It did so, in addition, not by eliminating discrimination "root and branch," as Burger put it, but precisely by discriminating among students on a racial basis. To what end? "To remedy past wrongs."

How could a court, via equitable remedies, "remedy past wrongs" associated with racial segregation? How, indeed, could a court identify segregation's effects? The Court assumed, as in *Green*, that one manifestation of segregation's harm was the pervasive racial identifiability of schools. But this was a false assumption: schools commonly are racially and/or ethnically identifiable throughout the country because neighborhoods commonly are identifiable. Typically this is the result not of any particular government policy but of the fact that people—whether Greek in Chicago, Puerto Rican in New York, Mexican in Austin, or Polish in New Britain—often prefer to live among members of the same ethnic group. Even where the affected groups are the same as those involved in the original "unconstitutional" decisions, the affected *families* may well be different from the original ones. This was especially important in *Swann*, because, as Burger noted, there had been significant population movement in Charlotte-Mecklenburg.

Burger's opinion overlooked the practical, everyday reality that jurisdictions that had never been intentionally segregated by government would still have racially identifiable neighborhoods and thus racially identifiable schools. Elected school board members could not ignore the fact that the racial makeup of particular neighborhoods reflected people's voluntary decisions. An unelected federal judge, however, could consider the newly concocted "constitutional" requirement that schools not be racially identifiable in isolation from people's preferences. As Burger explained, federal courts had the power to craft equitable remedies as extensive as they desired.

The problem here, of course, is that a "remedy" of this type could not, by its nature, be distinguished from a wide-ranging act of legislation. To redraw multiple school districts' pupil-assignment plans was far more a legislative function than a judicial one, and this in an area in which the qualifications of a typical federal district judge—a law degree and some connection to a powerful politician—were of little use. The Supreme Court's guidance in this case cannot have given much assistance, for even as Burger said that administrators must not discriminate among students on a racial basis in assigning them to schools, he added that they might attempt to achieve an equal black-white ratio in each school "in order to prepare students to live in a pluralistic society." Apparently Burger did not realize that one could not assign students on a racial basis with that goal in mind without inflicting a disadvantage on some students on the basis of their race.

Rewriting the Civil Rights Act

One of the more disturbing aspects of the Supreme Court's endorsement of forced busing was the fact that *the Civil Rights Act of 1964 had specifically forbidden court-ordered busing schemes to achieve racial balance.*

The North Carolina authorities had raised this very issue in the *Swann* case. As noted, the Civil Rights Act explicitly stated that desegregation could not be taken to mean "the assignment of students to public schools in order to overcome racial imbalance." Even beyond that, the act said:

> Nothing herein shall empower any official or court of the United States to issue any order seeking to achieve a racial balance in any school by requiring the transportation of pupils or students from one school to another or one school district to another in order to achieve such racial balance, or otherwise enlarge the existing power of the court to insure compliance with constitutional standards.

Chief Justice Burger tried to explain away this language. "On their face," he said, "the sections quoted purport only to insure that the provisions of Title IV of the Civil Rights Act of 1964 will not be read as granting new powers." He added that the "Nothing herein shall empower . . ." proviso was "designed to foreclose any interpretation of the Act as expanding the existing powers of federal courts to enforce the Equal Protection Clause. There is no suggestion of an intention to restrict those powers or withdraw from courts their historic equitable remedial powers."

Typically, Burger's explanation was false. The purpose of that section was to foreclose precisely the possibility that a federal court might order busing of students in an enormous area such as Charlotte-Mecklenburg (550 square miles, 101 schools) for racial balance.[9] During congressional debate over the Civil Rights Act of 1964, the act's proponents had insisted that southern opponents of the act had misconstrued it. This provision, they maintained, guaranteed that there would be no large-scale busing. That, they said, would involve "transporting children because of their race" and thus would be unconstitutional.[10]

Also untrue was Burger's claim that this section of the Civil Rights Act pertained only to situations in which "segregation" was not the result of government policy. Why, indeed, would southern members of Congress have been concerned to preclude race-based busing in such circumstances, when virtually their entire region had had a forthright policy of legal segregation, and so would not be protected by such a provision?

Having mischaracterized the Civil Rights Act in this way, Burger concluded that "there is nothing in the Act that provides us material assistance in answering the question of remedy for state-imposed segregation in violation of Brown I." So once again, unelected judges overrode the will of the people.

"Awkward, Inconvenient, and Even Bizarre"

Once he dispensed with the Civil Rights Act, Burger turned to the issue of the standards the Court intended to impose on school systems that formerly had been officially segregated. These requirements, the chief justice insisted, flowed from the Equal Protection Clause. "The first remedial responsibility of school authorities" in such jurisdictions, Burger said, "is to eliminate invidious racial distinctions."

Taking up a related case in Mobile, Alabama, Burger noted that that city's school board asserted that the Constitution (meaning *Brown*) required "that teachers be assigned on a 'color blind' basis. It also argues that the Constitution prohibits district courts from using their equity power to order assignment of teachers to achieve a particular degree of faculty desegregation. We reject that contention." It seems that the authorities in Mobile, like those in many other localities, had made the mistake of taking the language of *Brown* and the Civil Rights Act seriously.

The Court was about to correct this error.

It did so by restoring the lower court's order that the Mobile authorities adopt a quota for minority hiring of teachers in each school. The goal, the Court said, was to create "a unified, unitary, nondiscriminatory school system." So once again, a quota was necessary to create a "nondiscriminatory school system."

Turning to the issue at hand in *Swann*, Burger said that local authorities' decisions about where to build new schools or close old ones had reinforced the desired racial segregation. Locating new schools in expanding white areas far from black neighborhoods or closing schools in areas seemingly bound to become mixed-race over time may, "when combined with 'neighborhood zoning,' further lock the school system into the mold of separation of the races." Thus, Burger said, federal courts might use their equitable powers to "correct" this "problem" by dictating to local communities where their facilities should be located. Notably, the chief justice had already conceded that building new schools and closing old ones were "two of the most important functions of local school authorities." Apparently, silly matters such as the principles of federalism and republicanism, not to mention constitutionalism, can be dismissed when there is a higher ideal in mind.

Burger made a telling admission when he wrote, "Absent a constitutional violation, there would be no basis for judicially ordering assignment of students on a racial basis. All things being equal, with no history of discrimination, it might be desirable to assign pupils to schools nearest their homes." If there had not been segregation in the past, in other words, the Court perhaps would not think there should be discrimination in the future. Since there has been racial segregation, however, the Court will have remedies that "may be administratively awkward, inconvenient, and even bizarre."

Up Is Down

Soon after the Supreme Court handed down its decision in *Swann*, busing as a tool for accomplishing "desegregation" spread throughout the country—to southern cities where once there had been official school segregation, to northern cities where school segregation long ago had given way, and even to cities where segregation had always been banned.

Federal courts' use of "equitable" power—the power to issue orders unrelated to particular statutory language—spun completely out of control. In time, federal judges would take over entire school districts and would even order statewide tax increases in attempts to foster racial balance across school districts and metropolitan regions. Popular opposition to busing blossomed.

The first Supreme Court busing case involving a jurisdiction outside the South was 1973's *Keyes v. School District No. One, Denver, Colorado*.[11] Denver had always prohibited segregation, and in fact it had been well ahead of the Supreme Court in moving to implement integration.[12] How, then, could the federal courts be in the business of "correcting" bygone violations of the supposed Fourteenth Amendment ban on school segregation in Denver?

As legal scholar Lino Graglia shows, they could not. What happened instead was that a lower court held that the Court's "remedy" idea applied to part of Denver, and then the Supreme Court ruled that the entire city must be visited with the burden of race-based busing.

If, as the Court conceded, Denver had never had statutory segregation of schools, how had it violated the *Brown* mandate against segregation? By not intentionally integrating, the Court claimed. For example, in one instance, the city had built a school in a black neighborhood with full knowledge that locating it there would lead to its having a predominantly black student body. The decision to build a school in a neighborhood where its student body would be overwhelmingly black reinforced the tendency of schools in non-black neighborhoods to have non-black student bodies, Justice William Brennan reasoned; this amounted to willful segregation in violation of the Court's *Green-Swann* reading of the Equal Protection Clause of the Fourteenth Amendment.

What remedy recommended itself? Why, citywide busing of students for racial balance, of course. The federal district court had adopted such a plan, but the federal circuit court of appeals had vacated the order on the grounds that it violated the Civil Rights Act's ban on use of busing to achieve racial balance. The circuit court's opinion had, however, come before Chief Justice Burger's helpful explanation in *Swann* that the Civil Rights Act's limitation on the use of busing had not been intended to restrict federal courts' use of busing. Justice Brennan, then, had no difficulty in overturning the circuit court's action.

Brennan said that Denver had intentionally segregated a particular portion of the city, a black portion; in doing so, he relied on the finding of the district court. The district court had erred in that regard, though. Denver had not been involved in segregation, as defined in *Brown* and banned by the Civil Rights Act.

The district judge had based his decision chiefly on a single school out of more than one hundred in the Denver system.[13] The city had chosen a site for this institution, the Barrett Elementary School, in 1958; by the time the school opened two years later, intervening demographic changes had left it with a student body 89.6 percent black. The district court found that by locating Barrett there and failing to use it to relieve overcrowding in a predominantly white school nearby, the school board had "acted purposefully to create and maintain segregation at Barrett."

The Denver school board, of course, had done nothing more than assign children to neighborhood schools; it was only natural, and certainly not sinister, that the student bodies tended to reflect the racial makeups of the neighborhoods where the schools were located. But in the new up-is-down, in-is-out legal regime the Court had created in *Green* and *Swann*—in which "segregation" was suddenly defined as doing *anything* that tended to maintain the racial identifiability of schools—the school board was branded as a bunch of segregators.

Oddly enough, the reason Denver came before the federal courts in the first place was that early in 1969 the school board, acting on its own initiative, had investigated a busing plan. But then the city's voters threw out the board members responsible for that plan in the 1969 elections—that is, Denver's electorate decided against elected officials' plans for integration on the basis of race. Afterward, the board rescinded the busing plan. And one district judge, acting alone, ruled that this board decision amounted to acting intentionally to keep the races separate. As Lino Graglia puts it, "Under the unique system of American government, . . . a victory at the polls remains a victory only so long as it is not disapproved by the courts—a function performed in some other systems by the military."

So if Denver had either not built a new elementary school to serve black students in a black neighborhood or not considered busing to achieve racial balance before finally rejecting that idea, the city would not have been stigmatized as a haven for segregationists or penalized by the federal judiciary. In other words, good intentions joined to good deeds were Denver's crime.

And Denver's schoolchildren would pay the price for the board's dastardly deeds.

From Integration to White Flight

As a penalty for its supposed segregation, the entire Denver school system was placed under a federal receivership—a situation in which a federal judge would oversee the massive busing scheme. To help implement the Supreme Court's decision, the district judge called in a renowned expert on busing: none other than John Finger, the same fellow who had concocted the Charlotte plan. Soon enough, the Rocky Mountains' chief city had a busing plan much like that of North Carolina's chief city.

The unintended consequences of the *Keyes* decision ran directly counter to what the Supreme Court's integration policy was meant to achieve: by 1974, the schools in the Denver system had 30 per- cent *fewer* white pupils than they had in 1969. With forced busing, the Court had tried to force a specific mix of races in schools. But all the busing controversy ensured was a quick exodus of white students from the system.[14]

The busing issue was, if anything, more polarizing in other cities— and in the politics of the United States at large. It became a major element of Republican presidential candidacies from Richard Nixon through the elder George Bush, and it seriously divided communities at the local level. By the time busing began to be abandoned—by the time federal courts declared "victory" and retreated—white flight had left the majority of American cities mostly black.[15]

Members of Alaska's congressional delegation insisted that despite the recent devastation wrought on the Gulf Coast by Hurricane Katrina, their state was entitled to this expenditure. Mississippi's similarly absurd Railroad to Nowhere drew far less scrutiny than did the Alaska bridge, even though that price tag was more than $700 million.

Since Congress was dominated by Republicans at the time, critics in Democratic and media circles (if there was any distinction) responded with shock—shock!—that there should be prostitution in the bordello. But such wastefulness is a bipartisan vice. Just look at Boston's Big Dig, a highway/tunnel project approved when Democrats controlled Congress. Initially envisioned as a $3.3 billion project, by 2003 it had ballooned into a $14.3 billion boondoggle, and the end of the expense was nowhere in sight.[1]

Why did Congress spend so irresponsibly on these projects? Simply put, that is where all the incentives are. Since the vast majority of the funding for these projects is provided by the federal government (read: not by the hometown congressman's constituents), and since local media can be counted on to credit the congressman for "bringing home the bacon" to his district (read: his constituents), there is every reason for the self-serving congressman to maximize pork spending in his district. The more powerful the congressman, the more spending his district receives. Is it any wonder, then, that Boston's Big Dig was begun while Thomas P. "Tip" O'Neill (of "All politics is local" infamy) was Speaker of the House, or that Alaska's senior senator, Ted Stevens, was chairman of the Appropriations Committee when it funded the Bridge to Nowhere?

The outrage over these exorbitant taxpayer-funded projects is understandable. The simple fact that such dubious public works projects carry sky-high price tags at a time when other needed improvements—such as the Minneapolis bridge—are passed over is enough to disgust most Americans. But a much more fundamental question is no longer asked: is it even constitutional for the federal government to spend tax dollars on these public improvements?

5

Roads to Nowhere

On August 1, 2007, the eight-lane Interstate 35W bridge over the Mississippi River in Minneapolis, Minnesota, collapsed into the river. The Associated Press reported the next day that more than sixty people had been killed or hurt and as many as fifty vehicles had fallen into the river.

The public soon learned that the bridge had been identified as in need of extraordinary attention years earlier, and President George W. Bush's spokesman said that the state of Minnesota bore responsibility for the bridge's maintenance. Within days, politicians of both parties insisted that all "finger-pointing" should be avoided in reconstructing the bridge; the idea of responsibility, by bipartisan agreement, was passé.

This episode followed hard on the heels of controversies over federal pork barrel projects such as the "Bridge to Nowhere" and the "Railroad to Nowhere." In 2005–6 Americans discovered the extent to which members of Congress were inserting massive earmarks into federal appropriations bills. The example that sparked the most outrage was for a bridge connecting a 9,000-person village in Alaska to a 50-person island, which was already served by ferry service dozens of times per day. The cost to federal taxpayers: more than $200 million.

The very question seems perplexing today. But the fact is that for much of American history it seemed clear to most American leaders that such federal spending was *not* constitutional. Thomas Jefferson thought you needed to amend the Constitution if you wanted the federal government to spend tax dollars on roads. So did James Madison. So did James Monroe. So did Andrew Jackson.

These men and many others scrutinized road-building legislation for constitutionality; today, the subject of constitutionality is scarcely ever raised. That alone tells a story of what has happened to our government and the constitution that was supposed to bind it.

When and why did concern for the Constitution disappear?

Jefferson, Madison, and the Constitution

The idea of federal sponsorship of road building was raised by Presidents Thomas Jefferson and James Madison at the beginning of the nineteenth century. Jefferson, in his 1806 State of the Union address, urged the federal government to spend its surplus on road and canal projects and other public improvements, since "by these operations new channels of communications will be opened between the States, the lines of separation will disappear, their interests will be identified, and their union cemented by new and indissoluble ties."[2] But he stated explicitly that the federal government could not go forward with these public projects without "an amendment to the Constitution, by consent of the States," because "the objects now recommended are not among those enumerated in the Constitution, and to which it permits the public moneys to be applied."

Jefferson's successor as president, Madison, also called for such spending, and with exactly the same caveat. In his annual message of 1815, he declared:

Among the means of advancing the public interest the occasion is a proper one for recalling the attention of Congress to the great importance of establishing throughout our country the roads and canals which can best be executed under the national authority. No objects within the circle of political economy so richly repay the expense bestowed on them; there are none the utility of which is more universally ascertained and acknowledged; none that do more honor to the governments whose wise and enlarged patriotism duly appreciates them. Nor is there any country which presents a field where nature invites more the art of man to complete his own work for his accommodation and benefit. These considerations are strengthened, moreover, by the political effect of these facilities for intercommunication in bringing and binding more closely together the various parts of our extended confederacy. Whilst the states individually, with a laudable enterprise and emulation, avail themselves of their local advantages by new roads, by navigable canals, and by improving the streams susceptible of navigation, the General Government is the more urged to similar undertakings, requiring a national jurisdiction and national means, by the prospect of thus systematically completing so inestimable a work.[3]

Lest his audience misunderstand, President Madison reminded them of the amendment process outlined in Article V of the Constitution: "It is a happy reflection that any defect of constitutional authority which may be encountered can be supplied in a mode which the Constitution itself has providently pointed out."[4]

But his audience *did* misapprehend his message. Leading War Hawks in the House, the men who had only recently urged Madison into the War of 1812 and helped Madison follow up on that war by chartering a second Bank of the United States in 1816, pushed for the so-called Bonus Bill. This legislation would apply the government's share of the profit from the Bank toward internal improvements—what in our day would be called "infrastructure." Speaker of the House Henry Clay and Foreign Affairs Committee

Chairman John C. Calhoun believed that in pushing the legislation through the House of Representatives, they were implementing Madison's will. Imagine their surprise, then, when Madison, in his last official act as president, vetoed the bill.

Not only did Madison veto the Bonus Bill, but he also issued the Bonus Bill veto message, explaining how the Constitution was to be interpreted.

The Bonus Bill Veto Message

In his veto message, Madison set out a reading of the Constitution that seemed ripped out of the pages of history, echoing as it did the Madison of 1791. Here was Madison, the champion of the bill chartering the second Bank of the United States in 1816, harking back to the argument against the first bank bill's constitutionality he had used in the House in 1791.

According to the Madison of 1817, "I am constrained by the insuperable difficulty I feel in reconciling the bill with the Constitution of the United States to return it with that objection to the House of Representatives, in which it originated."[5] Why? As Madison put it, "The legislative powers vested in Congress are specified and enumerated in the eighth section of the first article of the Constitution, and it does not appear that the power proposed to be exercised by the bill is among the enumerated powers, or that it falls by any just interpretation within the power to make laws necessary and proper for carrying into execution those or other powers vested by the Constitution in the Government of the United States."

In plain English, Madison was saying that Congress had only a few powers. Those powers, his contemporaries knew, were listed in Article I, Section 8 of the Constitution. The power to build roads, bridges, and canals was not among them. Neither was it covered by the Necessary and Proper Clause at the end of Article I, Section 8, because road building was not incidental to the exercise of any of the enumerated powers. Thus Congress did not have the power to appropriate money for the construction of "internal improvements" projects.

Madison had heard the argument that the Commerce Clause of Article I, Section 8, which says, "The Congress shall have power . . . [t]o regulate commerce with foreign nations, and among the several states, and with the Indian tribes," gave Congress power to finance roads, bridges, and canals. He would have none of it. "'The power to regulate commerce among the several States' can not include a power to construct roads and canals, and to improve the navigation of water courses in order to facilitate, promote, and secure such a commerce," he wrote, "without a latitude of construction departing from the ordinary import of the terms strengthened by the known inconveniences which doubtless led to the grant of this remedial power to Congress."

As we shall see, this straightforward statement of the obvious by one of the Constitution's chief authors would eventually be rejected as a test for interpreting the Commerce Clause.

Perhaps the most significant passage in Madison's veto message came as he considered the idea that the General Welfare Clause provided Congress with power to fund roads and canals. Taking up the more general question of how the grants of power to Congress in Article I, Section 8 were to be read, he wrote: "To refer the power in question to the clause 'to provide for the common defense and general welfare' would be contrary to the established and consistent rules of interpretation, as rendering the special and careful enumeration of powers which follow the clause nugatory and improper." His point was that since the Constitution provided a list of specific congressional powers, it followed that Congress must not have a general power to do whatever it wanted to do. It would have made no sense for the Constitution's authors to say, "Congress may do a, b, and c, plus whatever it wants."

A broad reading of the General Welfare Clause, Madison held, "would have the effect of giving to Congress a general power of legislation instead of the defined and limited one hitherto understood to belong to them, the terms 'common defense and general welfare' embracing every object and act within the purview of a legislative trust. It would have the effect of subjecting both the Constitution and laws of the several States in all cases not specifically exempted to be superceded by laws of Congress," since the Supremacy Clause made congressional legislation "the supreme law of the land."

Most important in Madison's mind, it seems, was the effect that such a broad reading of the General Welfare Clause would have on the structure of the federal system. If Congress were empowered to do anything it judged to be conducive to the general welfare, Madison explained, the Supreme Court would be stripped of its intended role in maintaining the line between state and federal legislative authority. And the government could not succeed if the distinction between state and federal legislative authority collapsed, he said.

Madison concluded his message by saying he still supported a federal program of road building and canal digging and by recommending a constitutional solution to the lack of congressional power to initiate such a program. Echoing the call for a constitutional amendment he had made in his 1815 annual message, he counseled that a federal public improvements program "may be attained by a resort for the necessary powers to the same wisdom and virtue in the nation which established the Constitution in its actual form and providently marked out in the instrument itself a safe and practicable mode of improving it as experience might suggest." As we shall see, however, his endorsement of an amendment empowering the federal government never bore fruit.

Farewell to the Constitution

The Bonus Bill veto message was a kind of constitutional valedictory, one that would remain important in many people's understanding of the question of federally funded infrastructure projects through the rest of the nineteenth century. It remained dogma for the Virginia Republicans, and their heirs the Democrats, for generations after.

British historian Gabriel Roth calculates that at least eight of the fifteen pre-Civil War presidents adjudged federal road and canal projects to be unconstitutional. In addition to Jefferson and Madison, Roth points to the other presidents who vetoed internal improvements projects on constitutional grounds: James Monroe (one veto), Andrew Jackson (five), John Tyler (two), James K. Polk (two), Franklin Pierce (seven), and James Buchanan (one).

Of course, even in those days there were vocal proponents of unfettered federal spending on transportation projects. Then as now, however, those advocates were chiefly motivated by political empire building more than the common good. Consider Henry Clay's "American System."[6] In 1824, several years after co-sponsoring the Bonus Bill, Clay unveiled his grand program, a series of interlocking proposals for a federal bank, protective tariffs, and internal improvements for the Northeast and West. Clay conceded that the South would bear the chief burden of his program, but he forecast that southerners were patriotic enough to do so. He clearly thought that the American System would make him president. Although he miscalculated, his idea was not unique, as we see contemporary politicians continue to try to win popularity and power by spending federal tax dollars.

For the most part, Clay and his allies fought a losing battle until the South seceded. Only then did Congress, now dominated by northerners essentially hostile to the idea of constitutional limits on federal power, adopt an array of legislation providing federal funds for internal improvements.[7] Even then, however, this funding was very limited: only $17 million was spent on it by 1891.

Not until 1916 and 1921 did Congress set up the federal road program that remains essentially in effect today, with the states responsible for upkeep of their roads and the federal government providing the lion's share of the funding.

The truly profound change came in 1956 with the Federal-Aid Highway Act, when Congress set up the Interstate Highway System at the urging of President Dwight D. Eisenhower.

What of the traditional constitutional objections to such federal programs? They played precious little role in the congressional debate on the bill.

But is it possible that the seemingly inoffensive Interstate Highway System was actually unconstitutional?

"National Defense"?

The lack of congressional debate over the highway bill reflected the sea change in America's constitutional culture that had occurred in the twentieth century. Consider, for example, that early in the century it seemed obvious to those who championed prohibition of alcoholic beverages that the federal government could impose this novel policy on all the states only through a constitutional amendment, and so the Eighteenth Amendment was adopted and ratifed. Yet when various other products were banned later in the century, Congress felt perfectly at liberty to ban them without any amendment empowering it to do so.

The greatest impetus behind federal involvement in road building came, unsurprisingly, at the height of the New Deal. President Franklin Roosevelt thought in 1935 that construction of roads would be a logical addition to his public works program. After all, people had been paid for literally digging holes in the ground in the morning and filling them back in the same afternoon, so why not redirect their energies toward road construction?

According to a story in the *Washington Post* for February 20, 1935, "The President emphasized the self-liquidating phase of the road program. He explained the Government could buy broad tracts flanking the highways and obtain the benefit from the increased property valuation." This helped to explain, the article continued, the fact that the public works bill pending in Congress included an eminent domain provision authorizing the purchase of land.[8]

How would the government profit from purchase and resale of lands on projected highway paths it had purchased at market prices? It would not. Rather, it would condemn the properties under the power of eminent domain, pay sub-market prices for them, and then sell them at market prices. As was typical of New Deal measures, this idea was both economically and constitutionally dubious.

When Roosevelt proposed the matter publicly on February 15, 1936, he described his road-building scheme as "a national-defense and business pump-priming measure."[9]

National defense? Would spending federal money on roads serve some sort of military purpose?

No.

By 1939, an administration official would admit that the federal government had spent virtually nothing on military roads in the previous year.[10] Including the phrase "national defense" seems, then, to have been an attempt to put a constitutional gloss on the federal power grab. At that point the Supreme Court was still insisting that the Constitution actually did establish a boundary between state and federal legislative authority, but the courts long had been loath to impede the other two branches of the federal government from fulfilling their responsibility for national defense. Simply put, invoking "national defense" was a bit of clever packaging.

Roosevelt's real interest in building roads, it seems, was as part of his jobs program. The administration official who spoke of the lack of spending on military roads also revealed that federal expenditures on "roads and streets" had done precious little in regard to "betterments or pavement itself." Instead, "unemployment relief" often took pride of place in federal planning.[11]

When President Roosevelt presented Congress with a plan for a few regional superhighways, he couched it in an analysis of the problem of urban decay. He explained that the advent of automobiles had enabled people to move out of cities and commute to work.

"The former homes of the transferred population have descended by stages to . . . form the city's slums." If the federal government did not immediately undertake a road-building program, he claimed, it might later find that new construction aimed at clearing slums had obstructed the best routes for highway construction. Another benefit to be obtained by adopting his administration's program, Roosevelt concluded, was that the road construction projects would take employment to the affected areas, which tended to be depressed.[12]

In short, Roosevelt intended to build the entire highway network on the superstructure of his planned federal role in urban renewal. The president even admitted that there was no great need outside cities for augmenting American highways' capacity; as a Department of Transportation historian explained, "traffic demand was not the driving force behind the rural interstate beginnings."[13]

"Federal Paternalism"

From the early 1940s through the inauguration of Dwight D. Eisenhower in 1953, as the United States was distracted first by World War II and then by the Korean War, the federal government spent little on road programs. That changed in 1954, when Eisenhower proposed a marked expansion in federal highway spending. The president called for a national system of highways that encompassed some 41,000 miles of roads. He championed them as the "Interstate and National Defense Highways." Once again, we see the invocation of the phrase "national defense," which, as one scholar notes, was probably used "to strengthen the constitutional case for federal financing" of roads.[14]

What constitutional case could be made? Since it was Congress that would push through Eisenhower's plan (by means of the Federal-Aid Highway Act), one would have to believe that the power to build roads for military transportation might be seen as included in the "emanations" of "penumbras" of Congress's power to raise armies.[15]

On its own, this would be a dubious argument. But when Vice President Richard Nixon, speaking in Eisenhower's behalf, explained the president's case for the federal highway system, he said that the nation needed "a grand plan for a properly articulated system that solves the problems of speedy, safe, transcontinental travel—intercity communication—access highways and farm-to-market movement—metropolitan area congestion—bottlenecks and parking."[16] Notice what went unmentioned: the supposed military utility of the program that had been invoked to give federal road spending at least a patina of constitutionality.

Senator Harry F. Byrd of Virginia found much to decry in the president's proposal. To begin, he called Eisenhower's proposal to dedicate the gas tax to highway spending a nonstarter. Never before in American history had a federal tax been put in a "lockbox," dedicated to particular future expenditures. Not only that, Byrd said, but one Congress could not bind a later Congress to use money for any particular purpose.

In addition, Byrd said, "this substitute . . . turns over to the Federal Government absolute control over 40,000 miles of our most important roads heretofore under the control of the 48 states. This plan would be the greatest single step yet taken toward Federal paternalism."[17]

Despite such objections, Congress agreed to undertake a program very similar to the one Eisenhower had recommended. Which was very similar to that which Henry Clay had advocated 130 years before. And the constitutional reform that paved the way for this innovation was . . . nothing. What had changed between the time of Thomas Jefferson and James Madison and the time of Dwight D. Eisenhower? Only that federal officials had accepted the New Deal assumption that all a federal official needed to justify a particular act was the desire to undertake it. The Constitution, as a limitation on federal authority, as a guarantee of federalism, had died.

6

The Great Gold Robbery of 1933

IN MARCH 1933, the federal government declared the existence of a banking emergency that required a swift and sweeping response. It would not be the last time that American leaders used the pretext of emergency to consolidate their power. But the federal government's actions in this instance—confiscating American citizens' gold—amounted to an especially egregious power grab. Americans were forced to hand over all their gold, assuming it would be returned after the economic crisis had passed. The federal government, however, hid its intentions every step of the way, never returned the gold, and began its career of inflation that has harmed Americans ever since. And the average American high school student has no idea any of this even happened.

By seizing Americans' gold, the federal government committed yet another offense against the U.S. Constitution. This constitutional assault involved not merely a Supreme Court run amok, a foolish or evil Congress, or an activist president wielding extraordinary power, but all of these things. The much-ballyhooed "separation of powers" between executive, legislative, and judicial branches did nothing to protect the liberties of the people.

Saving the Banking System, or Destroying It?

As the standard tale would have it, President Franklin D. Roosevelt set about saving the banking system upon taking office in 1933. There is, however, one fairly important question normally passed over in discussions of this period in American history: *why* was there a banking emergency?

The answer, as simple and obvious as it is neglected, is that the banks had been operating on what in any other industry would be considered an unsound basis. They were lending out money that they were supposed to have on hand for depositors. That can work as long as the people's basic trust in the banks is not disturbed. But when something happens that alerts people to the unsoundness of the banks or that makes them think the banks may be especially shaky and vulnerable, people rush to withdraw their money, concerned that not all depositors' claims will be satisfied. That is what happened in the 1930s: the chickens had come home to roost, in the form of people demanding cash from their accounts, to which they had a clear moral claim.

When you put $100 in your checking account, you have access to that money on demand, whenever you want. These are *demand deposits*. When you put $100 in something like a certificate of deposit, on the other hand, you have access to that money only three months from now, or six months, or a year, or whenever the maturity date is. (You can access it earlier than the maturity date if you must, but only with a penalty.) This is a *time deposit*: you can get your money back not on demand but only after the passage of some specified amount of time. During that time, the bank lends out your money, but collects it back from lenders by the time of your maturity date so it will be available for you to withdraw.

What has taken place throughout much of American history is the conflation of these two different kinds of banking. Even though demand deposits are supposed to be available to depositors on demand, bankers lend 90 percent of them out anyway, confident that the 10 percent they keep on reserve will be enough to satisfy the typical demands for redemption—most people leave the bulk of their money in the bank, using checks to carry out financial transactions, and generally do not withdraw large sums of cash from their bank balances. But when a bank run occurs and an unusual proportion of depositors come demanding their money, all bets are off.

Throughout American history, the dollar had been defined as approximately one-twentieth of an ounce of gold. Strictly speaking, the gold was really the money, and the paper dollars that people generally used merely represented the money. These money substitutes were used for convenience in lieu of the precious metal. The paper notes could be redeemed for gold at any time.

Governments have often granted special privileges to banks, particularly the right to suspend specie payment. That is a technical way of saying that when more people come demanding their gold than the banks can satisfy with the gold on hand, the government declares it to be perfectly legal for the banks to refuse to honor their clients' legitimate demands for some period of time, sometimes years. No other industry is allowed to function like this: if a dry cleaner could not produce his client's clothes on demand, he would not be legally granted a two-year window to do so, with his customers simply out of luck in the meantime. If anything, state propaganda is usually able to persuade the general public that the real scoundrels are not the bankers but rather the depositors, whose perfectly justifiable and sensible desire to withdraw funds from an untrustworthy bank is made to appear wicked and unpatriotic.

Although you are liable to be considered a crank if any of this strikes you as strange, opposition to fractional-reserve banking has not been unusual at all throughout history, and critics of the practice today are actually in very good company. Roman law, one of the building blocks of Western civilization, made a clear distinction between demand deposits and time deposits, and penalized bankers who lent out demand deposits that were supposed to be

available to depositors at all times.[1] The Late Scholastics, sixteenth-
and seventeenth-century scholars who have been called the Founders
of modern scientific economics, generally opposed it.[2] In the eighteenth century, David Hume, the Scottish philosopher, economist,
and historian, wrote against the practice. Following the Panic of
1819 in the United States, many leading monetary theorists advocated a system of 100 percent reserve banking.[3]

Reforming this system, admitting that it might bear some responsibility for financial instability, or even just being honest with
the American population about how the banks operated were not
options that the political establishment was willing to pursue in
1933, when Franklin Roosevelt took office. To the contrary, Americans were told that still more sacrifices and transfers of power to
government and banks were called for in order to preserve what was
assumed to be a perfectly fine system.

It was then that the federal government ordered the confiscation
of Americans' gold on the spurious grounds that such action was necessary to fight the Depression. Trivial amounts could be retained for
ornamental or industrial purposes, but all monetary gold had to be
handed over to the government. If the government had suddenly imposed on Americans a paper currency that was not convertible into
any precious metal but that could be inflated at the whim of politicians, Americans would be liable to flee into gold if they still had access to it. With gold having been seized from them and ultimately
de-monetized, Americans would find it much more difficult to cope
when paper money inflation reduced the value of their earnings and
savings. And that is just the way the federal government, and indeed
all governments, liked it.

Grabbing for Gold

The process by which Americans were divested of their gold occurred
over the course of numerous legislative enactments and executive

orders, so we shall focus our attention only on some of the most pertinent. It began with the Emergency Banking Act, which Congress approved on March 9, 1933, after only the most trivial debate. Among other things, the act retroactively approved the president's closing of private banks throughout the country for several days the previous week, an act that he had not bothered to justify and for which he had possessed no constitutional or statutory authority. It gave the secretary of the Treasury the power to require all individuals and corporations to hand over all their gold coin, gold bullion, or gold certificates if in his judgment "such action is necessary to protect the currency system of the United States."

Furthermore, the Emergency Banking Act amended the Trading with the Enemy Act of 1917, which originally had been intended to criminalize economic intercourse between American citizens and declared enemies of the United States. One provision of the act granted the president the power to regulate and even prohibit "under such rules and regulations as he may prescribe . . . any transactions in foreign exchange, export or earmarkings of gold or silver coin or bullion or currency . . . by any person within the United States." In 1918, the act was amended to extend its provisions two years beyond the conclusion of hostilities and to allow the president to "investigate, regulate, or prohibit" even the "hoarding" of gold by an American.

Once the war had been over for two years, people naturally assumed that the Trading with the Enemy Act no longer possessed any force. The Supreme Court, on the other hand, later explained that no specific limitation restricted the act's provisions to World War I. Rather, the Trading with the Enemy Act "stood ready to meet additional wars and additional enemies" and could be called into service once again under those circumstances.[4] Little did anyone suspect in 1917 that these "additional enemies" would turn out to be the American people themselves, who would one day see the act used against them to confiscate their gold, permanently. As amended by the Emergency Banking Act of 1933, the Trading with the Enemy

Act no longer says that simply "during time of war" may the president prohibit the export of gold or take action against "hoarding" (i.e., holding on to your money). Now they can be done during time of war *or* "during any other period of national emergency declared by the President."

So cavalier was Congress in its deference to the president that both houses actually passed an unfinished version of Roosevelt's banking bill, the Emergency Banking Act. The Speaker of the House read his colleagues a rough draft of the legislation, while the Senate had nothing to work from at all. "Mr. Speaker," Representative Louis T. McFadden, Republican from Pennsylvania, vainly protested, "I regret that the membership of the House has had no opportunity to consider or even read this bill. The first opportunity I had to know what this legislation is was when it was read from the Clerk's desk. It is an important banking bill. It is a dictatorship over finance in the United States. It is complete control over the banking system in the United States."[5]

Senator Ernest Lundeen, Republican from Minnesota, had a similar reaction. "I am suspicious of this railroading of bills through our House of Representatives, and I refuse to vote for a measure unseen and unknown," he said. Senator Lundeen wondered at "the spectacle of the great House of Representatives of the United States of America passing, after a 40-minute debate, a bill its Members never read and never saw, a bill whose author is unknown. The great majority of the Members have been unable to get a minute's time to discuss this bill; we have been refused a roll call; and we have been refused recognition by the Chair." The bill's passage, he claimed, could "be accomplished only by rapid procedure, hurried and hectic debate, and a general rush for voting without roll call." Senator Lundeen continued:

> I want the RECORD to show that I was, and am, against this bill and this method of procedure; and I believe no good will come out of it for America. We must not abdicate our power to exer-

cise judgment. We must not allow ourselves to be swept off our feet by hysteria, and we must not let the power of the Executive paralyze our legislative action. If we do, it would be better for us to resign and go home—and save the people the salary they are paying us.[6]

House minority leader Bertrand H. Snell, Republican from New York, observed that it was "entirely out of the ordinary to pass legis lation in this House that, as far as I know, is not even in print at the time it is offered." Unusual though it was, however, he urged the bill's passage anyway:

The house is burning down, and the President of the United States says this is the way to put out the fire. [Applause.] And to me at this time there is only one answer to this question, and that is to give the President what he demands and says is nec-essary to meet the situation. I do not know that I am in favor of all the details carried in this bill, but whether I am or not, I am going to give the President of the United States today his way. He is the man responsible, and we must at this time follow his lead. I hope no one on this side of the aisle will object to the consideration of the request. [Applause.][7]

Another Republican, Senator James Couzens of Michigan, was likewise unconcerned about the irregular procedure; much less was he troubled about the actual content of the legislation. To the con-trary, he frankly acknowledged that "we are proposing to set up an autocrat to deal with our currency." But that autocrat, he assured his colleagues, was "one who has been selected by the people them-selves. What is there so terrible about selecting our own autocrat?"[8]

A month later, claiming authority from the Emergency Banking Act and its amendment to the Trading with the Enemy Act, President Roosevelt ordered all individuals and corporations in America to hand over their gold holdings to the federal government in exchange for an equivalent amount of paper currency. The people were not yet told that the gold they were delivering to the government would never be returned to them. That would come later. They were not told that the paper currency they would receive in return would be diluted in value. That also would come later. For now, people were told that it was their patriotic duty to obey the government's command to divest themselves of their gold, and they believed it would be returned to them at some future date. The paper currency they were receiving in exchange for the gold had always been redeemable into gold in the past, so few saw anything amiss in this coerced transaction, and most trusted the government's assurances that this was somehow necessary in order to combat the Depression.

"As If There Were No Constitution"

On June 5, 1933, at the behest of President Roosevelt, Congress passed a joint resolution that made it illegal to "require payment in gold or a particular kind of coin or currency, or in an amount in money of the United States measured thereby."[9] That meant that any provision in a private contract, or even in a public one (as when someone bought a government bond), promising payment in gold was nullified. Payment could be made in whatever the government had declared to be legal tender. Gold could not even be used as a yardstick for determining how much paper money would be owed. Creditors would be required to accept, in repayment of loans, a dollar that the government had now defined as being worth less than at the time the loan was made. For instance, leaving aside interest payments, if you lend someone one dollar you are fairly repaid when the borrower repays you either ten dimes or a one-dollar bill. But suppose dollar bills are suddenly forbidden as a medium of exchange, and six dimes are suddenly declared to be the equivalent of the now-defunct dollar bill. People will now repay you with six dimes even though you lent the equivalent of ten. It was this prospect that people were objecting to when gold contracts were banned. Senator Thomas P. Gore, Democrat of Oklahoma, told the president to his face what he thought of the policy: "Why, that's just plain stealing, isn't it, Mr. President?"[10]

For the next six months President Roosevelt pursued a highly erratic monetary course. Every day the president and Treasury Secretary Henry Morgenthau would meet and decide the gold price. In doing so, they were in effect announcing the dollar price, since the dollar at that time was equivalent to a fixed weight of gold. If they set the price of gold at $30 on day one and $34 dollars on day two, they were lowering the value of the dollar (from one-thirtieth of an ounce of gold to one-thirty-fourth of an ounce of gold).

Every day a new gold price was declared, and no one quite knew on what basis that price was being decided. Secretary Morgenthau relates an incident in which Roosevelt decided one morning that the gold price should be $21—that was a lucky number, the president said, since it was three times seven. Morgenthau wrote in his diary, "If people knew how we fixed the price of gold they would be frightened."[11]

The consequences are not difficult to predict. Private lending in effect came to a halt. What other outcome was possible? With the value of the dollar constantly changing, lenders had no way of knowing whether the dollars they would earn from repaid loans in the future would be worth less than the dollars they were lending in the present, and if so, roughly how much less. As Senator Carter Glass, Democrat of Virginia, put it, "No man outside of a lunatic asylum will loan his money today on a farm mortgage."[12] And thus the government could triumphantly announce that since the private sector was cruelly depriving Americans of credit, it would have to step in and provide relief.

Of all the supporters of the president's gold confiscation and devaluation, few were more accommodating and sycophantic than Senator William Borah, Idaho Democrat, who was then in his pro-FDR phase. According to Senator Borah, when it comes to the nation's monetary system "there is no limitation upon the power of Congress. It is not circumscribed in any respect whatever. It is given full and plenary power to deal with that subject; and therefore it is the same as if there were no Constitution whatever."[13] Borah also argued that "when an individual takes an obligation payable in gold" he does so "with the full understanding that the Government may change its monetary policy at any time and that he must accept whatever the Congress says at a particular time shall constitute money."[14]

That a politician should speak from ignorance or lie hardly even merits our attention any longer, but this is a lie so spectacular as to be a special case: *all* the evidence we have points to a very limited power over money on the part of the federal government, and *none* suggests that the power of Congress is open-ended, as Senator Borah claimed.

According to the Constitution, Congress has the power to "coin Money, regulate the Value thereof, and of foreign Coin, and fix the Standard of Weights and Measures." Coining money refers to the process of taking a precious metal, converting it into coins, and stamping those coins with an indication of their metal content. The phrase did not have any other meaning.

The power to regulate the value of money does not involve a power to dilute the value of money by inflation, an absurd and self-serving rendering. Regulation of the value of money is a power of declaration and comparison, whereby some monetary standard is compared to other coins in circulation and an exchange rate for these various kinds of currency is established according to the amounts of precious metals (with due allowance for the distinct values of different precious metals) in each. In the common law, "regulate" meant only "the process of properly comparing the coin needing regulat[ion] to the monetary standard, not falsifying that comparison or changing the standard."[15] (Blackstone said that "the king's prerogative seemeth not to extend to the debasing or inhancing of the value of the coin, below or above the sterling value.")[16]

At the time the Constitution was drafted there was a clear

American monetary standard: the silver Spanish milled dollar, which was in widespread use in the United States. In 1785, two years before the Constitution was drafted, the Congress declared the American monetary unit to be the dollar. The Board of Treasury then clarified that the reference to the dollar must be to "the common Dollars that are Current in the United States." "The Money Unit or Dollar," it went on, "will contain three hundred and seventy-five grains and sixty-four hundredths of a Grain of fine Silver. A Dollar containing this number of Grains of fine Silver, will be worth as much as the New Spanish Dollars."[17]

The Constitution thus authorizes Congress to take this preexisting "dollar" standard and use it to "regulate"—that is, declare the value of—other silver coins in circulation in terms of the standard, or of gold coins in terms of the standard, or of copper or other coins in terms of the standard. Although the values of these metals vis-à-vis one another are always in some kind of flux, the idea behind the congressional power of regulation is to make the various coins in circulation into roughly equivalent means of making payment for some good or in satisfaction of a debt. If gold sells on the market for sixteen times as much as silver does, then the regulation of coin consists of declaring a sixteen-to-one ratio between silver and gold coins.

That is why this power appears in the same constitutional clause with the power to "fix the Standard of Weights and Measures," which involves the measurement of fixed standards in order to assure uniformity throughout the country. That power does not give Congress the authority to declare that one-tenth of a pound is now a pound; like the power of regulation, it authorizes Congress merely to take an already existing standard and codify it.

Other evidence makes clear that the Constitution did not give Congress the power to declare that money possesses some arbitrary value that suits the whims of politicians or central bankers. The Constitution twice refers to the dollar—in Article I, Section 9, Clause 1, a clause that everyone understood to involve a tax on the import of slaves, and in the Seventh Amendment, which protected the right to a jury trial in civil cases involving at least $20. If the dollar had been something that Congress could manipulate at will, or if "dollar" had been merely a generic term to refer to whatever Congress should arbitrarily choose to recognize as currency, the South never would have accepted that clause, or the Constitution itself. Congress might have manipulated the dollar so as to make the tax on slave imports prohibitively expensive. It could also have effectively abolished trial by jury in civil cases by making $20 an astronomically high amount of money.[18]

Just as significant, every single monetary statute enacted from the ratification of the Constitution until the 1930s understood the congressional power to regulate the value of money in the modest sense described here.[19]

It would be a stretch, but the claim could be made that the gold seizure was merely an exercise of the government's power of eminent domain, by which it may seize private property for an alleged public purpose. But in the American legal tradition the idea of eminent domain takes for granted that the purpose for which the seized property is used must itself be constitutional. Since the gold seizure helped establish a monetary system at odds with the constitutional design, it does not qualify as a legitimate exercise of eminent domain. (That is only one of many difficulties with an eminent domain defense.)[20]

The constitutional case against what the federal government did in the 1930s, and what it continues to do today, is actually far stronger and could go on at much greater length than a book of this size permits. But let us turn now to what the Supreme Court had to say about all this.

"Monstrous" Decisions

For reasons that we shall consider in a moment, the Court never pronounced upon the constitutionality of the gold seizure, whose legality it simply took for granted. The cases it did hear involved the cancellation of gold clauses in public and private contracts. The three Gold Clause Cases were argued in January 1935 and decided the following month: *Norman v. Baltimore & Ohio Railroad Co.*, *Nortz v. United States*, and *Perry v. United States*. In each case Chief Justice Charles Evans Hughes wrote the opinion for the Court; Justice James Clark McReynolds composed a single dissent that he applied to all three.

In the first two of these cases the Court declared that the federal government had been absolutely entitled to cancel all private contracts in gold, and that the perpetuation of gold clauses would have amounted to the "attempted frustration" of "the constitutional power of the Congress over the monetary system of the country . . . [T]hese clauses interfere with the exertion of the power granted to the Congress." Not a stitch of evidence existed for any aspect of this argument.

Perry involved a man who had purchased in gold a U.S. bond that was payable in gold and who was seeking payment either in gold or in the equivalent in paper currency. The government intended to pay in depreciated dollars, and thus he would have received far less than he was entitled to under the terms of the bond. The bond had a face value of $10,000 in gold, but in the inflated dollars of post-gold-standard America it would have taken nearly $17,000 in paper currency in order to satisfy what the government had contracted to pay him.

The Supreme Court held that in the case of a public gold clause, as in the case of a government bond, the government had an obligation to live up to its promises. The plaintiff was entitled to his gold. But then the Court followed with this twisted argument: since gold was now illegal to hold, the plaintiff had not really been wronged after all. For even if the government did redeem his bond in gold, it would have to confiscate that gold from him.

Speaking for the minority, Justice McReynolds declared:

Just men regard repudiation and spoliation of citizens by their sovereign with abhorrence; but we are asked to affirm that the Constitution has granted power to accomplish both. No definite delegation of such a power exists; and we cannot believe that the farseeing Framers, who labored with hope of establishing justice and securing the blessings of liberty, intended that the expected government should have authority to annihilate its own obligations and destroy the very rights which they were endeavoring to protect. Not only is there no permission for such actions; they are inhibited. And no plenitude of words can conform them to our charter.

To the ludicrous argument that the bondholder had suffered no damage in being denied payment in gold since it was now illegal for people to own gold, McReynolds's dissent sensibly replied: "Obligations cannot be legally avoided by prohibiting the creditor from receiving the thing promised. . . . There would be no serious difficulty in estimating the value of [the plaintiff's] gold in the currency now in circulation." The contract to pay in gold having been broken, the holder was at least morally entitled to receive in currency not just the nominal amount of the bond but an amount in paper dollars equivalent to what he would have earned if the payment could have been made in gold. "For the government to say, we have violated our contract but have escaped the consequences through our own statute, would be monstrous. In matters of contractual obligation the government cannot legislate so as to excuse itself." Suppose a private individual tried to do the same thing, "secreting or manipulating his assets with the intent to place them beyond the reach of creditors." Any such attempt "would be denounced as fraudulent, wholly ineffective."

"Loss of reputation for honorable dealing," the dissent concluded, "will bring us unending humiliation; the impending legal and moral chaos is appalling."

Yet the minority, blunt and confrontational as it was, was not nearly as confrontational as it might have been. Nowhere was the constitutionality of the gold seizure itself ruled upon. Even the dissent shrugged off major issues with the suggestion that "any abstract discussion of congressional power over money would only tend to befog the real issue." In fact, of course, a sound, constitutional discussion of the government's power over money would have been a refreshing note of clarity for a government that had been egregiously dishonest about the extent of its authority over money.

The Court had had an opportunity to face the gold seizure issue directly. In late 1932 Frederick Barber Campbell had deposited some gold bars for safekeeping at New York's Chase Manhattan Bank. In 1933, after the federal government had handed down various instructions regarding gold ownership, Chase contacted Campbell and informed him that the bank and he had to file with the government regarding his ownership of the gold, and that within thirty days the bank would have no choice but to hand over Campbell's gold to the government. Campbell sought an injunction against Chase to prevent it from delivering his gold to any party other than himself. Meanwhile, the government tried to punish him for evading the various requirements associated with the termination of gold ownership.

A district court sorted out the matter in November 1933. Naturally, it found the federal government to be perfectly within its rights to seize people's gold, holding this to be a corollary of its alleged currency power. The court sided with Campbell only on a technicality: the secretary of the Treasury, not the president, had been authorized to seize gold. The president had been given the power merely to prevent "hoarding." Seizing people's gold from them was not a legitimate way to combat hoarding, the Court declared. A month after the decision, perhaps in order to maintain a façade of legality, the secretary of the Treasury officially called on Americans to hand over their gold, thereby addressing the court's trivial complaint about the gold seizure.

Although Campbell appealed his case, the Supreme Court refused to hear it. Monetary historian Edwin Vieira speculates that the Supreme Court deliberately avoided ruling on the gold confiscation one way or the other. Those who might have been inclined to favor the administration would have had the unenviable task of showing that such a seizure, which lacked any kind of precedent in American history, was a reasonable exercise of the federal government's monetary powers under the Constitution. (The precedents referred to even in the Gold Clause Cases either had made far more modest claims than the 1935 Court alleged or had themselves been based on absurd legal and historical arguments.) The minority would have faced an equally difficult assignment. Once the government was found to have seized the gold illegally, it surely would not be permitted to keep it. Were the confiscation to be ruled unconstitutional, the government would confront the serious logistical difficulty of tracking everyone down and returning the correct amount of stolen gold. The justices may have feared that they would put the government in an embarrassing or even impossible situation. Likewise, they may not have relished the prospect of being blamed for the continuation of the Depression, which the snake oil salesmen in the Roosevelt administration foolishly attributed to the gold standard.

And so the confiscation stood.

By the 1970s the federal government had once again permitted Americans to hold gold, even in the form of commemorative coins. But just to make sure these coins could never circulate and displace the constantly depreciating paper currency printed by the U.S. government, the law required that such coins could circulate only at a value of $50 an ounce. Since gold (as of early 2008) sells for about $1,000 an ounce, no one in his right mind would exchange a one-ounce gold coin for a mere $50. The coins are thereby kept out of general circulation.

The Endless Emergency

There is an important footnote to all this, which reveals just how pliable is the "emergency" rationale for government power. In late 1950, President Harry Truman issued a proclamation stating the existence of a "national emergency" in light of hostilities in Korea. After the Korean War ended in 1953, several cases arose involving people who had acquired gold bullion. The pretext for criminalizing the possession of gold bullion had been the alleged economic emergency, long since over, of the 1930s. And with peace having been established in Korea, the owners of the bullion were sure that no emergency existed that could justify criminalizing their ownership of such property.

They were wrong, of course: in the district court decision of *United States v. Briddle*, Americans learned that there would always be some emergency or other to which the government could appeal to justify continuing criminal sanctions on gold ownership. Presidents Truman, Eisenhower, and Kennedy had all declared the existence of emergencies—related, respectively, to the Korean War, the general threat of Communism, and the balance-of-payments deficit. Any one of these, the plaintiffs learned, suffices to maintain in effect the emergency legislation of the 1930s. Other courts followed suit.[21]

Looting

Over the years a number of arguments have been advanced to persuade us that the gold standard is a ridiculous idea, and that we are better off with a currency that politicians can manipulate at will.[22] We are likewise told that the gold standard was responsible for a host of economic downturns—even though, upon closer inspection, every one of these was preceded by some form of government manipulation of the monetary system.

This is not the place to reply in detail to these various arguments, so we shall simply observe that people have supported the gold standard because compared with an irredeemable paper currency of the kind we have now, gold severely restricts the ability of government to manipulate the money supply on behalf of the politically well connected (who receive newly created paper money first, before prices have commensurately risen) at the expense of the rest of the population (who receive it only later, while meanwhile having to pay the higher prices it brings in its wake). Irredeemable paper money also gives the government an easier time of financing war and welfare, which can be portrayed as essentially costless. The government pays for these by silently looting its subject population, in the form of diluting the value of everyone's dollar. Meanwhile, the general public blames rising prices and the fall in the dollar's value on greedy businessmen and labor unions, while believing that government gives them things for free. Likewise, there is very little understanding among the public about financial bubbles, boom-bust cycles, monetary depreciation, and inflation-driven wealth transfers, all of which are attributable to the fiat currency that replaced the precious-metal standard under which Americans had lived for centuries.

For our purposes, we can appreciate the importance of the gold standard to a free society even without the assistance of economic arguments. Consider the opinion of Joseph Schumpeter, one of the twentieth century's great economists. Writing in the early 1950s, Schumpeter observed that people had been taught to look upon the idea of the gold standard as

> wholly erroneous—as a sort of fetishism that is impervious to rational argument. We are also taught to discount all rational and all purely economic arguments that may actually be adduced in favor of it. But quite irrespective of these, there is one point about the gold standard that would redeem it from the charge of foolishness; even in the absence of any purely economic advantage. . . . An automatic gold currency is part and parcel of a laissez-faire and free-trade economy. It links every nation's money rates and price levels with the money rates and price levels of all the other nations that are "on gold." It is extremely sensitive to government expenditure and even to attitudes or policies that do not involve expenditures directly, for example, to foreign policy, to certain policies of taxation, and,

in general to precisely all those policies that violate the principles of economic liberalism [i.e., the free market]. *This* is the reason why gold is so unpopular now and also why it was so popular in the bourgeois era. It imposes restrictions upon governments or bureaucracies that are much more powerful than is parliamentary criticism. It is both the badge and the guarantee of bourgeois freedom—of freedom not simply of the bourgeois *interest*, but of freedom in the bourgeois *sense*. From this standpoint *a man may quite rationally fight for it, even if fully convinced of the validity of all that has ever been urged against it on economic grounds.*[23]

The constitutional offense we have discussed in this chapter is all but unknown to most Americans. On top of that, Washington politicians, when they are forced to mention the subject of monetary policy at all, assure everyone that it is perfectly fine for government to be able to inflate the money supply at will, and that only a crank could possibly object to a currency backed by nothing. Looting the public and then persuading them that their expropriation was really for their own good—that is a neat trick, even for government.

7

The Court's "Wall of Separation": Banning Prayer from Public Schools

ONE OF THE most controversial developments in the history of "constitutional law" was the Supreme Court's decision to ban prayer from public schools. When the Court handed down its ruling in *Engel v. Vitale* (1962), the response was electric: all but one governor joined in immediately denouncing the decision, and opponents in Congress for decades thereafter repeatedly attempted to negate the Court's newly minted policy.[1] Yet still the decision stands. This reflects the extraordinary power that the Supreme Court has granted itself, as well as the deference the other branches of the federal government traditionally extend to the judiciary.

The key question in this instance is, how did the Court arrive at this pass? How did it decide to regulate state policies touching on religion in the first place, and then how did it move to the conclusion that a nondenominational prayer was an establishment of religion?

In reaching this decision, the Court claimed to be "interpreting" the First and Fourteenth Amendments. A better way to put it would be that the Court completely remade American governments' relationship to religion, and in the process inverted the Constitution.

A Miraculous Discovery, Seventy-two Years Late

The First Amendment had been understood from the beginning as having no bearing on the policies of state (including local) governments. As Chief Justice John Marshall wrote for a unanimous Supreme Court in *Barron v. Baltimore* (1833), the Bill of Rights was adopted entirely in response to the idea that the federal government might be a threat to traditional individual rights and to state governments' traditional powers.[2] Marshall said that opponents of ratification of the Constitution had provoked unfounded fear of federal overreaching, and that the addition of the first ten amendments to the Constitution was among the results. Mr. Barron, then, could not go to federal court for relief from an uncompensated taking of his property by the city of Baltimore, since the Fifth Amendment did not apply to the city; he had instead to seek his remedy at the state level.

While history would prove—indeed, Marshall's own opinions in *McCulloch v. Maryland* (1819), *Martin v. Hunter's Lessee* (1816),[3] *Gibbons v. Ogden* (1824), and other cases had *already* proved—that fears of federal overreaching were well founded, in *Barron* Marshall clearly had gotten the outcome right, and for the right reasons: the purpose of the Bill of Rights was to guard against the advent of an all-powerful federal government. Thanks to Marshall's decision in *Barron*, the First Amendment's religion clauses never formed the basis of any Supreme Court decision for the next century.

In the mid-twentieth century, however, came an abrupt change. In *Cantwell v. Connecticut* (1940), the Supreme Court announced that the Fourteenth Amendment's Due Process Clause ("Nor shall any state deprive any person of life, liberty, or property without due process of law") made the First Amendment's religion clauses applicable against state governments.[4] Since the First Amendment had existed for 149 years without being held to bind the states, and since the Fourteenth Amendment had been in place for 72 years without being held to bind states in this way, this proclamation required more than an *ipse dixit*, more than a mere statement from the Court that what it had not known—indeed, what it had denied—was true.[5]

How, then, did the *Cantwell* court explain its holding, which was at odds with 149 years' experience under the First Amendment? It did not. It merely said, "The fundamental concept of liberty embodied in [the Fourteenth] Amendment embraces the liberties guaranteed by the First Amendment. The First Amendment declares that Congress shall make no law respecting an establishment of religion or prohibiting the free exercise thereof. The Fourteenth Amendment has rendered the legislatures of the states as incompetent as Congress to enact such laws." It offered no historical demonstration whatsoever of what truly was a radical proposition—that the Fourteenth Amendment had inverted the American federal system in regard to religion, but that no one had realized this was so until now, seventy-two years later.

The Court's reference to "the liberties guaranteed by the First Amendment" also assumes that the First Amendment was intended to establish an individual right, a right good against government—an assumption completely at odds with Chief Justice Marshall's decision in *Barron*. Marshall said in *Barron* that the Bill of Rights was intended solely to limit the powers of the federal government. When it came to religion, then, the Establishment and Free Exercise Clauses of the First Amendment were to be understood as reserving control over policies in that area to the states—where such control had always been.

So how could a federal court enforce the First Amendment's reservation of control over religion policy to the states against the Connecticut legislature, as it did in the *Cantwell* case? Put more simply, how could a federal court enforce a state's right against a state?

It could not.

But 1940 was a high-water mark of federal authority and a low-water mark of state autonomy. There is no evidence that the

Supreme Court justices even considered the issue of local communities' power or rights in drafting the *Cantwell* decision.

Seismic Shift

In 1873, soon after the adoption of the Fourteenth Amendment, the Supreme Court said that it could not imagine how the amendment's provisions ever could be held to apply to any situation other than that of freed blacks.[6] Yet by the turn of the twentieth century, they were being put to many different uses. In cases such as *Lochner v. New York* (1905), the Court used the Fourteenth Amendment's Due Process Clause as a vehicle for reading its laissez-faire preferences into the Constitution—that is, for writing libertarian economics into "constitutional law" insofar as distasteful state economic regulations were concerned.[7] (Doing the same thing in regard to federal policy did not require similar derring-do, because the Tenth Amendment clearly reserved matters such as wage and hours regulation to the states.)

Soon after Franklin Roosevelt became president in 1933, he reneged on his campaign vows of traditional Democratic laissez-faire economic policy. In its place, he offered up a series of European-style centralized economic planning measures such as the National Industrial Recovery Act (NIRA) and the Agricultural Adjustment Act (AAA), as well as acts establishing federal wage minima, regulating the coal industry, and aiding indebted farmers. The Court said that the Congress could not delegate so much legislative authority to the president or regulate any activity it wanted to regulate under the guise of regulating commerce.

In 1937, however, the Court abandoned its attempt to set limits to the Commerce Clause power and to enforce the Tenth Amendment. No longer would the Court be in the business of drawing a line between federal and state authority, as it had been intended to do. Instead, it would allow Congress to do almost anything it wanted to do on the basis of the Commerce Clause.[8]

The year after the seismic shift of 1937, the Court staked out a new role for itself: protecting the free operation of the electoral process and protecting "discrete and insular minorities."[9] Soon enough, the Court also set itself the task of defining the contours of certain substantive rights it said had been "incorporated" into the Due Process Clause of the Fourteenth Amendment—and thus had come to be enforceable against the states.

That is how the Court claims to enforce the First Amendment's Establishment Clause against the states, even though the Establishment Clause says that "*Congress* shall make no law respecting an establishment of religion" (emphasis added). Some of the justices recognized that the Incorporation Doctrine was at odds with the intentions of the Fourteenth Amendment's authors and ratifiers, as when Justice Felix Frankfurter said, "The relevant historical materials demonstrate conclusively that Congress and the members of the legislatures of the ratifying States, did not contemplate that the Fourteenth Amendment was a shorthand incorporation of the first eight amendments making them applicable as explicit restrictions upon the States."[10]

But no matter: in time, the Court would declare its favorite Bill of Rights provisions "incorporated" anyway.

Law Office History

The Court's process of "incorporating" the Establishment Clause that began with *Cantwell* came to full fruition in *Everson v. Board of Education of the Township of Ewing* (1947). That case, like many others in this area, had its origin in an old American suspicion of Catholicism—more specifically, of Catholic education.

The city of Ewing, New Jersey, had implemented a 1941 New Jersey law providing public busing of children to schools public and private. Arch R. Everson insisted that this plan, as it affected children bused to Catholic schools, constituted a violation of the principle of separation of church and state—which he said the Fourteenth Amendment made enforceable against the states.

The Court, through Justice Hugo Black, agreed that the Establishment Clause mandated a "separation"—as he put it, a "wall of separation"—between church and state. How did it come to that conclusion? Through some classic law office history. Law office history is partisan history based on evidence carefully chosen to support an advocate's agenda—the kind of history one expects to find in the arguments an attorney offers to a judge on behalf of his client.

Black begins his historical discussion in *Everson* by positing that "a large proportion of the early settlers of this country came here from Europe to escape the bondage of laws which compelled them to support and attend government-favored churches." What can he mean by this? Virginia, the first English colony in North America, was founded by monarchist Anglicans (adherents of the state church, the Church of England) in 1607, and the Church of England was the established church of Virginia throughout the colonial period. The General Assembly, which first met in 1619, legislated on behalf of Anglicanism from the start.[11] The next colonies founded by the English in North America, the New England colonies, were founded by separatists not to escape the principle of church-state alliance but to establish societies in which their preferred form of Protestantism, instead of the king's, would be the one the state supported and enforced. Far from pushing for separation of church and state, the Puritans believed that if one did not appreciate the New England Way, one could avoid New England altogether.[12] Religious dissenters from Massachusetts, such as Roger Williams and Anne Hutchinson, found themselves expelled to Rhode Island; several Quakers who returned to New England after being banished for their nonconformity were executed. By the time the Revolution began, nine states had established churches and others had various religious requirements. Indeed, the colonies that had policies of religious nonestablishment and tolerance throughout the colonial period— Rhode Island (the "Isle of Errors," receptacle of lapsed Puritans),

Quaker New Jersey, and Pennsylvania—were the exceptions. British North America was founded, in the main, by people who accepted the long-standing tradition of state support for Christianity.

Black admits (inconsistently) in his next paragraph that various church-supporting practices, such as requiring attendance at services and punishing blasphemy, were transplanted to British North America in the colonial period. He continues, "These practices became so commonplace as to shock the freedom loving colonials into a feeling of abhorrence. The imposition of taxes to pay ministers' salaries and to build and maintain churches and church property aroused their indignation. It was these feelings which found expression in the first amendment."

Black then launches into an account of the adoption of the Virginia Statute for Religious Freedom, written by Thomas Jefferson and shepherded to adoption in the General Assembly by James Madison, which established Virginia as the first officially secular republic in history. According to Black, Madison's sponsorship of Jefferson's statute proved that Madison's and Jefferson's thoughts on government and religion were interchangeable; since Madison played the leading role in securing congressional passage of the First Amendment, his understanding of the proper relationship between government and religion underlay that amendment's religion clauses; and thus, Jefferson's statement in a letter to the Danbury Baptists penned January 1, 1802, that the First Amendment had established "a wall of separation between church and state" should guide application of that amendment.

Black's reasoning is faulty in several respects. First, Jefferson had no role in securing the adoption of either the Statute for Religious Freedom or the First Amendment. He did write the Statute for Religious Freedom, but only for Virginia. It was a state law, and, as we have seen, the Supreme Court noted in *Barron v. Baltimore* (1833) that the Bill of Rights was intended to circumscribe only the powers of the federal government.

We do not have to rely simply on John Marshall's say-so in accepting that the Establishment Clause applied only to the Congress and not to state governments. An early version of the First Amendment read, in pertinent part, "no religion shall be established by law, nor shall the equal rights of conscience be infringed."[13] During the congressional debate on the proposed amendment, Representative Peter Silvester of New York said that he "feared it might be thought to have a tendency to abolish religion altogether." Massachusetts's Elbridge Gerry interjected that "it would be better if it was, that no religious doctrine shall be established by law." Roger Sherman of Connecticut opined that the amendment was "altogether unnecessary, inasmuch as congress had no authority whatever delegated to them by the constitution, to make religious establishments," and that he would therefore "move to have it struck out."

In response to these observations, Madison explained that he "apprehended the meaning of the words to be, that congress should not establish a religion, and enforce the legal observation of it by law, nor compel men to worship God in any manner contrary to their conscience." He noted that "some of the state conventions" had thought such language was needed because they feared Congress might take advantage of the Constitution's Necessary and Proper Clause to pass laws that "infringe[d] the rights of conscience, or establish[ed] a *national* religion" (emphasis added). Therefore he defended the amendment as preventing such problems. When called on to elaborate, Madison even suggested that to ease concerns about infringing on the states, Congress might insert the word "national" before "religion" in the amendment. (He withdrew this motion after an objection from Gerry, who observed that the government was not national but federal; Madison conceded Gerry's point.)

Moreover, in that same First Congress, Madison also proposed an amendment reading, "No state shall infringe the equal rights of conscience, nor freedom of speech, or of the press, nor of the right of trial by jury in criminal cases."[14] This amendment was rejected despite Madison's characterization of it as "the most valuable amendment on the whole list." In other words, Congress had considered the idea of empowering the federal government to interfere in the states' religion policy, and the idea had been defeated.

How, then, did the First Amendment come to be the basis of Black's opinion in *Everson* 158 years later? How, in other words, did the Supreme Court—a group of unelected justices—decide to undo the intention of the First Amendment's authors and ratifiers and give us the policy the First Congress—the people's elected representatives— had *rejected*?

The Klan

The notion of a federal separation of church and state, of separation of church and state as an American right instead of a right of citizenship in some states (such as Virginia), first came into vogue as a by-product of the large influx of Catholics resulting from the Irish potato famine.[15] That mid-nineteenth-century wave of immigration spurred large numbers of devout Protestants, atheists, and nativists to organize politically on behalf of "Americanism."

This organization took the form of advocacy of an Americanism amendment—of an amendment intended, among other things, to make separation of church and state part of the Constitution. Otherwise, Americanism advocates feared, followers of the pope might tie the government to their religion and thus undo the traditional American tolerance of a multiplicity of different forms of Protestantism, as well as of irreligion.

Thus, for example, Francis Abbot's Toledo Liberal League complained in an 1871 broadside that "it is clear that the absolute separation of Church and State is a principle neither fully understood nor faithfully obeyed by the people of the United States."[16] He was certainly right about that: they had never understood it, let alone adopted it, and so had no intention to obey it.

The Free Religious Association's newspaper in 1874 several times ran the text of their proposed constitutional amendment, which read:

SECTION 1.—Congress shall make no law respecting an establishment of religion, or favoring any form of religion, or prohibiting the free exercise thereof; or abridging the freedom of speech or of the press, or the right of the people peaceably to assemble and to petition the Government for a redress of grievances.

SECTION 2.—No state shall make any law respecting an establishment of religion, or favoring any particular form of religion, or prohibiting the free exercise thereof; or abridging the freedom of speech or of the press, or the right of the people peaceably to assemble and to petition the Government for a redress of grievances. No religious test shall ever be required as a condition of suffrage, or as a qualification to any office or public trust, in any State; and no person shall ever in any State be deprived of any of his or her rights, privileges, or capacities, or disqualified for the performance of any public or private duty, or rendered incompetent to give evidence in any court of law or equity, in consequence of any opinions he or she may hold on the subject of religion.

SECTION 3.—Congress shall have power to enforce the provisions of the second section of this Article by appropriate legislation.[17]

As the text of their proposed amendment makes clear, the secularists—also known as "Liberals"—did not believe that the First Amendment or the Fourteenth Amendment's Due Process Clause barred states from adopting any legislation they saw fit on the question of religion. Instead, they believed that an amendment was necessary to write separation of church and state into the American federal constitutional system.

Although the Liberals failed to achieve adequate political force to amend the Constitution, they did achieve a measure of popularity. In large part because of their influence, the notion of separation of church and state as part of America's cultural and constitutional inheritance became a more common part of the discourse.[18]

For Protestants, advocating the separation of church and state remained essentially an anti-Catholic position. Thus, for example, many saw no inconsistency between separation and Bible reading in school. Separation, to them, meant the absence of the organized Catholic Church from government institutions; since Protestants acted only as individuals in these matters—since the Protestant conscience was not beholden to higher ecclesiastical authority—Protestant influence on public schools was not a problem.[19]

Another organization leading the fight for separation of church and state was that most powerful of American nativist groups, the Ku Klux Klan. The Klan's leading role in these matters is not widely recognized. As Philip Hamburger, the outstanding historian of church-state separation, explains, "Leaping from Jefferson's 1802 letter to Hugo Black's *Everson* opinion in 1947, the modern myth of separation omits any discussion of nativist sentiment in America and, above all, omits any mention of the Ku Klux Klan. Yet nativists had popularized separation in America in the nineteenth century, and, during the first half of the twentieth, they continued to distinguish themselves as the leading proponents of this ideal."[20]

The Ku Klux Klan, born out of anti-black, anti-Republican sentiment in the post–Civil War era, was revived in 1915, and by 1926, according to Hamburger, it had "about five million members and innumerable sympathizers. It exerted profound political power in states across the country and, probably more than any other national group in the first half of the century, drew Americans to the principle of separation." By this point the Klan was directing much of its attention to Catholics, who, as an organized mass directed by their hierarchs, were thought to represent a profound threat to American government. The nub of the problem was the involvement of their church in politics, and the solution advocated by the Klan's leader was separation of church and state.[21]

The "Klansman's Creed" included a statement that "I believe in the eternal Separation of Church and State," as well as an article echoing traditional Anglophone anti-Catholic test oaths: "I hold no allegiance to any foreign government, emperor, king, pope or any other foreign, political or religious power."[22] Catholicism was un-American, in this view. As one nativist put it, "To be a good Roman Catholic you must give up liberty of conscience, all civil and political rights, and even the privilege of THINKING for yourself."

It was from the Klan that Justice Hugo L. Black emerged. The Alabama native was a Baptist and thus suspicious of Catholicism. As early as 1921, lawyer Black took a Klan case and used a flagrantly racial appeal to win his client's acquittal. The accused, a Methodist minister, had shot a Catholic priest for marrying the accused's daughter to a Hispanic Catholic. Black called the new son-in-law, a Puerto Rican, to stand before the jurors so that they might ponder the likelihood that he had some "negro ancestry," and he insinuated that the priest had deserved death for proselytizing a Protestant minister's daughter into a mongrel marriage. Since the majority of jurors were Klansmen, Black flashed them a Klan hand signal. He won his man an acquittal.[23]

In 1923, Black officially joined the Klan, and he soon was Kladd of his Klavern—the official responsible for administering the oath about "white supremacy" and "separation of church and state." Soon he ran for senator as, in the words of the *Montgomery Advertiser*, "the darling of the Ku Klux Klan." A major component of his campaign was his tour of state Klan Klaverns, "nearly all 148 Klaverns," where he gave speeches on the history of the church—that is, anti-Catholic lectures. His tour guide was the leader of the Alabama Klan. While making this tour, Black also addressed a Baptist convention on the First Amendment's religious liberty guarantees.[24]

After winning the Democratic primary, which in those days in Alabama was tantamount to being elected, Black gave a public speech expressing his thanks to the Klan. "I know," he said, "that without the support of the members of this organization I would not have been called, even by my enemies, the 'Junior Senator from Alabama.' [Applause.] I realize that I was elected by men who believe in the principles that I have sought to advocate and which are the principles of this organization." He concluded by saying, "I thank you from the bottom of a heart that is yours."[25]

In 1937 the Senate confirmed Black's nomination to the Supreme Court, but almost immediately thereafter his membership in the Klan became public knowledge. Calls for his resignation resounded throughout the country. Black responded with a radio address in which, as Hamburger notes, he raised "the old allegation of a Catholic plot" and "suggested to Protestants that the accusations against him were evidence of a Catholic conspiracy." He went on to say that if the furor did not die down, anti-Catholic boycotts and social ostracism would harm innocent Catholic businessmen throughout the country.[26] Within minutes of his speech, crosses were alight in New Jersey and Massachusetts.

So when Black encountered the case of *Everson v. Board of Education of Ewing Township* in 1947, the *Cantwell* case and his own Klan background had prepared him to carve out a completely novel understanding of the Constitution's meaning in regard to church-state relations. The widespread appeal of nativist messages such as the Klan's had prepared the intellectual elite, including lawyers, for Black's unfounded claims about the colonial history of the country and about the significance for federal constitutional law of Madison's and Jefferson's state-level reforms in Virginia. Significantly, the chief quarrel between the Black majority on the Court and the dissenters was simply how strongly the Black principles should be imposed on the states.

And the Court devised an answer the very next year, in *McCollum v. Board of Education*.[27] The case involved a Champaign, Illinois, program for children whose parents wanted brief, weekly release time from school for sectarian instruction by local religious instructors on public school grounds. The Court held this to be an establishment of religion. Justice Black, again writing for the majority, rejected the schools' contentions that the Fourteenth Amendment did not make the Establishment Clause applicable against state governments and that "the First Amendment was intended to forbid only government preference of one religion over another, not an impartial governmental assistance of all religions." Black's opinion offered no argument to support his position beyond reference to *Everson*.

The Final "Interpretation"

The stage was set, then, for *Engel v. Vitale* (1962), the school prayer case.[28] The facts of the case were simple: New York State had a policy of encouraging local public school districts to adopt prayers to be recited each morning by those students who chose to participate. New Hyde Park, New York, had adopted an anodyne prayer: "Almighty God, we acknowledge our dependence upon Thee, and we beg Thy blessings upon us, our parents, our teachers and our Country." The plaintiffs asserted that this practice violated the Fourteenth Amendment's Establishment Clause—as Justice Black put it in his majority opinion, that it "breache[d] the wall of separation between Church and State."

The Court concluded, "We agree with that contention since we think that the constitutional prohibition against laws respecting an establishment of religion must at least mean that in this country it is no part of the business of government to compose official prayers for any group of the American people to recite as a part of a religious program carried on by government." Then Black launched into a recapitulation of his *Everson* account of the background of the First and Fourteenth Amendments, an account that was, once again, a confused jumble.

Without addressing the question of whether the Establishment Clause really had been made applicable to the states by the Due Process Clause of the Fourteenth Amendment, Justice Potter Stewart in dissent noted that he could "not see how an 'official religion' is established by letting those who want to say a prayer say it." He went on to note that the inclusion of religious lyrics in "The Star-Spangled Banner" did not make designation of that hymn as the national anthem an establishment of religion, and that adding "under

God" to the Pledge of Allegiance in 1954 had not made recitation of that oath an establishment, any more than putting "IN GOD WE TRUST" on American coinage was an establishment.

Americans at large found the *Engel* outcome lamentable. They tried instantly, and they still try now, to undo what the Court did in that case. But thanks to the difficulty of the amendment process outlined in Article V, it is far easier for the Court to amend the Constitution through "interpretation" than for the people to undo the Court's work through the legitimate amendment process. No matter how unpopular the ban on prayer in schools proves to be, it is unlikely ever to be reversed.

8

The Power to Draft

ON HIS EIGHTEENTH birthday, the average American man registers for the draft. This requirement, instituted by President Jimmy Carter in 1979 in response to the Soviet invasion of Afghanistan, is a rite of passage, much as taking the driver's test is. While the U.S. government has not conscripted soldiers since 1973, Carter's requirement that young men register for Selective Service has never been eliminated. And periodically we hear calls to reinstitute the draft, particularly as the United States has deployed hundreds of thousands of volunteer soldiers abroad since September 11, 2001. In 2006, for example, Congressman Charles Rangel, the New York Democrat who now chairs the House Ways and Means Committee, presented a plan to require all Americans between the ages of eighteen and forty-two, men and women, to perform military service.[1]

Some public intellectuals would have young Americans directed into other types of service as well. The late conservative publicist William F. Buckley Jr., in his 1990 book *Gratitude: Reflections on What We Owe to Our Country*, proposed that high school be followed by a year of government-approved public service. Buckley's rationale was that if government is entitled to require that people complete twelve years of schooling, why may it not require a year of labor of them as well? He would have had the program be administered chiefly by the states, with federal guidelines, and would have penalized nonpartici- pants via such mechanisms as withholding driver's licenses—which in many parts of the country would make them essentially unemployable.

Where did people such as Buckley get the idea that the federal government was entitled to drive American citizens into involuntary service to the government? For one thing, he seems to have believed that if Americans are blessed to be Americans, they should be thank- ful to the government for that blessedness. Instead of serving soci- ety, or God, by being productive citizens, then, they should repay the government by serving the government.

The Thirteenth Amendment to the federal Constitution says:

SECTION 1.—Neither slavery nor involuntary servitude, except as a punishment for crime whereof the party shall have been duly convicted, shall exist within the United States, or any place subject to their jurisdiction.

SECTION 2.—Congress shall have power to enforce this arti- cle by appropriate legislation.

One might have thought that this provision answered the ques- tion: there could be no involuntary service to the government in the United States.

But it did not. In fact, quite the opposite: the Supreme Court has given its approval to the draft. It says that the government has a power to force men to serve in the military, and it reads that power very broadly. Far from an involuntary servitude, to be drafted is a wonderful obligation.

The First Take

While the constitutionality of military conscription is barely ques- tioned today, it was not always so. When a congressional bill to institute conscription was being considered during the War of 1812, Daniel Webster of Massachusetts took to the floor of the House of Representatives to offer a rousing defense of the Constitution: "Is this, Sir, consistent with the character of a free Government? Is this civil liberty? Is this the real character of our Constitution? No, Sir, indeed it is not. The Constitution is libeled, foully libeled. The people of this country have not established for themselves such a fabric of despotism. They have not purchased at a vast expense of their own treasure and their own blood a Magna Carta to be slaves. Where is it written in the Constitution, in what article or section is it contained, that you may take children from their parents, and parents from their children, and compel them to fight the battles of any war in which the folly or the wickedness of government may engage it?"[2]

The draft was not instituted then, but it became an issue again during the Civil War. President Abraham Lincoln had already spurred the secession of Middle South states Arkansas, North Carolina, Tennessee, and Virginia by calling for volunteers to enlist in an army to invade the Deep South without Congress's approval. Then, in March 1863, his fellow Republicans in control of Congress adopted a conscription act, making all able-bodied male citizens ages twenty-one to forty-five the "national forces."

In doing this, as in so much else, the Republicans merely imitated the French revolutionaries, institutors of the dreadful *levée en masse*. By instituting universal service, the French Revolution was able to sweep million-man armies across Europe, raping and looting as they went. The monarchies of Europe responded in kind, and the modern era of total war had been launched. The prospect was similar in 1863.

In response to the Conscription Act of 1863, the chief justice of the United States, Democrat Roger B. Taney of Maryland, wrote a memorandum on the draft's constitutionality.[3] Taney, virtually the judicial voice of Jacksonian Democracy, offered a classic Jeffersonian analysis of federal conscription's constitutionality.[4] In his memorandum, Taney began by considering the Constitution as a federal one

(one granting the new government only certain powers) rather than a national one (one creating a central government with whichever governmental powers it wished to exercise).

As Taney put it, to answer the question whether a federal draft law was constitutional, "we should fix clearly in our minds the relative powers of the general and State governments, and the attitude in which they stand to each other when exercising their respective powers." He would rely on the Constitution to provide the measure of the federal government's authority, bearing in mind the line between the legislative authority of Congress and the powers reserved to the states.

This did not mean that the states could do everything and the federal government could do nothing. Taney contrasted the federal Constitution to the old Articles of Confederation, under which the states had been able essentially to stifle any impulse the central government might have. The Confederation was an agency of the state governments, always responsible to them. Under the Constitution, however, the federal government had certain powers it could exercise independently of the state governments.

Taney noted that the Necessary and Proper Clause at the end of Article I, Section 8 says that Congress shall have power to pass the laws necessary and proper to execute the powers expressly granted in the Constitution; the Supremacy Clause of Article VI, Clause 2, says that the Constitution and laws made in pursuance of it shall be the supreme law of the land; and the Tenth Amendment reserves to the states the powers not delegated by the Constitution to the federal government. These three provisions, Taney said, establish that the extent of the federal government's sovereignty (that is, supremacy) "is confined to the powers delegated by the Constitution."

The Tenth Amendment in particular, Taney continued, was adopted after the ratification process to underscore the fact that the states remained sovereignties—that is, that they remained the final authorities in the areas the Constitution did not delegate to the fed-

eral government. Thus, any congressional attempt to legislate beyond the known bounds of Congress's authority would be "a usurpation of State sovereignty—and consequently illegal." While this
Jeffersonian assessment of the limitations on federal power would
have been totally alien to the Republican majority then in control of
Congress and the executive branch, it was the same explanation of
the Constitution that the Federalists offered during the ratification
dispute, and thus was the basis on which the Constitution was instituted in the first place.[5]

When it came to the Conscription Act, the key question was
whether the power to force men into the military was one the Constitution granted the federal government. Taney noted that the
Constitution includes provisions relating to two kinds of military
organization: the army and the militia. The army is to be raised, organized, and equipped by the Congress, as it sees fit; the militia, on
the other hand, is beyond the general government's control in peacetime and subject only to limited congressional authority in wartime.

As to the army, Taney noted, the Constitution gives Congress a
"general" power, in peace and in war. "It is a body of men separated
from the general mass of citizen [sic]—subject to a different code
of laws liable to be tried by Military Courts instead of the Civil
Tribunals—and may be employed at all times in or out of the United
States, at the pleasure of Congress—and willing or not willing forced
to obey the orders of their superior officers. . . . The control of the
whole body is exclusively and absolutely in the general government.—
They compose the national forces—or what is called in the Constitution the land forces of the United States."

While the Constitution empowers Congress to raise armies,
Taney said, it treats the militia as always existing, as "needing no law
to bring it into existence and merely requiring organization, discipline and training." The power to appoint officers in the militia and
to train it according to Congress's regulation is reserved expressly to
the states, Taney noted, while Congress is given power to call forth
the militia to execute the laws of the Union, suppress insurrection,

and repel invasion. When called into federal service, he said, militia members are to be treated as citizens of the distinct states from which their units hail. (After all, the Second Amendment begins, "A well regulated militia being necessary to the security of a free State. . . .")

The problem with the Conscription Act, Taney found, was that it would render all of the constitutional provisions for the militia inoperative. Why? Because the Conscription Act purported to make all male American citizens of military age members of the army; it left no one to be a member of the militia. When called into service, they were to be members not of the distinct states' militias but of the United States Army. Besides that, all of the militia officers, from the highest grade to the lowest, would be reduced from their ranks to that of mere privates in the United States Army. If they refused to surrender their civil rights and to be exposed to the rigors of martial courts, they might be tried for desertion.

Taney concluded that the Constitution's elaborate set of provisions giving the federal government limited control over the militia in certain carefully enumerated circumstances, along with the Second Amendment's statement that "a well regulated militia" was "necessary for the security of a free State," could not be read to empower Congress to wipe out the militia whenever it felt like it. The simple principle that no provision of the Constitution should be read as rendering another inoperative meant that the congressional power to raise armies must not have been intended to empower Congress to conscript people.

What, then, is one to make of the Constitution's statement in Article I, Section 8 that Congress will have the power to raise and support armies? Did it support the reading that it empowered Congress to conscript? Once again, Taney offered a characteristically Jeffersonian answer:

> The words themselves, even if they stood alone, will not, according to their known and established use and meaning in the English language, justify this construction.

During the period when the United States were English Colonies, the Army of England—the standing army—was always raised by voluntary enlistments—and the right to coerce all the able bodied subjects of the Crown into the ranks of the Army and subject them to military law, was not claimed or exercised by the English government—and when the power to raise and support armies was delegated to Congress, the words of the grant nececcarily implied that they were to be raiced in the usual manner.—And the general government has always heretofore so understood them and has uniformly by its own officers recruited the ranks of its "land forces" by voluntary enlistments for a specified period.

Taney went on to say that it would be far more convincing to argue that the power to raise a navy included the power to coerce men into naval service, as coercion for that purpose had long been the English custom. Yet he doubted that northeastern fishermen and sailors would accept this construction, and it certainly seemed to be contrary to the general spirit of the Constitution.

Taney also rejected the common arguments for the Conscription Act that the United States faced an emergency and that a draft was simply a more efficient, more reliable way of tapping into the manpower needed to cope with that emergency. He stated that where the Constitution granted a limited power (the power to call the militia into federal service) in enumerated circumstances (including suppression of insurrection), Congress could not simply say, "We find this power inadequate to our needs, and so we are going to exercise a more far-reaching power instead." If Congress could do that, it would "make the Constitution of no higher authority than an act of Congress." The rule that Congress could ignore relevant constitutional provisions whenever it felt justified in doing so would mean the death of the Constitution, the chief justice concluded. Congress would be transformed from a federal legislature of limited powers into a national legislature of unlimited powers.

Moreover, Taney disputed the claim that war is an emergency requiring resort to extraconstitutional means. Since the Constitution grants the federal government several war powers (for example, the power to raise armies, the power to establish a navy, and the power to embargo) but no others, one may rightly conclude "that they are all that were deemed necessary, and that it was not deemed safe or prudent to trust more in the hands of the new government." Even if it had not been obvious before that the list of war powers was exhaustive, he added, the Tenth Amendment made it clear. To ignore this principle in the name of emergency would be to set aside the Constitution and establish a provisional government, he averred.

Even more significant, the chief justice added, was the concern that a federal government empowered to draft could disrupt the state governments by depriving them of citizens—including officials serving in those state governments. The Conscription Act seemed to assume, Taney observed, that the federal government had the power to conscript even governors if it had a mind to do so, as the legislation included provisions explicitly exempting governors from the draft. He noted that the functions of the state governments, including protection of life, liberty, and property on a daily basis, are as important as those of the federal government, and that the Constitution was not meant to empower the federal government to prevent the states from fulfilling them. While the Constitution's provisions for federal employment of state militias in certain circumstances were consistent with the continued existence of the state governments, then, a federal power to draft men into the military was not.

For these reasons, Taney held that "this Act of Congress is unconstitutional and void—and confers no lawful authority on the persons appointed to execute it."

The chief justice expressed all these ideas in a memorandum, not in a Supreme Court ruling. Although the Conscription Act was highly controversial, leading ultimately to an enormous race riot in New York City in the summer of 1863, Taney never had an opportunity to issue a legal ruling on the subject.[6] Indeed, the Supreme

Court would not consider the federal draft's constitutionality until World War I.

White's Sleight of Hand

Chief Justice Edward White wrote the Court's opinion in the *Selective Draft Law Cases* of 1917.[7] The issue, as he put it, was the conscription policy adopted by Congress in response to "the war then and now flagrant." The conscription legislation incorporated the National Guard and National Guard Reserve into the service of the United States. These units had already been put under federal supervision with the Dick Act of 1903, which was itself constitutionally questionable. Now Congress converted the states' self-defense organizations into federal agencies.

The Conscription Act of 1917 also subjected all male citizens ages twenty-one to thirty (with only a few exemptions provided) to duty in the United States Army "for the period of the existing emergency after the proclamation of the President announcing the necessity for their service." It left to the president the option of drafting up to 1 million men in 500,000-man increments.

The defendants in these cases had refused to present themselves for the draft when President Woodrow Wilson called on them to do so. They asserted that the draft law was unconstitutional on various grounds, among them that the Constitution had not given Congress a draft power. The lower appellate courts upheld their convictions.

Chief Justice White wrote that the law would have to find its basis in several military clauses of Article I, Section 8 of the Constitution. The relevant language said Congress had power

> to declare war; . . . to raise and support armies, but no appropriation of money to that use shall be for a longer term than two years; . . . to make rules for the government and regulation of the land and naval forces.

Besides those, he added, was the Necessary and Proper Clause at the end of Article I, Section 8.

White simply scoffed at the defendants' constitutional claims, writing, "As the mind cannot conceive an army without the men to compose it, on the face of the Constitution, the objection that it does not give power to provide for such men would seem to be too frivolous for further notice." He likewise dismissed the defense counsel's argument that a power to force people into the military was "repugnant to a free government and in conflict with all the great guarantees of the Constitution as to individual liberty" and that the power to raise armies was solely a power to seek voluntary enlistments. Pointing to "the almost universal legislation" allowing conscription then in effect, White marshaled the examples of Asian and European imperial republics, monarchies of various stripes, and a number of Latin American banana republics to disprove the assertion that Americans were supposed to be free and that the Constitution had not negated that intention.[8] In other words, if the kaisers, the tsar, the sultan, and various generalissimos exercised power to force their subjects to fight, surely the American president could, too. In the Supreme Court's view, it seems, World War I was a contest to see who had the best imperial model, the Central Powers or the Allies. Here we have an early warning of the probable effect of a heightened judicial reliance on foreign precedents to rationalize granting new power to the federal government.

Much of White's decision was an exercise in sleight of hand. For example, he said there was no need to consider the fact that the English militia had not been subject to conscription for service outside the kingdom, since no one had denied that Parliament had authority to deploy Britons outside the context of the militia. In essence, he was saying that the British government exercised arbitrary authority over subjects in the home islands, so the United States Constitution must have given the federal government arbitrary authority over American citizens.

White said that during the American Revolution at least nine states recognized the obligation to serve as a conscript, and he offered as an example this provision of Pennsylvania's 1776 state constitution:

> That every member of society hath a right to be protected in the enjoyment of life, liberty, and property, and therefore is bound to contribute his proportion towards the expense of that protection, and yield his personal service when necessary, or an equivalent thereto.

White overlooked two aspects of this provision: that it is perfectly consistent with Taney's idea that service in the militia was citizens' sole military obligation, and that even this provision provided for making payment or procuring a substitute as a legitimate alternative to personal military service.

Turning to the other state legal provisions to which White referred, one finds little support for his position. For example, Section XXVIII of the Massachusetts Bill of Rights of 1780 says that no one may be subjected to court-martial in peacetime except members of the army, navy, and militia when called into service.[9] It is unclear how this provision in any way indicates that Massachusetts men were to be subject to conscription. Section 13 of the Virginia Declaration of Rights of 1776 said, "That a well-regulated militia, composed of the body of the people, trained to arms, is the proper, natural, and safe defence of a free State; that standing armies, in time of peace, should be avoided, as dangerous to liberty; and that in all cases the military should be under strict subordination to, and governed by, the civil power."[10] Again, one is hard pressed to determine how this casts any light on the meaning of Congress's power to raise armies.

Did the states actually exercise a drafting power during the Revolution? Chief Justice White noted that Congress had called on them to do so. Although the states were "sometimes slow in exerting the power in order to fill their quotas"—to the point that General

George Washington importuned Congress to compel the states to draft—White explained that "a default in exercising a duty may not be resorted to as a reason for denying its existence."

What kind of "duty" did White have in mind here? It seems that he believed the states had a duty to Congress. But the congresses of the Revolution were, as John Adams of Massachusetts put it, simply meeting places of ambassadors. How could South Carolina, say, have a duty to do what its own ambassadors to Congress—its congressmen—asked it to do? It could not. In fact, it was not responsible to Congress in any sense, since Congress was no more than a group of people delegated by the state legislatures to coordinate their policy.

Perhaps, then, White had in mind that the states had a duty to comply with General Washington's requests. This idea is, if anything, even more outlandish than the idea of a duty to Congress. Washington was not dictator, king, or any other kind of chief executive. He was, instead, the functionary of Congress, which was, as we have just seen, simply a group of ambassadors of what first the Continental Congress (in the Declaration of Independence) and then the Articles of Confederation (in Article II) recognized as the sovereign states. Since the states were sovereign—that is, since they each had ultimate authority, standing on a par in the international system with Sweden, Spain, and Great Britain—they arguably had no legal duty to anyone. They certainly had no moral or legal responsibility to comply with requests made of them by a general who had been entrusted with his high station by their Congress—their conclave of ambassadors. In saying that they did have such responsibility, White must have assumed that the Congress was a sovereign entity and the states merely local administrative units—which was entirely inaccurate.[11]

White next said that one motive behind the movement to create a new federal constitution in the 1780s was the desire to right the situation in which Congress was entirely dependent upon the states to raise an army. It is true, indeed, that the states did not provide Congress and General Washington with the manpower it and he would have liked to have. And it is true that this was seen as an element of what nationalists such as James Madison called the "imbecility" of Congress. But does this mean that the power to raise armies, rather than simply to ask the states to raise armies as during the Revolution, included a power to conscript?

White also made short, unsatisfactory work of the relationship between the Constitution's army clauses and militia provisions. Recall that Chief Justice Taney had insisted that any valid reading of the Constitution must give effect to all of its provisions, not allow one of them to vitiate another. According to White, however, "To argue that, as the state authority over the militia prior to the Constitution embraced every citizen, the right of Congress to raise an army should not be considered as granting authority to compel the citizen's service in the army is but to express in a different form the denial of the right to call any citizen into the army." His attitude was that the states' militias exist only so long as Congress wants them to do so, which, among other things, makes them incapable of performing the defensive function they had performed during the Revolution and that Federalists had promised they would be able to perform under the new Constitution.

The idea that Congress must exercise its power to raise armies consistently with the continued existence of the militia, White insisted, does not make sense. He pointed to Secretary of War James Monroe's calls for conscription during the War of 1812 as evidence that Congress had the power to conscript—though he then conceded that Congress opposed Monroe's suggestion on the grounds of "the incompatibility of compulsory military service with free government." White argued that he did not need to consider this incompatibility because he had already resolved it.

The first (real) precedent for the World War I legislation to which White could point was the Conscription Act of 1863—the law so powerfully criticized by Chief Justice Taney. White omitted any mention of Taney's criticism from his opinion. He also did not mention that President Lincoln's initial proclamation calling for volunteers, which he issued without congressional authorization, was an unconstitutional presidential exercise of a power—the armies power—that the Constitution clearly lodges in the Congress. Congress did then authorize Lincoln to enroll 500,000 volunteers and also passed a law augmenting militia forces to be trained by the states and called into federal service. It finally passed the Conscription Act when Lincoln could not find enough citizens willing to volunteer for his forces. White noted that the Act was very similar to the proposal offered by Monroe and rejected by Congress during the War of 1812.

All told, Chief Justice White assembled an extremely weak argument to legitimate the draft law. While he cited "the text of the Constitution," the Constitution, as we have seen, says only that the federal government will have power to raise armies and may in certain circumstances call the militia into federal service; this does not answer the question of how those armies will be raised, and—as Taney developed—does not seem to leave it at the federal government's discretion effectively to abolish the state governments, including the militias, by drafting their most important officers. It was similarly unconvincing to argue, as White in essence did, that the Russian, Austrian, German, Japanese, and Chinese emperors drafted their subjects into their military establishments, and so the United States Congress may draft people, too. The third factor White mentioned, historical practice, came down to the argument that the Lincoln administration did it, and so Wilson's may, too. Congress and the executive during the Lincoln administration felt empowered to do essentially anything they wanted to do to win the war and to perpetuate southern subjugation thereafter.[12] This, then, does not make a very persuasive argument for anyone who believes in constitutional government.

With the last factor he cited to justify the World War I draft law, White clearly signaled that the Supreme Court was not interested in the limitations on federal power. In his reading, the Fourteenth Amendment gave the federal government even more power to adopt a policy of conscription than the central government had possessed in Lincoln's day. By adopting that amendment, White said, the people had elevated the significance of federal citizenship above that of state citizenship. So much for the reservation of powers to the states.

While Chief Justice White relied on the Fourteenth Amendment in his ruling, he did not pay much heed to the Thirteenth. The argument that the prohibition of slavery and involuntary servitude barred the government from forcing men into the military (or as White put it, exacting "from the citizen . . . the performance of his supreme and noble duty of contributing to the defense of the rights and honor of the nation, as the result of a war declared by the great representative body of the people") was, he declared, "refuted by its mere statement."

Ipse dixit, pure and simple: "because we say so."

Unmoored

Since 1917, the federal government has felt perfectly at liberty to draft men into the military. Yes, it ceased actually to do so at the end of the Vietnam War, but the reason for that forbearance was not constitutional but practical: President Richard Nixon recognized that the widespread opposition to the war resulted chiefly from college students' exposure to the draft, and so he decided to cut off the protest movement at its source. As he had expected, the mass protests of the war ended at the moment he canceled the draft.

In 1979, after President Carter required all eighteen-year-old males to register for the draft, Ronald Reagan condemned conscription by noting that it "rests on the assumption that your kids belong to the state. If we buy that assumption then it is for the state—not for parents, the community, the religious institutions, or teachers—to decide who shall have what values and who shall do what work, when, where, and how in our society. That assumption isn't a new one. The Nazis thought it was a great idea."[13]

The fact that so few Americans today question the constitutionality of the draft—even as every eighteen-year-old male must register for Selective Service, and even when politicians raise the specter of reinstituting the draft (for men *and* women)—is another telling, and troubling, reminder of how we have become unmoored from the Constitution. The Supreme Court's weakly argued opinion in the *Selective Draft Law Cases* cries out for someone to insist that the draft is unconstitutional. Conscription is inconsistent with what the Founding Fathers called "the genius of republican government."

Nonetheless, thanks to the Supreme Court's characteristic decision giving Congress the green light, Congress can draft as it pleases.

9

Do Americans Have a Constitutional Duty to Suffer? The Case of Medical Marijuana

IN AUGUST 2002, agents of the Drug Enforcement Administration (DEA), along with Butte County sheriff's deputies, raided the home of Diane Monson, a California woman who suffered from severe back pain and spasms.

The problem? At her physician's direction, Monson was using cannabis to treat her condition.

A surprised Monson showed the law enforcement officials her cannabis plants and explained that she was growing them in accordance with her rights under Proposition 215, the popular referendum that led to the passage of California's Compassionate Use Act of 1996. That law directed that physicians may not be "punished, or denied any right or privilege, for having recommended marijuana to a patient for medical purposes."[1] As of this printing, similar legislation has been passed in twelve other states.

At first it seemed as if the raid would be over quickly. The local deputies "were quite willing to leave [the plants] there because I'm working within the confines of the state law and the county guidelines," Monson later recalled. "So they said, 'Well, there's only six plants here. She's totally within her rights to be doing this cultivation, so we're leaving.'"[2]

But the standoff didn't end there. According to Monson, the two federal agents "refused to leave without taking the plants, and the sheriffs refused to let them do so. So it got kind of ugly, and it went on for about three hours." After some phone calls back and forth, the federal agents prevailed.

"I stood with the sheriffs while the federal agent chopped down the plant, and I read to him the text of Prop. 215," said Monson.

Federal agents thus confiscated her marijuana plants—and then brought no charges against her.

Angel Raich, another medical marijuana patient who made national news, insists that she owes her life to the treatment. "I actually don't like smoking or vaporizing or using cannabis," Raich told PBS's *NewsHour*, "but it's the only way that I can keep from dying."[3]

Raich suffers from a variety of serious afflictions, including fibromyalgia, seizures, nausea, and an inoperable brain tumor. She endures chronic pain resulting from scoliosis, endometriosis, and temporomandibular joint dysfunction. She suffers from a mysterious wasting syndrome that causes her to lose a life-threatening amount of weight. She has tried traditional pain medication but has either found no relief or suffered from intolerable side effects. Only cannabis—which she needs to ingest every two hours, or she loses a pound of weight a day—has ameliorated her condition in any significant way.

The raid on Diane Monson's home occurred against the backdrop of a wave of federal arrests that had taken place over the previous several months. As a result, Monson and Raich went to district court to get an injunction to stop the federal government from initiating legal action against patients who were using medical marijuana. They argued that the federal government's harassment and threatened imprisonment of medical marijuana users was an unconstitutional exercise of power, and that the government's Commerce Clause rationale for it was legally indefensible.

(Raich more than Monson became the public standard-bearer for the case and for the issue it embodied, in large part because

Monson, in her own words, wanted only "to be left alone to pursue my health and happiness. I feel very much forced into my legal actions by the federal government. I led a very private life until the raid on my house.")[4]

Although they lost in district court, Raich and Monson later got exactly what they had hoped for when a panel of the U.S. Circuit Court of Appeals for the Ninth Circuit ruled in their favor, issuing an injunction forbidding any federal agent from confiscating the women's marijuana. The Justice Department appealed the case, which wound up in the United States Supreme Court.

The "Hey, You Can Do Whatever You Feel Like" Clause

The Supreme Court heard the case of *Gonzales v. Raich* in the fall of 2004.[5] The women again premised their case on their interpretation of the Constitution's Commerce Clause. That clause, found in Article I, Section 8, Clause 3 of the Constitution, grants Congress the power to "regulate Commerce with foreign Nations, and among the several States, and with the Indian Tribes."

All the evidence we have suggests that the word "commerce" was meant to be understood narrowly and precisely. At the Constitutional Convention, no reference to "commerce" clearly refers to anything other than trade. The same goes for the sixty-three times the word appears in the *Federalist Papers*.[6] And the same is also true with regard to the state ratifying conventions.[7] James Madison later observed that "if, in citing the Constitution, the word trade was put in the place of commerce, the word foreign made it synonymous with commerce. Trade and commerce are, in fact, used indiscriminately, both in books and in conversation."[8]

The other words crucial in the *Raich* case were "among the several states." This phrase referred to commerce between one state and another. The words were not meant to refer to commerce that occurred in one state and merely concerned or had effects upon other states.[9] According to Madison, the phrase "'*among* the several States' . . . grew out of the abuses of the power by the importing states in taxing the non-importing, and was intended as a negative and preventive provision against injustice among the States themselves, rather than as a power to be used for the positive purposes of the General Government."[10] In other words, it established a giant free-trade zone throughout the United States and prevented the states from obstructing this free flow of commerce.

In *Gibbons v. Ogden* (1824), Chief Justice John Marshall introduced the idea that the Commerce Clause empowered the federal government to regulate activities that occurred within a single state if they affected other states. Absolutely nothing in the language or the history of the clause supported that position. Marshall created it out of thin air. By the twentieth century the doctrine had been modified to the claim that the federal government could regulate intrastate activities that had a "*substantial* effect" on other states, but this, too, was a legal fabrication.[11] And since practically any activity, when taken in the aggregate, could be said to have a "substantial effect" on interstate commerce, this interpretation of the clause deprives the federal government of the limited character it was intended to have. Listing the federal government's specific powers in Article I, Section 8 seems superfluous and absurd if the federal government has the essentially unlimited powers that this interpretation of the Commerce Clause would grant it.[12] No wonder Ninth Circuit judge Alex Kozinski called it the "Hey, you-can-do-whatever-you-feel-like Clause."[13]

In 1942, the Supreme Court outdid itself in its Commerce Clause jurisprudence with *Wickard v. Filburn*, which found that a farmer growing wheat for his own use on his own land was subject to federal regulation because he affected interstate commerce: had he not grown his own wheat, he might have purchased it from another state. Thus his abstention from purchasing wheat from other states affects interstate commerce, and thereby makes his activity subject to federal control. Justice Robert Jackson, in the course of deliberation in *Wickard*, suggested that the best course might be to admit frankly that the Commerce Clause imposed no limits on the federal government at all, apart from those the Congress might choose to acknowledge. "A frank holding that the interstate commerce power has no limits except those which Congress sees fit to observe might serve a wholesome purpose," he said. "In order to be unconstitutional by the judicial process if this Act is sustained, the relation between interstate commerce and the regulated activity would have to be so absurd that it would be laughed out of Congress." Since Congress is not exactly known for bursting out in laughter at the powers with which it proposes to clothe itself, this is not the most robust defense against the expansion of government.[14] But Justice Jackson's suggestion gives a good indication of how the federal government had begun to think about the liberty of action it might enjoy if it in effect ignored the Commerce Clause.

"Rootless and Malleable" Standards

Given a precedent such as *Wickard*, the Court's finding in *Gonzales v. Raich* can hardly come as a surprise: under the interstate Commerce Clause, it said, the federal government could ban the use of a substance (medical marijuana) that was grown and consumed in a single state and never bought or sold (just like the wheat in *Wickard*). In its ruling against Raich and Monson, the Court argued that marijuana, even if originally intended for medical purposes alone, could make its way into the interstate market for recreational marijuana. Such leakage from the medical marijuana community to society at large could have a substantial effect on the interstate market in marijuana, the Court said. Since the federal government was assumed to have the right to regulate (more precisely, to prohibit) the use of marijuana, it also had the right to regulate (or, again, to prohibit) the use of marijuana even for medical purposes. After all, the argument went, medical marijuana diverted into the market would disrupt the federal drug (prohibition) policy, known as the Controlled Substances Act. In fact, the Court ruled, failing to ban medical marijuana would make the government's larger regulatory scheme banning marijuana in general less effective, and harder to operate. (In its ruling the Court did not directly overturn state laws allowing medical marijuana, but by ruling that such patients and their suppliers were subject to prosecution under federal drug statutes, it made the continuation of such treatment difficult and risky, and may have undermined the progress of medical marijuana initiatives in other states.)

Now suppose that the Court's speculation had merit, and that leakages of medical marijuana into the marijuana supply as a whole would probably disrupt the overall policy of marijuana prohibition. If that were so, we should expect to see amicus briefs in defense of the federal government's position coming from state governments concerned that federal sanction of state medical marijuana laws could add to the drug traffic in their own states. But no state filed a brief in support of the federal government. To the contrary, three states that outlaw medical marijuana—Alabama, Louisiana, and Mississippi—actually filed amicus briefs in support of Angel Raich.[15]

"Whether California and the other compassionate-use states are 'courageous'—or instead profoundly misguided—is not the point," reads Alabama's brief on behalf of these three states. "The point is that, as a sovereign member of the federal union, California is entitled to make for itself the tough policy choices that affect its citizens." The federal government may not "displace the States from their traditional role as the enforcers of local criminal law and assume the States' police power to provide for the health, safety, welfare, and morals of their citizens." The states filing amicus briefs find themselves "in complete agreement with the Federal Government as a matter of drug-control policy, but in complete disagreement as a matter of constitutional principle." Since the latter trumps the former, the brief concludes, the decision of the court of appeals in support of the patients should be upheld.[16]

In other words, the states that would be affected do not believe they are in any danger from medical marijuana that might make its way into their jurisdictions. They consider themselves far more threatened by a federal government so unhinged from constitutional restraints that it believes itself authorized to arrest people on drug charges in defiance of state laws exempting them from prosecution.

The principle claimed by the federal government is indeed a dangerous one. In case the implications of the government's case are not clear, consider some analogies. According to the principles set forth in *Raich*, a comprehensive federal regulatory regime covering commercial day care services could also lead to federal regulation of child care in the home. A comprehensive regulatory regime covering store-bought TV dinners could justify the regulation of food prepared in the home. And so on.[17]

If the Court's argument really held water, argued Justice Sandra Day O'Connor in her dissent, then under the interstate Commerce Clause, Congress could regulate just about anything, no matter how purely local or noncommercial, as long as it was part of a larger regulatory scheme. The Court was telling Congress, albeit unintentionally, that if it wanted to regulate a local practice but felt confined by the Commerce Clause, all it needed to do was pass a larger regulatory scheme of which the local practice would be a subset. The federal prohibition on guns in schools that was overturned in *United States v. Lopez* (1995), for instance, could have been upheld if only Congress had established a larger regulatory scheme prohibiting firearm ownership and transfer throughout the country—for in that case the possession of firearms in a school would have been a subset of this larger regulatory scheme and thus subject to federal regulation.[18]

Useful as Justice O'Connor's dissent was (a dissent on which she was joined by Chief Justice William Rehnquist), by far the better dissent came from Justice Clarence Thomas, who revisited the question of how, in the name of regulating "interstate commerce," the federal government could gain control over homegrown marijuana that had never crossed state lines and was immediately consumed rather than sold. He also wondered how a definition of interstate commerce that was broad enough to include what was so obviously an intrastate activity could be compatible with the limited government that the Framers plainly intended to construct. What activity could possibly escape federal scrutiny if even homegrown marijuana for the relief of suffering could be defined as "interstate commerce"?

Beyond all this, Thomas even raised the forbidden question of whether the "substantial effects" test should be retained at all. He cited the majority's decision as "further proof that the 'substantial effects' test is a 'rootless and malleable standard' at odds with the constitutional design." Hardly anything could be exempt from federal control or left to the people of the states under that standard. "One searches the Court's opinion in vain for any hint of what aspect of American life is reserved to the States," Thomas said.[19]

Are we overstating the dangers and foolishness in the Court's reasoning? If anything, we have understated it. As we have seen, the majority contended that the states' allowance for medical marijuana could have a substantial effect on interstate commerce. Justice O'Connor, sensibly enough, noted that there is "simply no evidence that homegrown medical marijuana users constitute, in the aggregate, a sizable enough class to have a discernible, let alone substantial, impact on the national illicit drug market." But according to the Court, *no evidence of such effects need be shown.* It is enough if Congress rationally could have *believed* that the activity substantially affected interstate commerce, even if it made no findings to that effect and even if the Court itself disagreed.[20] "In assessing the scope of Congress's authority under the Commerce Clause," the Court explained, echoing legal reasoning dating back to the 1960s, "we stress that the task before us is a modest one. We need not determine whether respondents' activities, taken in the aggregate, substantially affect interstate commerce, in fact, but only whether a 'rational basis' exists for so concluding."[21]

Even Justice Antonin Scalia, who is usually portrayed as a supporter of federalism and original intent, voted with the majority in *Raich*, though using his own rationale. According to Scalia, the Commerce Clause alone could not reach activities that substantially affect interstate commerce but are not part of interstate commerce themselves. But he said that the Commerce Clause in this case worked in tandem with the Necessary and Proper Clause, according to which Congress has the power to "make all Laws which shall be necessary and proper for carrying into execution the foregoing Powers, and all other Powers vested by this Constitution in the government of the United States, or in any Department or Officer thereof." According to Scalia, then, this pairing of constitutional clauses permits the federal government to reach intrastate economic activity that has substantial effects on interstate commerce, and to reach intrastate *non*economic activity if—and here we return to a familiar formulation—doing so is necessary in order to carry out a larger scheme of regulation. The federal government's power to ban medical marijuana that the states have permitted is "necessary and proper" in order to carry out the regulation envisioned by the Controlled Substances Act. Medical marijuana, after all, is "never more than an instant from the interstate market."[22]

In the end, Scalia's reasoning—notwithstanding his protests to the contrary—is just as open-ended as that of the majority, and just as feckless in imposing restraints on the federal government. How does Scalia propose to determine whether a particular regulation of noneconomic intrastate activity is really "necessary" in order to "make the interstate regulation effective"? His answer is that Congress needs to show that its regulation is "reasonably adapted to the attainment of a legitimate end under the commerce power." But Scalia nowhere suggests that Congress should be required to provide *evidence* of a connection between banning medical marijuana and carrying out the goals of the Controlled Substances Act. As law professor Ilya Somin concludes, "Failure to require at least some substantial evidence that regulation of intrastate noneconomic activity really is 'necessary' to effectuate the government's attempt to regulate interstate commerce ensures that Scalia's approach has the same tendency to legitimate unlimited federal power as the majority's use of the broader regulatory scheme exception."[23]

A "rational basis" test, the Necessary and Proper Clause—the justification doesn't matter. The toothless restraints allow the federal government to operate unfettered.

"The Dirty Little Secret of Constitutional Law"

Its Commerce Clause challenge having failed, Raich's legal team had another avenue to pursue in light of modern constitutional law: the Due Process Clause. By using medical marijuana, Raich was taking an action necessary to preserve her life. By refusing to allow her access to marijuana, the federal government was in effect depriving her of life without due process of law. Even though this is surely to stretch the Due Process Clause, the fate of this argument reveals a lot about the current state of the Constitution.

Here we need to recall the important principle the Court established in *United States v. Carolene Products* (1938). In that case the Court declared that federal legislation was to be *presumed constitutional*. The only caveat to this extraordinary allowance came in the form of footnote 4, whose first paragraph described the conditions that would need to be met in order for claimed violations of the Constitution to be taken seriously. There we learn that the federal government could be restrained only on the basis of "certain expressed prohibitions" in the Constitution. In other words, federal action might be declared unconstitutional only if it violated one of these expressed prohibitions. But the federal government need not look for any expressed *permissions* in order to *exercise* all manner of power. What the federal government cannot do is summed up in a few prohibitions; what it *can* do is left undefined—and all of its acts are presumed constitutional.

Since the 1960s, the formula that courts and legal scholars have adopted in light of footnote 4 runs as follows: notwithstanding this presumption of constitutionality, the Court can still strike down a federal law, but only if the right that the law is alleged to violate is a "fundamental" one.[24] What makes a right fundamental? A fundamental right, according to the reasoning in *Washington v. Glucksberg* (1997), is one that is "deeply rooted in this Nation's history and traditions" and "implicit in the concept of ordered liberty."[25]

Now consider: the right at issue in *Raich* could, on one hand, be described as the right to preserve one's life and avoid unnecessary pain and suffering. That sounds fundamental. On the other hand, the principle at stake could also be described as the right to smoke marijuana for health reasons. That, by contrast, does not sound so fundamental. So which description is correct? The answer is that *both* truthfully and accurately describe the right in question. This is what Randy Barnett, who represented Angel Raich and Diane Monson in court, called "the dirty little secret of constitutional law": both descriptions are right, so whether a petitioner will find relief in federal court "depends on which accurate description a court chooses to accept." Barnett summed up: "[A] court may rule however it wishes simply by choosing how to describe the right."[26]

Thanks to this doctrine, Americans wishing to challenge federal power find themselves up against an essentially arbitrary and possibly insuperable obstacle: a court may simply word their complaint in such a way as to make it impossible for them to prevail. That's probably not what the Constitution's Framers had in mind.

In a speech at Washington University School of Law in February 2006, Barnett predicted the outcome of the case. "Unless we prevail on our claim that the liberty in question is fundamental," he warned, "the irrebuttable presumption of constitutionality will kick in and we lose."[27]

And that is precisely what happened.

On March 14, 2007, the Ninth Circuit Court of Appeals handed down its decision: the federal government could indeed prohibit medical marijuana in the face of state laws to the contrary, and Angel Raich's right to use it was not sufficiently "fundamental" to challenge this federal power. The court acknowledged the gravity of Raich's condition and the uncontroverted testimony of her physician that she "cannot be without cannabis as medicine" because she would very rapidly suffer "precipitous medical deterioration" and "could very well" die. The court recognized that prior to the pain management regime she received by means of medical marijuana, Raich had been confined to a wheelchair, unable to walk. The court likewise admitted that if Raich obeyed the Controlled Substances Act she would have to endure

> intolerable pain, including severe chronic pain in her face and jaw muscles due to temporomandibular joint dysfunction and bruxism, severe chronic pain and chronic burning from fibromyalgia that forces her to be flat on her back for days, excruciating pain from non-epileptic seizures, heavy bleeding and severely painful menstrual periods due to a uterine fibroid tumor, and acute weight loss resulting possibly in death due to a life-threatening wasting disorder.[28]

The Ninth Circuit even agreed that Raich "does not appear to have any legal alternative to marijuana use." The side effects of other treatments, it conceded, had included "violent nausea, shakes, itching, rapid heart palpitations, and insomnia."[29]

When it came time to define the precise nature of the right Raich was claiming, however, the court rejected her description and accepted that of the government—thereby dooming her case. "Raich," the court began, "asserts that she has a fundamental right to 'mak[e] life-shaping medical decisions that are necessary to preserve the integrity of her body, avoid intolerable physical pain, and preserve her life.'" The court conceded that several fundamental rights that the judiciary has upheld in the past are indeed contained in Raich's description of her claim. But according to the court, she had not phrased her claim quite narrowly enough. What she was really claiming, said the Ninth Circuit, was "the right to use *marijuana* to preserve bodily integrity, avoid pain, and preserve her life . . . Accordingly, we will add the centerpiece—the use of marijuana—to Raich's proposed right."[30]

The following section of the court's decision begins with the heading "Whether the Asserted Right Is 'Deeply Rooted in This Nation's History and Tradition' and 'Implicit in the Concept of Ordered Liberty.'"[31] One could hardly be in suspense as to the contents of that section.

Naturally, then, Angel Raich lost her case. (Diane Monson had dropped out of the process by this point.) The Ninth Circuit concluded that "federal law does not recognize a fundamental right to use medical marijuana prescribed by a licensed physician to alleviate excruciating pain and human suffering." So that was that. "When the Ninth Circuit accepted the government's description of the right in question," Barnett wrote in the *Wall Street Journal* after the decision, "the outcome followed like night follows day."[32]

A Modest Shift

It was not entirely implausible to suggest that the cause of medical marijuana might have had a fighting chance in the Supreme Court. Since 1995, legal commentators had been reporting on a shift in the Court's thinking away from deference toward the other branches and toward a more confrontational stance. More specifically, the Court once again seemed to be taking seriously the idea that the Constitution established a limited federal government with fixed powers, rather than an unlimited one with indefinite powers. No longer could the federal government, with barely a nod in the direction of the Constitution, automatically assume its legislation would pass constitutional muster with the Court, or that it wouldn't be told that the power it sought to exercise belonged to the states instead.

Much of this reaction was overblown: government partisans typically respond to even the tiniest retrenchment of government power by wildly exaggerating what is actually happening.[33] Something *was* happening, but it was something more modest than most political observers suggested. Over the course of half a century the Supreme Court had not once found the Congress to have exceeded its powers under the Commerce Clause. Not even once. Suddenly, the Gun-Free School Zones Act of 1990 (GFSZA), which criminalized the possession of a firearm within a thousand feet of a school, was overturned in *Lopez v. United States* (1995) on precisely those grounds. The federal government had claimed, in part, that the presence of guns in or near schools was a proper subject of federal regulation because it affected interstate commerce. The argument ran as follows: The presence of guns in schools interfered with education because it made students nervous and afraid, and thus less apt to learn. If students learned less, they would be less productive as adults. And if they were less productive as adults, production would be lower and there would be less traffic in interstate commerce.

That was too much of a stretch even for the normally indulgent Supreme Court.

If a law regulating guns in or near schools were to be made, said the Court, our constitutional system required that it be made at the state level—and in fact forty states had already adopted such laws at the time. The Court gave no precise account of how far the federal government's power could extend under the Commerce Clause, but it made clear for the first time in decades that such a limit, whatever it was, certainly existed and would perhaps even be enforced.

Lopez was followed in 2000 by *United States v. Morrison*, which expanded on the Court's evolving position on the Commerce Clause. That case overturned provisions of the 1994 Violence Against Women Act (VAWA), again on the grounds that violence against women was not related to interstate commerce in any substantial way, and that the Constitution left police powers over such matters to the states.[34]

These decisions were indeed surprising, given the Court's previous reluctance to challenge the other branches' claims to power under the Commerce Clause. Still, although the Court suggested in *Lopez* and *Morrison* that there must be *some* limit to federal power under the Commerce Clause, it never precisely described what that limit was. *Lopez* and *Morrison* also preserved the "substantial effects" test intact, arguing only that the test had not been passed in these cases. *Lopez* maintained the exception that Congress could regulate even local matters if they were "an essential part of a larger regulation of economic activity, in which the regulatory scheme could be undercut unless the intrastate activity were regulated."[35] Both decisions argued that Congress could regulate only "economic" or "commercial" activity under the Commerce Clause, but without defining those terms. The way was thus left open for the majority in *Raich* to argue that the use of any substance for which an interstate market existed amounted to commercial activity—and could therefore be regulated by the federal government.

Therefore, even in the midst of a much-touted "revolution" in favor of federalism and states' rights, the ingredients that could be used to reach an absurd decision such as *Raich* were sitting there in plain sight, waiting to be exploited. The sober commentators were closer to the truth than the hysterical ones: *Lopez* had been a "particularly modest opinion," said Jonathan Adler.[36] According to Robert Pushaw, it is "impossible to determine whether the majority or the dissent [in *Raich*] correctly applied the *Lopez* and *Morrison* standards, because they are so malleable as to justify either result."[37]

A Sickening Pattern

What happened here fits exactly with the pattern we have described so often in this book: time after time, the Court's finding gives the federal government the broadest latitude possible for the exercise of power, so the possibility of meaningful limits on that power essentially disappears. In this instance, many commentators were prematurely celebrating a return to some sort of judicial acknowledgment that the federal government possessed only the powers enumerated in the Constitution, only to see the American people hit with the *Raich* decision, which once again undermines the idea of limits on what government can do. Ilya Somin is surely correct when he concludes that the decision in *Raich* has placed "insurmountable obstacles" in front of efforts to limit the federal government's exercise of power under the Commerce Clause.[38]

Yet again, however, this was not simply a case of a Supreme Court run amok. It was a Supreme Court ratifying the policy of the executive branch, whose DEA launched the raids in the first place. And the legislative branch played its role, too. Nine days after the ruling in *Gonzales v. Raich*, Congress failed—for the third year in a row—to support a measure that would have denied funds to the Justice Department for the purpose of prosecuting medical marijuana cases.[39] In other words, Congress had a golden opportunity to use its power of the purse to make right an obvious constitutional wrong. It chose instead to let the offense against the Constitution stand.

preceding decades. It was a vision of government at odds with the Constitution and destined to have earth-shaking results.

Is It Right? Better Question: Is It Constitutional?

Justice Oliver Wendell Holmes's short majority opinion in the case of *State of Missouri v. Holland* (1920) does not on its face seem significant.[2] But in fact it addressed a crucial constitutional question: could congressional legislation that would have been void because it violated the Tenth Amendment become constitutional if adopted in fulfillment of a treaty? In other words, if the U.S. Constitution reserved power in a certain area to the states, might the federal government get around this limitation on its power by using its power to make treaties?

Congress had adopted a law in 1913 intended to protect endangered migratory birds.[3] Opponents of the bill had asserted that the Constitution did not give Congress power over migratory birds and so this power had been reserved to the states.[4] In response, the bill's chief Senate sponsor, Senator George McLean, introduced a constitutional amendment to empower Congress to adopt his legislative proposal. Later, however, he concluded that an amendment was unnecessary, because the federal government had "implied attributes of sovereignty" in areas the individual states acting separately could not adequately address.[5]

What McLean was saying was that the U.S. government was a national one, on the model of the government of France or of Britain, and not a federal one possessing only the few powers carefully delegated to it by the states through the Constitution. The Tenth Amendment's explicit reservation of all powers not delegated to the federal government through the Constitution was, then, inoperative in those areas that federal officials felt the need to address. This would mean that the federal government's powers were not limited at all, since an official who has only the powers he feels the need to exercise is an official with unlimited power.

10

From Chief Executive to Prince: The Presidency and Foreign Policy

Y NOW WE have become accustomed to the idea that the president serves as the chief national legislator. Just watch what happens in any presidential campaign, as the candidates tout laundry lists of legislative proposals that they promise to enact as soon as they enter the Oval Office. This legislative role of the executive is at its most uninhibited in the area of foreign relations. In fact, the president has come to exercise almost complete discretion in making American foreign policy.

How in the world did this happen? This is certainly not the plan that the federal Constitution lays out. The Constitution leaves nearly all powers to the states. When it delegates power to the federal government, it makes Congress the policy-making body and assigns the executive branch responsibility to, well, execute policy.

So when did the Constitution become an afterthought in the conduct of foreign affairs? The answer, as is so often the case, is the twentieth century.[1] In the 1920s and 1930s a triad of Supreme Court rulings completely upended traditional constitutionalism regarding foreign policy and installed the federal government as the unchecked authority. But these decisions did not arise in a vacuum. They reflected a new conception of government developed over the

At the Constitutional Convention in 1787 the Framers actually considered the version of the Constitution that Senator McLean described—and they rejected it. The Virginia Plan, which was chiefly the work of James Madison, proposed that Congress have power to legislate in areas in which the separate states were incompetent. Instead of this national legislature, however, the Convention agreed to a federal Congress—with a specified set of powers listed mainly in Article I, Section 8. In the ratification process, Federalist proponents of the new Constitution—Alexander Hamilton in New York, William Cushing in Massachusetts, Charles Cotesworth Pinckney in South Carolina, James Wilson in Pennsylvania, and Edmund Randolph and George Nicholas in Virginia—pointed to this feature of the Constitution to assure doubters that the new government would not subvert the principle of local self-government for which the Revolution had been fought. As Governor Randolph of Virginia put it, the federal government was to have only the powers it was "expressly delegated."[6]

The Supreme Court had remained committed to this traditional federal structure, even in regard to foreign affairs, throughout the nineteenth century and into the twentieth. As recently as 1907 it had upheld this reading of the Constitution. In *Kansas v. Colorado*, Justice David Brewer wrote for the majority:

> The powers affecting the internal affairs of the states not granted to the United States by the Constitution, nor prohibited by it to the States, are reserved to the States respectively, and all powers of a national character which are not delegated to the National Government by the Constitution are reserved to the people of the United States.[7]

So when Congress took up the migratory birds legislation just six years later, advocates of the bill had to get over this constitutional hurdle. The proponents' true attitude was perhaps expressed most clearly by the supporter who said, "I do not know whether [the bill] is constitutional, but I do know that it is eternally right and in the end right will prevail." The House and Senate committee reports in favor of the bill provided different constitutional justifications for the legislation. The House committee said that an "interstate bird" was in interstate commerce and thus could be regulated by Congress under its Commerce Clause power. The Senate report likened this bill to the "power of the Federal Government to regulate by treaty the taking of migratory seals and fish." (This analogy seems inappropriate, since there was no treaty concerning migratory birds yet.)[8] Despite the absence of agreement concerning its constitutional basis, the bill was enacted.

But that did not end the dispute. Two lower-level federal courts invalidated the act in 1914 and 1915. The law's supporters joined Senator McLean in urging a treaty to cover the matter, as legislation to enforce a migratory birds treaty seemed more likely to be constitutional than the free-standing legislation was. As Senator Elihu Root put it, "It may be that under the treaty-making power a situation can be created in which the Government of the United States will have constitutional authority to deal with this subject."[9]

In 1916 a treaty was concluded with Britain (which at the time controlled Canada's foreign relations). Next, in 1918, Congress adopted legislation to implement that 1916 treaty addressing the same issues as the invalidated 1913 law. It was this 1918 legislation that the Supreme Court considered in *Missouri v. Holland* as it addressed the question of whether the federal government had constitutional power to enact such legislation.

The Federal Government Trumps All

Justice Holmes's majority opinion in *Missouri v. Holland* is typical of his work on the Supreme Court. He offers unproven assertions as if they were incontestable, when actually they get at the very point that is in dispute. "It is obvious that there may be matters of the sharpest exigency for the national well being," he says, "that an act of Congress could not deal with but that a treaty followed by such an act could, and it is not lightly to be assumed that, in matters requiring national action, 'a power which must belong to and somewhere reside in every civilized government' is not to be found."[10]

Holmes tacitly conceded that the Constitution had not originally been understood as enabling the federal government to strip the states of power in the pursuit of foreign policy goals. "We may add," he intoned, "that when we are dealing with words that also are a constituent act, like the Constitution of the United States, we must realize that they have called into life a being the development of which could not have been foreseen completely by the most gifted of its begetters. It was enough for them to realize or to hope that they had created an organism; it has taken a century and cost their successors much sweat and blood to prove that they created a nation."

As in many of his decisions, it may be unclear exactly what Holmes is saying, so here is the gist of it: All civilized governments must have unlimited power to make treaties. Perhaps the federal government did not always have such power, but the federal government may claim powers it was not delegated in the first place by referring to the idea of its unpredictable "growth." Far from a federation of sovereign states, the United States is a nation with the powers of a nation. A nation can do things such as the one at issue here. No puny claim that the states reserved some powers when they created the federal government will be allowed to stand in the way of the federal government's ineluctably evolving purposes and powers, its ever-growing strength. Missouri, therefore, loses, and the congressional legislation will be enforced.

Holmes's position is that over time, the federal government will be able to do more and more things. In the end, then, one infers, there likely will be no area of legislation that will be reserved to the states. The discretion of the executive branch and the Senate is the sole limitation on the federal government's power to enter into treaties on Americans' behalf.

One authority on constitutional history says that Holmes avoided the "horrifying" conclusion that "the treaty power was not limited by other provisions at all."[11] But since Holmes concluded that the Tenth Amendment's reservation of certain powers to the states—the principle underlying the Constitution—must yield to the treaty power (despite the fact that the Tenth Amendment was added to the Constitution after the language conveying the treaty power was ratified), it is hard to see which sections of the Constitution the treaty power does not trump. Why, logically, would the reasoning leading to the conclusion that it trumps the Tenth Amendment *not* apply to the other provisions of the Bill of Rights as well?

In Holmes's day, reaction to this decision was generally positive. What else could the rule be? asked one commentator.[12] If the federal government could not make treaties touching on questions reserved to the states, the ban on state treaty-making would leave many areas of legislation regarding which no American government could make treaties. (One might have thought that it was for just such cases that two mechanisms for formally amending the Constitution had been included in Article V.)

Another writer, after noting that the treaty in question had been entered into in response to the court decisions striking down the earlier statute, contended, "It is within the power of the federal government by treaty to remove from state control any matter which may become the subject of negotiation with a foreign government"—thus implying that the federal government could circumvent the Tenth Amendment at will through the use of the treaty power.[13]

In 1920, in response to the Court's decision, an author in the *University of Pennsylvania Law Review* asked whether the president and Senate might use the treaty power to give some or all of a state's territory to another country and concluded, not very reassuringly, that "there are but few who go that far."[14] Yes, really, it was just a matter of opinion, and only some went that far! To reach such a conclusion, scholars had to ignore the plain statements by Federalist proponents of ratification in the 1780s that the treaty power concerned only external matters, not internal ones (such as, perhaps, the movements of migratory birds).[15]

For the author writing in the *University of Pennsylvania Law Review*, the issue was the same whether the treaty purported to surrender a state to a foreign country or simply to strip the state of its power over migratory birds within its territory: would the Tenth Amendment reservation continue to limit the federal government's powers vis-à-vis the states, or were the states going to be entirely subject to the federal government? He concluded that in *Holland*, as in his hypothetical case, the Supreme Court should have ruled in favor of the state: the federal government did not have all of the constitutional power that it was claiming. After all, the states were integral to the federal Constitution, and so that document should not be read as permitting the abolition of all (or even one) of them.[16]

Not only did the Court reject this argument, but so did the majority of legal commentators. Since these developments came in the immediate wake of the adoption of the Seventeenth Amendment (1913), which transferred the power to elect U.S. senators from the state legislatures to the people of each state, *Missouri v. Holland* can be understood as an enormous incursion on the now-defenseless states' traditional reserved powers. Holmes's notion that the executive's treaty power is bounded only by the requirement that the Senate give its consent by a two-thirds vote runs contrary to the consensus in the 1790s that treaties could not contravene the Constitution—including the Tenth Amendment.[17]

An "Indefinitely Flexible" Constitution?

The twentieth-century revolution in the Supreme Court's foreign affairs jurisprudence did not end there, however. It culminated in the decision in *United States v. Curtiss-Wright Export Corporation* (1936), in which the Court considered the constitutionality of a congressional attempt to delegate to the president broad discretion in one aspect of foreign affairs.[18]

In *Panama Refining Co. v. Ryan* (1935), the Court had struck down the Fair Trade Commission Act as an invalid delegation of legislative authority to the president, so the notion that legislating was Congress's responsibility and not the president's had not died by then.[19] At least, that is, when it came to domestic affairs.

The law in question in *United States v. Curtiss-Wright* was Congress's response to the bloody war between Paraguay and Bolivia that had raged since June 1932. American arms manufacturers had found lucrative markets for their wares in the two South American countries. Both Great Britain and the League of Nations had begged the United States government to call a halt to American arms sales to the combatants.

Congress, through a joint resolution of May 28, 1934, had resolved, "That if the President finds that the prohibition of the sale of arms and munitions of war in the United States to those countries now engaged in armed conflict in the Chaco may contribute to the reestablishment of peace between those countries, and if after consultation with the governments of other American Republics and with their cooperation, as well as that of such other governments as he may deem necessary, he makes proclamation to that effect, it shall be unlawful to sell, except under such limitations and exceptions as the President prescribes, any arms or munitions of war in any place in the United States to the countries now engaged in that armed conflict, or to any person, company, or association acting in the interest of either country, until otherwise ordered by the president or by Congress." President Franklin Roosevelt made it applicable to Bolivia and Paraguay through a proclamation issued that day. Although he repealed this proclamation by another dated November 14, 1935, the defendants in the case were charged with selling machine guns to Bolivia in the interim. In other words, the Curtiss-Wright Export Corporation was supposed to have violated Roosevelt's proclamation.

Among the defenses raised by Curtiss-Wright was that the congressional resolution underlying Roosevelt's proclamation was unconstitutional, since it delegated legislative power to the president. Congress's resolution did not make a policy, but instead said that

Roosevelt could make a policy in case he found that the situation required it. According to Curtiss-Wright, Congress could not constitutionally give Roosevelt power to exercise Congress's legislative (that is, policy-making) discretion. The Constitution had given the power to legislate to the Congress, not to the president, and Congress could not hand that power and responsibility off to anyone else, even him.

A federal district court agreed with Curtiss-Wright's argument and acquitted the corporation. When the government appealed to the Supreme Court, Curtiss-Wright offered four arguments why the congressional delegation was unconstitutional. Justice George Sutherland, in his majority opinion, described the four arguments as follows: (1) the resolution's effectiveness depended on the president's judgment concerning the desirability of implementing it; (2) the resolution's effectiveness depended on his arbitrary exercise of discretion to make a proclamation, which meant that his will, not Congress's, governed; (3) the resolution's validity depended on the president's decision to withhold a proclamation canceling it; and (4) the resolution's effect could be shaped or limited by the president at his discretion.

Sutherland followed his summary of the corporation's arguments by making an interesting distinction. The issue, he said, was not Congress's delegation of legislative power over an internal matter. The matter at hand was "entirely external to the United States, and falling within the category of foreign affairs."

Why did this matter? According to Sutherland, the federal government's powers regarding external affairs were to be understood differently from those in relation to internal affairs. "The two classes of powers are different, both in respect of their origin and their nature."

Sutherland had long advocated the idea that the federal government, and in particular the executive branch, had more latitude in formulating policy in regard to external matters than to internal affairs. As a senator, he had written a report in 1909 in which he said that if the Constitution had denied a power necessary to government either to the states or to the federal government, the power must implicitly have been granted to the other. It was impossible, then, that no American government had powers the Supreme Court dubbed "essential." The states had been denied various foreign affairs powers by the Constitution, and those powers must be somewhere, so they must be in the federal government.[20]

What of the Revolution's fear of abuse of power? Wasn't the invention of written constitutions intended to circumscribe the authority of everyone in office on the ground that, as James Madison had put it in *Federalist* no. 51, only angels can be trusted? In his 1909 report, Sutherland flatly rejected the Madisonian notion that it is better to have inefficient government than unlimited government, with its corollary that American governments had only the powers they had actually been delegated. "The exigencies of governmental administration," he explained, "cannot be foreseen and consequently cannot be enumerated; and it is better to risk occasional abuse of power (which is, after all, under our system of representative responsibility, very slight) than it is to incur the inconveniences and dangers arising from lack of effective power."[21] He thus concluded that the federal government had inherent power to undertake executive agreements—binding international agreements not ratified by the Senate, or what one might have thought were unconstitutional substitutes for treaties—despite the absence of express constitutional warrant. (Sutherland was at pains, however, to deny that this was an inherent power; he said that it was the federal government's power resulting "from the application of a legitimate and logical rule of construction.")

So it does not come as a surprise that in his opinion for the Court in *Curtiss-Wright*, Sutherland made the rather astounding assertion that "the broad statement that the federal government can exercise no powers except those specifically enumerated in the Constitution, and such implied powers as are necessary and proper to carry into effect the enumerated powers, is categorically true only in respect of our internal affairs."

According to Sutherland, the states never had foreign affairs powers, and so the Constitution cannot have been intended to carve some foreign affairs authority from among the states' powers and reserve the rest to the states, as in the case of domestic powers. After all, he said, in the colonial period it was the Crown, not the colonies, that had foreign affairs powers. Independence vested such powers not in the states as separate entities but in "the United (not the several) Colonies."

This is an inaccurate account of the Revolutionary understanding of the situation of the states in the world. According to Richard Bland's 1766 *An Inquiry into the Rights of the British Colonies*, as elucidated further in Thomas Jefferson's 1774 *A Summary View of the Rights of British America*, the colonies were constitutionally separate from the British Parliament from the beginning.[22] The American Declaration of Independence did not randomly use the word "states" to describe them, then: a "state," in the eighteenth century, was not a province in a larger entity but a sovereign entity itself. The states may have been united in declaring independence, then, but that union was a marriage, not a merger.[23]

Thus the basis of Sutherland's argument was incorrect. And so, of course, was his conclusion.

Sutherland's false account of the Revolution allowed him to conclude that sovereignty in regard to foreign affairs resided in the federal government itself. Like other nationalists before and since, Sutherland seems to have been unfamiliar with the Revolution's underlying idea: that final authority—indivisible, supreme authority; "sovereignty"—lay in the peoples of the separate states. Instead, his description of the situation sounds much like the great British royalist Sir William Blackstone's description of Parliament's sovereignty in the British system.

Sutherland said that before the federal Constitution, "the Union . . . was the sole possessor of external sovereignty, and in the Union it remained without change save in so far as the Constitution in express terms qualified its exercise. The Framers' Convention was called and exerted its powers upon the irrefutable postulate that though the states were several their people in respect of foreign affairs were one."

This account of the federal government—as one empowered in foreign affairs to do anything its officials felt impelled to do—is contrary to the statement in Article II of the Articles of Confederation (1777/1781) that the states retained sovereignty under that charter: a state could not have retained sovereignty (indivisible, ultimate authority) if it had not had it. This account of the federal government was also entirely at odds with the explanation of the Constitution offered by proponents (Federalists) at the time it was being considered for ratification. They said that each state would be as one of thirteen parties to a compact, and that the federal government would have only the powers it was "expressly delegated."[24] Of course, this principle, said to be implicit in the unamended Constitution, was also made explicit by the ratification of the Tenth Amendment.

Why did Sutherland make this unhistorical argument for presidential discretion in the realm of foreign affairs? Ultimately, he believed that the events of the first third of the twentieth century demonstrated that more federal power in the area of foreign affairs was desirable. Rather than a constitutional amendment, then, he opted for an argument that the federal government already inherently had the power he thought it needed to have.

Justice Sutherland's view, like Holmes's, was that the Constitution did not create an unchanging framework of government. "As the Nation goes forward," he wrote, "the government, which has been organized to put the will of the Nation into operation, must go forward with it and in aid of it; but if the activities of the government are too strictly limited, a drag upon, instead of an aid to this forward progress will result." He admitted that "the meaning of the Constitution does not change," but he added that "its capacity for adaptation is indefinitely flexible."

What this distinction between "change" and "adaptation" meant is unclear.[25]

The Final Blow

In 1937 the Supreme Court ruled in the case of *United States v. Belmont*, and Justice Sutherland once again commanded a majority. This case concerned the extent to which a federal executive agreement—that is, presidential conclusion of an international agreement without Senate concurrence—could countermand the policy of one of the United States. Unsurprisingly, Sutherland concluded that the state policy must yield—in other words, that the Tenth Amendment's reservation of power in certain areas to the states did not affect the respect American courts were to pay to such executive actions.

What this meant was that when the president extended formal recognition to the Soviet Union, it no longer was up to New York courts to decide what effect Soviet nationalization decrees would have in New York. Rather, the decrees—by which the Soviet Communist government had nationalized (that is, stolen) much private property—had to be respected as valid, as that was the U.S. government's policy. No other country had admitted the validity of these confiscations.[26]

New York's position was that the Soviet confiscation decrees were contrary to New York's public policy. This particular case arose because a Russian corporation, the Petrograd Metal Works, had deposited funds in the hands of New York banker August Belmont, and the Soviet government said that its confiscation decree had made the corporation's property the property of the Soviet state. The executive agreement said that the United States succeeded to the Soviet government's supposed title.

In his ruling, Justice Sutherland noted that the Supreme Court's policy was that "the courts of one [sovereign state] will not sit in judgment upon the acts of the government of another, done within its own territory." The reason was that "to permit the acts of one sovereign state to be reexamined and perhaps condemned by the courts of another would very certainly 'imperil the amicable relations between governments and vex the peace of nations.'"

There were two objections to this position. First, by recognizing the validity of Soviet confiscation decrees, the United States had become the only country that granted those decrees power *outside* Soviet territory.[27] Second, it was not obvious that state policies constitutionally must give way to international agreements that the federal government entered into without the formality of treaties. The Senate has a role in the treaty power, and thus the separate states have a check on treaties potentially harmful to their interests; they have no role, however, in making executive agreements.

Despite these objections, the Court asserted in *United States v. Belmont* that state policies must yield to executive agreements. In support of this conclusion, Sutherland offered first an irrelevant quotation from James Madison to the effect that the treaty power—which was not at issue in this case—would be of no use to the federal government if treaties did not supersede contrary state policies, and then a reference to his own reasoning in *Curtiss-Wright* concerning the "complete power over international affairs . . . in the national government."

Sutherland stated his position as baldly as possible. When it comes to foreign affairs, he said, the constitution, laws, and policies of New York do not exist. Citing *Missouri v. Holland*, he said: "It is inconceivable that any of them can be interposed as an obstacle to the effective operation of a federal constitutional power." Even in case of the constitutional injunction against taking property without just compensation, New York's public policy had to yield to that of the federal executive in case of an international agreement.

The outcome in *United States v. Belmont* was entirely at odds with the original understanding of the Constitution. Even the Senate's role in concluding treaties with foreign countries seemed to critics of the proposed Constitution in 1787–88 to be an inadequate check on the federal government's tendency to sacrifice the interests of particular states and regions. John Jay, America's diplomat in

Spain, had requested authority to sacrifice American access to the Mississippi River, which then belonged to Spain, for twenty-five years in exchange for trade access to Spanish colonies in the Western Hemisphere. Congress divided over the issue in 1786, with the North (potential beneficiaries of Spanish trade) voting for it and the South (likely loser if the Mississippi were closed to the United States) against. The proposition carried, despite the protests of southern politicians.

As a result of the Confederation Congress's action, Patrick Henry, Virginia's leading revolutionary politician, became skeptical of reform of the federal system. At the 1788 Virginia ratification convention, Henry noted that the North had proved willing to surrender an interest, the right to use the Mississippi River as a route for exporting midwestern and Upper South agricultural products, that was essential to Virginia—in particular, to the areas that are now West Virginia and Kentucky. Consequently, delegates from Kentucky voted overwhelmingly against ratifying the Constitution.

James Madison and other proponents of ratification (Federalists) insisted that Virginia's interests actually would be safer under the proposed Constitution: the federal government would need both a president who favored a treaty and a two-thirds vote in the Senate to make a treaty. Imagine how the outcome in Virginia, where Federalists won by a vote of 88–78, would have been affected if one of Madison's opponents could have stood up and said, "Yes, but the president will be able to give up the Mississippi navigation without the Senate's approval merely by labeling what he is doing an 'executive agreement.'"[28]

Unchecked Federal Power

The Supreme Court has joined with the president and Senate in radically restructuring the government in the area of foreign relations. As it stands, it is unclear exactly what, if anything, the president *cannot* do via executive agreement. The states' reserved powers have ceased to exist when foreign policy is involved.

Of course, this problem affects areas other than foreign policy, too. In general, the organic metaphor of a growing national government has taken hold in contemporary America. The idea of carefully enumerated delegation of power to the federal government—the foundation of the Constitution, after all—is a quaint anachronism in the minds of federal government officials. That is, if they think about the idea at all.

11

The Phony Case for Presidential War Power

IN THE FIRST half of the twentieth century the Supreme Court and an aggressive executive, along with an acquiescent Senate, denied the states any authority in foreign relations. But the consolidation of power did not stop there. Just like the states, Congress has now been cut off from a role in foreign affairs.

For more than half a century Americans have been told that the president has all but exclusive control over foreign affairs, and that it is perfectly constitutional for him to deploy troops all over the world without the consent of Congress. The executive branch has made these claims so often that they have become second nature to most Americans. In fact, ever since the 2001 terrorist attacks we have been assured that the president has even more powers that Congress is constitutionally helpless to control, from interrogation practices to surveillance methods.

The one problem with these arguments is that they are absolutely false as statements of constitutional intent.

Original Intent

A brief overview of the Constitution's original intent in apportioning war powers might go something like this. At the time of the Constitution's drafting, many Americans deeply distrusted executive power, and essentially no one wanted to endow the president with the power to take the country to war. At the Constitutional Convention, George Mason urged that the president was "not to be trusted" when it came to initiating war, and that such power needed to reside in the Congress, the branch of government closest to the people. Alexander Hamilton, who favored a strong executive, nevertheless conceded that "the Legislature alone" can "plac[e] the nation in a state of war." The president's commander-in-chief authority, he said, had to do with directing "war when authorized or begun," not with beginning war himself.[1] Reflecting this general suspicion of executive authority, James Madison even proposed excluding the president from the negotiation of peace treaties, on the grounds that he might obstruct a settlement out of a desire to derive "power and importance from a state of war."[2]

In *Federalist* No. 4, John Jay warned that executives (monarchs, in this case) had a penchant for making war for petty, frivolous, or frankly wicked reasons. They will, he said, often "make war when their nations are to get nothing by it, but for purposes and objects merely personal, such as a thirst for military glory, revenge for personal affronts, ambition, or private compacts to aggrandize or support their particular families or partisans." These wars, Jay said, were generally "not sanctified by justice or the voice and interests of [the] people."

Although the Constitution withholds from the president the power to commence hostilities, the Framers did envision a defensive presidential power to *respond* to attacks in extreme cases that will admit of no delay. The Framers were thinking of genuine life-or-death situations. Even when Japan attacked Pearl Harbor in 1941,

President Franklin Roosevelt did not retaliate on his own authority but went to Congress for a declaration of war. Any action beyond the most unavoidable defensive measures requires congressional approval.

American history affords ample support for this position: until 1950, it was taken for granted that Congress had to approve offensive military operations. After 1950, the year President Harry Truman chose not to consult Congress before intervening in the Korean War, the executive branch felt it necessary to produce some kind of legal cover for this obvious departure from American tradition and the original understanding of the Constitution. Government spokesmen began claiming that there was nothing unusual about this at all, and that in fact the president had sent troops into harm's way without congressional approval more than one hundred times in the past. Few took these contrived and self-serving arguments seriously: according to presidential scholar Edward Corwin, these so-called precedents for presidential wars consisted mainly of "fights with pirates, landings of small naval contingents on barbarous or semi-barbarous coasts, the dispatch of small bodies of troops to chase bandits or cattle rustlers across the Mexican border, and the like."[3]

While essentially unchecked presidential power in foreign affairs has become the norm, the evidence that this was *not* part of the constitutional design is so overwhelming that it is difficult to see how anyone could argue otherwise. But it is not difficult to see *why* they might so argue; presidential supremacy has not exactly been an unwelcome philosophy to most modern presidents.

This is where John Yoo enters the picture.

A Breathtaking Assault

Born in 1967, Yoo graduated from Harvard in 1989 and Yale Law School in 1992. He has since enjoyed a distinguished career in government and academia. In addition to clerking for Supreme Court justice Clarence Thomas, Yoo served as general counsel for the Senate Judiciary Committee and, from 2001 until 2003, in the Office of Legal Counsel as deputy assistant attorney general. He has since returned to private life and is currently a professor at Boalt Hall School of Law at the University of California, Berkeley.

In 1996, Yoo published an article in the *California Law Review* in which he advanced the astonishing claim that the Framers of the Constitution had given us a system that would "encourage presidential initiative in war" and that "the Constitution gives the President the initiative in war." The Framers, he said, "were not excessively worried by the prospect of unilateral executive action." Congress had essentially no power to rein in the president apart from its control of the purse strings and its power of impeachment.[4]

The article, in other words, was a breathtaking assault on the received understanding of the allocation of war powers. Louis Fisher, an authority on war powers and the Constitution at the Library of Congress, suggests that a law review was the perfect venue for such an article: unlike other scholarly journals, law reviews are run by students and the articles submitted to them are not subject to peer review by other scholars. The students themselves, who typically possess no expert knowledge of the subject matter involved, choose which articles to publish. Naturally, they will have a particular interest in articles that advance bold and original theses and buck the conventional wisdom. They are also liable to be impressed by sheer heft, another area in which Yoo's article distinguished itself—it ran some 139 pages and included 625 footnotes.[5]

The arguments Yoo advanced in his article (and in others that followed) amounted in the long run to far more than a mere academic exercise. He brought them to his unusually influential career as deputy assistant attorney general, where they became justifications for administration policies. In 2002 testimony before the Senate Judiciary Committee, Yoo declared: "The President has the constitutional authority to introduce the U.S. Armed Forces into hostilities when appropriate, with or without specific congressional authorization."[6] In a now-famous memo dated September 25, 2001, Yoo proclaimed that the president "has the constitutional power not only to retaliate against any person, organization, or State suspected of involvement in terrorist attacks on the United States, but also against foreign States suspected of harboring or supporting such organizations . . . The President may deploy military force preemptively against terrorist organizations or the States that harbor or support them, whether or not they can be linked to the specific events of September 11." Moreover, no congressional statute can "place any limits on the President's determinations as to any terrorist threat, the amount of military force to be used in response, or the method, timing, and nature of the response. These decisions, under our Constitution, are for the President alone to make. . . . In the exercise of his plenary power to use military force, the President's decisions are for him alone and are unreviewable." This was so, Yoo explained, because "during the period leading up to the Constitution's ratification, the power to initiate hostilities and to control the escalation of conflict had long been understood to rest in the hands of the executive branch."[7] In support of this extraordinary claim he cited . . . his 1996 article in the *California Law Review*.[8]

Yoo contends that the Framers of the Constitution intended to mimic the British model when allocating foreign affairs authority among the branches of the federal government. Since the British king had the power to initiate war, so, too, did the American president. To those who would deny the president this power on the grounds that the Constitution assigns the power to declare war to Congress, Yoo replies that such critics misunderstand what it means to declare war. According to Yoo, declaring war in the eighteenth century was a merely rhetorical and communicative act—a "courtesy to the enemy," he wrote—and did not involve the initiation or authorization of hostilities. Thus in granting Congress the power to declare war, the Constitution had merely given it the power to communicate to an enemy people (as well as to neutrals and to the country's own citizens) that a state of war existed; the president, on the other hand, retained the power actually to bring the United States into war by commencing military action. The Declare War Clause "does not add to Congress' store of war power at the expense of the President," Yoo argues. "Rather, the Clause gives Congress a judicial role in declaring that a state of war exists between the United States and another nation, which bears significant legal ramifications concerning the rights and duties of American citizens."[9]

Yoo is partly correct, as in the eighteenth century "declare war" could indeed mean what he says it means: to make a formal announcement to the enemy and the world. But a review of eighteenth-century usage reveals that to "declare war" *also* could mean to begin a war. Even if we leave that historical background aside, Yoo's position raises an obvious question: why would the Framers have assigned Congress the power of issuing proclamations that had only rhetorical and communicative purposes? That would have made no sense, since the executive is the branch that is understood to communicate the American position to other countries. Moreover, the president's control of the channels of diplomatic communication allows him to utter whatever statements he chooses. The arrangement would be unworkable: each presidential statement would have to be scrutinized to see if it had risen to the level of a declaration of war, such that the Congress would have to intervene and overrule him.[10]

Yoo tries to claim that the declaration of war did serve a substantive purpose apart from informing the enemy of the existence of a state of war: it caused the laws of war, international and domestic, to be invoked. But this argument also misfires; although the Dutch international lawyer Hugo Grotius advanced that view in the seventeenth century, it no longer held a century and a half later, when the Constitution was being drafted.[11] In fact, the laws of war went into effect for wars that existed de facto and not simply for those that had been formally declared.[12] On the domestic side, whatever augmented powers the government exercises during war (constitutionally or otherwise) turn on the existence of hostilities themselves, not the issuance of a formal declaration. The Third Amendment's allowance of quartering troops in homes can be invoked when hostilities are actually under way, not simply when war has been officially declared.[13]

Consider also that as the Constitution was being debated, Federalists sought to reassure skeptical Anti-Federalists that the president's powers were not so expansive as the latter feared. For one thing, the Federalists said, the president lacked the power to declare war. In order for their argument to hold any weight, "declare war" must have been taken to mean the power to initiate hostilities[14]—for no Anti-Federalist would have been appeased by "Sure, the president can take the country to war on his own initiative, but the power to draft declaratory statements will rest with Congress!"

Another solution to the puzzle of what the Framers meant by the phrase "declare war" is, as Michael Ramsey of the University of San Diego School of Law suggests in the *University of Chicago Law Review*, to examine the policy of the U.S. government in the years following ratification of the Constitution. If declarations of war were in fact merely rhetorical, as Yoo argues, we should expect presidents to initiate military force boldly and not to be concerned about the will of Congress.[15] Unfortunately for Yoo, the historical testimony of the early republic provides important evidence that the congressional power to declare war was a power to initiate war. George Washington specifically disclaimed the power to take the country to war without congressional authorization, and for that reason he confined his operations against the Indians to purely defensive measures. President John Adams complied with congressional statutes in the limited Quasi War with France. Thomas Jefferson's moves against the Barbary pirates were confined to the defense of American citizens and commerce; Jefferson said he would need the consent of Congress for anything beyond that. James Madison went to Congress for the declaration of war that brought about the War of 1812. Countless other early examples could be cited.[16]

Yoo's further claim that Congress might have some power over major wars but that lesser uses of force are surely reserved to the president alone is also contradicted by the evidence of the 1790s. Supreme Court justice Samuel Chase summed it up in 1800 using this formula: "*Congress* is empowered to declare a general war, or *Congress* may wage a limited war; limited in place, in objects and in time."[17] The 1804 case of *Little v. Barreme* involved a ship commander who, during the Quasi War with France in the late 1790s, had seized a ship that he thought was illegally trading with France. The commander was following a directive from President John Adams in seizing this ship, which had been coming from France. But Congress had authorized President Adams only to seize ships going *to* France; in short, the president's directive ventured beyond what Congress had called for in this limited war. In a unanimous decision, the Court declared that the commander was liable for damages even though he had acted in accordance with a presidential directive. No presidential directive could override the authority of Congress, said the Court.[18]

The case of *United States v. Smith* (1806) yielded a similar result. Accused of trying to launch a military expedition against Spanish America, the two defendants argued that President Thomas Jefferson and members of his cabinet had authorized the ill-fated incursion. The Court held that since a statute was on the books prohibiting private military adventurism of this kind, the president and his cabinet had no right to authorize it, and if any such authorization existed it would not exonerate the two men. The author of the decision was Justice William Paterson, who had been a delegate to the Constitutional Convention.[19]

Still other examples could be cited, but the point is made: numerous precedents from the earliest years of the republic make clear that Congress's claims to be able to bind the president in foreign affairs are nothing new; neither are they unlawful infringements on a field of presidential power that the chief executive is supposed to hold exclusively.

Yoo does not deny this evidence suggesting a common understanding that Congress alone may initiate offensive military operations; he responds simply that the evidence does not settle the argument. He maintains that this apparent impression on the part of statesmen from the 1790s cannot be tied to any specific constitutional language, and it is the constitutional language that matters. But this argument will not do. For one thing, the text of the Constitution, as we have seen, can be tied to the idea that Congress alone may take the nation to war, since that is indeed one of the two possible meanings of "declare war." For another, if the idea that only Congress could commence military action was constitutionally incorrect, how had it become the unquestioned consensus just a few years after the Constitution was ratified?

Yoo will concede one institutional mechanism Congress can use to rein in executive war making: the power of the purse. By withholding funds for a military operation, Congress can bring about a swift end to any conflict. But as important a power as that is, it leaves much to be desired as the exclusive congressional instrument for exercising control over matters of war and peace. Just one of its shortcomings is that although Congress yields power to the president through a simple majority vote (50 percent plus one), a veto-proof (two-thirds) majority is necessary in order to wrest that power back, since the president is likely to veto attempted congressional reversals of his policies.[20] The net result is a ratchet effect in the direction of war.

Clumsy Rationalizations

Another argument that executive supremacists have tried involves the so-called Vesting Clause, which comes from Article II, Section 1 of the Constitution: "The executive Power shall be vested in a President of the United States of America." According to this view, the Vesting Clause bestows on the president a host of unspecified powers in addition to the specific ones listed in the rest of Article II. The Framers of the Constitution, they say, thereby showed that they wanted the president to exercise all powers that would have been recognized in the eighteenth century as being fundamentally executive in nature, even if those powers are not actually mentioned in the Constitution. Congress, on the other hand, is assigned no such open-ended authority but is instead limited by the Constitution to all "legislative Powers *herein granted*" (emphasis added), a reference to the specific list of powers that then follows. The conclusion: the president may rightly exercise all powers relating to foreign affairs (since such powers are by their nature executive) except those specifically assigned to Congress.

Yoo, who has adopted the Vesting Clause argument in some of his own scholarship, made precisely this argument as deputy assistant attorney general, in a draft memorandum he co-authored for the Department of Defense dated January 9, 2002: "While Article II, § 1 of the Constitution grants the President an undefined executive power, Article I, § 1 of the Constitution limits Congress to '[a]ll legislative Powers herein granted' in the rest of Article I."[21]

But the Vesting Clause argument is nothing more than a clumsy rationalization of executive supremacy. The textual evidence for the meaning that Yoo and other executive supremacists wish to attach to the Vesting Clause is actually far weaker than they suggest. Far from recognizing such an expansive meaning of executive power, the Founders took the phrase to refer to the mere execution of the laws and nowhere suggested that it meant anything else. Much less did they say it conferred a bundle of unspecified powers on the president. Given the talk at the Constitutional Convention about whether the executive should be singular or plural, the Vesting Clause could have meant simply to clarify that point: executive power shall be vested in a single president of the United States.[22]

There is also the little problem that Article II lists specific powers that the Constitution confers upon the president. Since supporters of the Vesting Clause thesis generally concede that these powers—including the commander-in-chief power, the power to request written reports from heads of executive departments, and the power to issue pardons—naturally fall under the scope of executive power, then what is the point of listing them? Such a list would be superfluous if these powers were already contained under the more general category of executive power, and would therefore contravene "the general presumption against redundancy."[23]

In other words, the constitutional text itself does not demand the interpretation that John Yoo places on it.

Yoo also argues that a consensus existed among seventeenth- and eighteenth-century political thinkers regarding what constituted executive powers, and that this general understanding was incorporated into the Constitution when that document vested the executive power in the president. There was no need to list all the president's powers, the argument goes, since everyone at the time knew what powers were inherently executive ones. But other scholars have concluded that no consensus on the proper allocation of war powers existed among thinkers of that period and that it is therefore impossible to draw sweeping conclusions from them. Some have even argued that, if anything, the force of seventeenth- and eighteenth-century argument tends in the other direction.[24]

Yoo will not find any help for his views on executive power and the Vesting Clause in the state constitutions drawn up after 1776, in the *Federalist Papers*, or in the state ratification debates. Nowhere in the state constitutions do we see any indication of an intent to vest the executive with an array of unspecified powers beyond those that were expressly mentioned.[25] In *Federalist* no. 69, Alexander Hamilton argues that the American president would be much weaker than the British king, and to do so he specifically points to the list of specific powers the Constitution grants the president. That argument would have been absurd and dishonest if the Vesting Clause had given the president a reservoir of powers in addition to the ones Hamilton catalogued. As for the ratification debates, two students of the subject conclude that "in the thousands of pages recording these debates, the argument that the Vesting Clause grants the president a general foreign affairs power simply does not appear."[26]

So evidence to support the Vesting Clause thesis is, in effect, altogether absent.

Was It Illegal?

The foreign affairs powers that the president is said inherently to enjoy are quite expansive. For instance, President George W. Bush has argued, following the trail blazed by John Yoo, that by virtue of being commander in chief and the nation's "sole organ" in foreign affairs, he possesses (among other things) an inherent power to engage in wiretapping without a warrant, even in the face of a congressional statute to the contrary. Moreover, according to Bush, Congress in fact approved the exercise of this and a host of other sweeping powers when it voted for the 2001 Authorization of Use of Military Force Act, which gave the president the power to use "all necessary and appropriate force" against any entity involved in the September 11 attacks. In so doing, Congress provided statutory support for the exercise of what the administration describes as the president's inherent powers as commander in chief.

In December 2005, the *New York Times* reported that in the months following the September 11 attacks, President Bush secretly authorized the National Security Agency (NSA) to eavesdrop on domestic communications without first obtaining warrants. This was a significant departure for the NSA, which had previously listened in only on conversations overseas. It was also a departure from settled law: the Foreign Intelligence Surveillance Act (FISA) of 1978 had laid out a fairly modest set of rules that had to be obeyed before surveillance of Americans could be undertaken. As usual, the "liberal media" revealed itself to be more of an establishment media, with the *Times* breaking the story only a full year after learning of the secret NSA program, per an agreement with the White House.

John Yoo apparently had a hand in justifying this decision as well, both at the time and after the fact. He told a PBS interviewer, "I can't go farther than what's been released publicly. As the White House has said, the National Security Agency intercepts communications from abroad coming into the country where someone on the calls is a suspected member of Al Qaeda. The press has reported and I haven't denied that I worked on the legal authorization for those programs."[27] At a Federalist Society luncheon in September 2007, Yoo said the warrantless surveillance program was justifiable.[28]

A PBS interviewer once asked Yoo about a memo he had written while in the Office of Legal Counsel that had been quoted by the *New York Times*, to the effect that the federal government could use "electronic surveillance techniques and equipment more powerful and sophisticated than those available to law enforcement agencies in order to intercept telephone communications and observe the movements of persons but without obtaining warrants for such uses." Although Yoo claimed not to remember the memo, he also said he agreed with it and that it sounded like something he would have written. He likewise defended the decision by major telephone companies to give the government access to telephone and Internet traffic. Was any of that illegal? "It depends on why the government wants the information, but I don't think it's inherently always wrong for communications providers to give the government access to the networks."[29]

Fair enough, said the interviewer, but was it illegal?

"No. I don't [think] it's a violation of the law if by the law you mean the Constitution. The Constitution includes the president's commander-in-chief authority. No, I don't think it's a violation of that law." If the president's commander-in-chief authority permits him to carry out unchecked surveillance, then FISA was an unconstitutional infringement on an inherent presidential power—a position that would have been news to just about everyone involved in the debating and passage of FISA.

FISA was established in the wake of the Church Committee

hearings of the 1970s, in which four decades' worth of executive branch surveillance came to light. An American television audience was treated to a history of (among other things) illegal mail openings, burglaries, and various other abuses, including the use of the federal spying apparatus to gather intelligence and potentially damaging information about an administration's political opponents.

When we consider how relatively toothless the FISA requirements are and how accommodating the act is to a president facing an emergency under severe time constraints, claims that President Bush needed to evade the law for security reasons become less and less credible. FISA allows the president to carry out physical searches for up to fifteen days before approval is received from a FISA court, and to engage in electronic surveillance for three days before approval. And over the course of thousands of requests, the FISA courts have denied only a handful.

But even if the administration's case against FISA had been accurate, alleged defects in the law do not justify the president in defying it. If he needed amendments to the law, he could simply have gone to the Republican-controlled Congress for the appropriate remedy. In the wake of 9/11, Congress has been more than cooperative in granting the executive the additional powers he requests.[30]

Why, then, was FISA evaded and the secret NSA program approved? The president's motivations, speculates Bruce Fein, deputy attorney general under Ronald Reagan, were "to gather political intelligence against his domestic critics, to chill dissent by creating an aura of intimidation, to cripple Congress as a check on presidential power, to warn courts against second-guessing national security decisions of the commander in chief, and to concoct an appearance of toughness on terrorism."[31] Paul Craig Roberts, who served as assistant treasury secretary under Reagan, is certain that the warrantless wiretapping program was intended to spy on the president's political opponents. The "only possible reason for violating FISA," according to Roberts, "is to collect information that can be used to silence critics. The administration's claim that bypassing FISA was essential to the 'war on terror' is totally false." Some conservatives tried to argue that Bush's disregard for the FISA courts was a matter of slight importance, given how accommodating those courts typically are. But that's precisely what makes the president's behavior so suspicious: why, if these courts were so easy to satisfy, were they circumvented?[32]

If correct, Roberts's explanation would account for the Bush administration's refusal to go even to the compliant FISA courts for warrants. It could not do so because it was engaged in spying that would not have been considered legitimate under the terms of FISA. "Could it be that the Bush administration used the spy apparatus of the U.S. government in order to influence the outcome of the presidential election?" Roberts asked. "Could we attribute the feebleness of the Democrats as an opposition party to information obtained through illegal spying that would subject them to blackmail?"[33]

Columnist George Will has protested what he called the president's "monarchical doctrine" and criticized

> the administration's argument that because the president is commander in chief, he is the "sole organ for the nation in foreign affairs." That non sequitur is refuted by the Constitution's plain language, which empowers Congress to ratify treaties, declare war, fund and regulate military forces, and make laws "necessary and proper" for the execution of all presidential powers. Those powers do not include deciding that a law—FISA, for example—is somehow exempted from the presidential duty to "take care that the laws be faithfully executed."[34]

Even if the president's power to gather foreign intelligence is granted as a plausible reading of Article II of the Constitution, it is surely constitutional for Congress to impose limits on the manner in which such activity is carried out. The executive branch's forty-year record of abuse when its intelligence-gathering power was unchecked does not inspire confidence. FISA could thus be considered a "necessary and proper" mechanism for protecting First and Fourth Amendment rights.[35]

The infamous "torture memo" of August 1, 2002 (leaked to the press in 2004), which authorized the use of torture even in the face of congressional action to the contrary, also bears Yoo's imprint. Yoo interpreted existing statutes relating to torture very narrowly, arguing that it was legally acceptable, and thus not torture, to inflict pain on a suspect as long as that pain fell short of what one might experience from "serious physical injury, such as organ failure, impairment of bodily function, or even death." More interesting is Yoo's allowance for torture itself if the president found even this accommodating definition too constraining. Should Congress attempt to restrain the president's powers of torture, it would thereby violate "the Constitution's sole vesting of the Commander-in-Chief authority in the President."[36] The memo was signed by Jay Bybee, Yoo's superior, and delivered to Attorney General Alberto Gonzales.

When Yoo wrote that no law passed by Congress could restrain presidential behavior in this area, he meant it. In December 2005, Yoo debated Doug Cassel, director of Notre Dame Law School's Center for Civil and Human Rights. Cassel, seeking clarification of Yoo's 2002 memo, asked Yoo: "If the president deems that he's got to torture somebody, including by crushing the testicles of the person's child, there is no law that can stop him?"

"No treaty," Yoo responded.

"Also no law by Congress," Cassel reminded him. "That is what you wrote in the August 2002 memo."

"I think it depends on why the president thinks he needs to do that," came the reply.[37]

Some Things Never Change

American liberals, by and large, have had a field day with John Yoo (as have a few constitutional conservatives). But this is not exactly the first time a scholar's work has provided contrived constitutional cover for legally dubious actions the executive branch intended to take anyway. Liberals themselves, who for the most part have supported a strong executive, jumped at the chance to invent constitutional justification for Harry Truman's deployment of troops to Korea in 1950 without congressional authorization. In 1951, Senator Robert Taft, known in his day as "Mr. Republican," argued on the Senate floor that Truman's deployment of American troops in major hostilities without the consent of Congress violated both the Constitution and unbroken American tradition. Historian Henry Steele Commager, an establishment liberal, took the senator to task, claiming that his arguments had "no support in law or in history" and citing previous examples of presidential action that were obviously not comparable to what Truman had done. Truman's action was perfectly normal, according to Commager, and surely not a cause for concern: "There is, in fact, no basis in our own history for the distrust of the Executive authority."[38]

Arthur Schlesinger Jr., another establishment liberal, joined the attack on the heretic Taft. According to Schlesinger, Taft's remarks were "demonstratively irresponsible." He accused "Senator Taft and his friends" of "rewriting American history according to their own specifications."

By the 1960s, both Commager and Schlesinger had stepped forward in the wake of Vietnam to apologize for their earlier views, implicitly (and in Schlesinger's case, explicitly) acknowledging that Senator Taft—whom both of them had smeared viciously—had been right all along. Congress was not supposed to be eclipsed in war and foreign policy after all, they suddenly discovered.

This is all well and good, but rather too late. "Reconsideration is always valuable and needs to be encouraged," says Louis Fisher, "but independent scholarly checks are needed at the time of constitutional violations, not two decades later."

Whatever political party occupies the White House, therefore, there is usually a John Yoo prepared to rationalize the president's unconstitutional exercise of power. According to Bruce Fein, "Mr. Bush has adamantly refused to acknowledge any constitutional limitations on his power to wage war indefinitely against international terrorism, other than an unelaborated assertion he is not a dictator." In the name of fighting terrorism, says Fein, Bush has not ruled out arguments that the president possesses the inherent authority to "break and enter homes, to intercept purely domestic communications, or to herd citizens into concentration camps reminiscent of World War II."[39] That some conservatives consider this normal or desirable says rather a lot about the present condition of the conservative movement. But that's a subject for another book.

12

The President Enforces the Law . . . Right?

IF THERE'S ANYTHING most schoolchildren learn about the Constitution, it's the idea of "checks and balances." There is, we are taught at a young age, a separation of powers among the three branches of the federal government: the legislative branch makes the law, the executive branch enforces the law, and the judicial branch interprets the law. The checks and balances are the safeguards the Constitution includes to ensure that each branch remains limited to its proper role. This is among the most elementary of civics lessons.

The lesson is entirely correct, as far as what the Constitution says. According to Article I, Section 1, "All legislative Powers herein granted shall be vested in a Congress of the United States, which shall consist of a Senate and House of Representatives." Article II, Section 3 explains that it is the president's task to "take Care that the Laws be faithfully executed." Congress makes the law, and the president is to "take Care" that the law is executed. In terms of checks and balances, the president may recommend bills to Congress, and he may veto those to which he objects. But the language of the Constitution does not support the interpretation that he may approve of some parts of a bill and disregard others. President George Washington told Virginia Supreme Court of Appeals judge Edmund

Pendleton in 1793, "From the nature of the constitution I must approve all the parts of a bill, or reject it *in toto*."[1] Nor is the veto power insuperable: Congress can overturn the president's veto by a two-thirds vote.[2]

Of course, what the Constitution says has less and less to do with how the federal government actually operates.

In the late nineteenth century, President Rutherford B. Hayes observed that American presidents typically had been cautious and conservative men. What he feared was the accession to power of a would-be Napoleon, who would transform the presidential office into an engine of unaccountable power of which the Constitution's Framers could not have dreamed.[3]

Hayes's warning was sound, as events later demonstrated. It was not long before presidents began usurping the powers of Congress and attempting to make laws themselves, or even refusing to enforce laws passed by Congress. It takes little imagination to figure out what the Framers would have thought of this.

TR's Demagoguery

One of the most familiar instruments available to presidents is the executive order. An executive order, stated simply, is a directive issued by the president. Presidents may issue executive orders in pursuit of constitutional objectives, exercising powers that the Constitution assigns to them. The president may issue pardons by executive order, for instance. He may likewise use executive orders to implement policies for which Congress has granted him discretionary authority.

At the same time, executive orders can be abused, as when presidents employ them as a way of carrying out objectives for which congressional authorization is required. In October 1942, for example, Franklin Roosevelt capped all salaries in the United States at $25,000 by executive order. Roosevelt's initiative did not last: by

March of the following year Congress had forced its repeal, arguing both that it impeded the war effort and that it was incompatible with American principles.[4]

With an executive order the president can carry out some initiative he favors and then present Congress with a fait accompli. If sufficient legislative strength is lacking to force him to back down, the president can get away with his misuse of power. All too often, Congress actually winds up authorizing the president's action after the fact. After the Senate failed to ratify a treaty with the Dominican Republic, for instance, Theodore Roosevelt simply renamed the treaty an "executive agreement" (the diplomatic counterpart of an executive order) that he could enforce on his own authority. The Senate later approved Roosevelt's decision. That hardly mattered: TR recalled in his autobiography that he would have maintained the agreement with the Dominican Republic even if the Senate had withheld its approval for the rest of his term.[5]

Such a position was typical of Theodore Roosevelt, who explained his philosophy of the presidency as follows: the president's power is limited only by express prohibitions, and since the president occupies a political office for which the entire country votes (unlike senators and representatives, whose votes come only from their own states or districts), he is the unique representative of the American people. The president thus embodies the will of the people and must do what is necessary to carry it out.

Thus speak all of history's demagogues.

It is not surprising, then, that TR issued dramatically more executive orders than his predecessors had: 1,006 in his nearly two terms in office, whereas Rutherford B. Hayes had issued exactly zero; James A. Garfield, zero; Chester A. Arthur, 3; Grover Cleveland (first term), 6; Benjamin Harrison, 4; Grover Cleveland (second term), 71; and William McKinley, 51.[6] This exponential increase in executive orders reflected not merely a quantitative change but also a qualitative shift in governing style and philosophy.

The presidency would never be the same.

A New Presidential Weapon

Beyond executive orders, more recent presidents have picked up another tool to expand their own power dramatically and circumvent the separation of powers the Framers intended. The new instrument is the presidential signing statement.

A signing statement is exactly that: a statement the president issues alongside his approval of a bill. To be sure, presidential signing statements are nothing new in modern American history; they can be traced back to the first half of the nineteenth century. These statements for most of American history tended to be largely rhetorical, though, or provided the president an opportunity to single out people or groups for their efforts in making the legislation possible. Signing statements were also used occasionally to indicate the executive's displeasure with some aspect of the legislation, up to and including its alleged unconstitutionality. But everyone understood those statements to be legally toothless and more or less ceremonial, rather than legal or ideological position papers that laid out the president's intent to disregard provisions of the law. In fact, when President John Tyler in the 1840s issued a mild and diffident signing statement involving the constitutionality of a bill apportioning congressional districts, a House of Representatives committee, in a protest written by John Quincy Adams, shot back that such a statement ought never to have been made in the first place and that it should "be regarded in no other light than a defacement of the public records and archives."[7]

Even into the late twentieth century, signing statements were rare. Presidential scholar Christopher May counted 101 statutory provisions that presidents had challenged by means of signing statements through 1981. Of those provisions, he found that eighty-nine were nevertheless enforced, and only twelve were actually set aside in practice.[8]

The Reagan administration was the first to explore the legal possibilities of signing statements as instruments for expanding executive power. One of the architects of the idea was Samuel Alito, then serving as deputy assistant attorney general in the Office of Legal Counsel. An important potential virtue of the presidential signing statement, according to Alito, was that the president would thereby have the chance to record his own views of the statute in question—and those views, having been added to the record, could someday guide future interpretation of laws when controversy about their meaning should arise. "Since the president's approval is just as important as that of the House or Senate," Alito wrote, "it seems to follow that the president's understanding of the bill should be just as important as that of Congress." Congress, on the other hand, was "likely to resent the fact that the president will get in the last word on questions of interpretation."[9]

Alito, of course, would go on to become a Supreme Court justice. The president who appointed him, George W. Bush, would embrace his arguments—and take them much further.

The Bush Revolution

The administration of George W. Bush introduced two critical innovations into the presidential signing statement. First, the sheer number: no other president had used this instrument to challenge anywhere near the number of legislative provisions that President Bush did. "From the inception of the Republic until 2000," reports an American Bar Association task force on presidential signing statements, "Presidents produced signing statements containing fewer than 600 challenges to the bills they signed. According to the most recent update [mid-2006], in his one-and-a-half terms so far, President George W. Bush . . . has produced more than 800."[10] That number continued to increase: by December 25, 2006, Bush had issued 147 signing statements that included a total of 1,132 challenges to various provisions of law. According to Professor

Christopher Kelley, "The administration does a shuck and jive with the figures, suggesting that they have issued fewer signing statements than previous presidents, which is true. But the devil is in the details—he has blown the lid off the number of challenges—1,132."[11]

The second innovation, at least as important as the first, was that the Bush administration used signing statements as a tool to push its expansive theory of the executive branch. Just as Theodore Roosevelt transformed the executive order (and used it much more frequently) to create a radically stronger executive branch, George W. Bush dramatically expanded the use and the purpose of signing statements in the pursuit of a more powerful presidential office.

Phillip Cooper, a professor of public administration at Portland State University who has written a book on signing statements, contends in *Presidential Studies Quarterly* that "the George W. Bush administration has very effectively expanded the scope and character of the signing statement not only to address specific provisions of legislation that the White House wishes to nullify, but also in an effort to significantly reposition and strengthen the powers of the presidency relative to the Congress. This tour d' force has been carried out in such a systematic and careful fashion that few in Congress, the media, or the scholarly community are aware that anything has happened at all."[12] Professor Cooper categorized Bush's signing statements according to the rationale offered for them. On eighty-two occasions the president targeted provisions of bills on the basis of his power "to supervise the unitary executive." In seventy-seven cases he appealed to his "exclusive power over foreign affairs" as president. In forty-eight instances he referred to his "authority to determine and impose national security classifications and withhold information."[13]

In short, the Bush administration devised a way around the constitutional requirement that, as George Washington aptly summarized it, the president "approve all the parts of a bill, or reject it *in toto*." Wielding the signing statement as a weapon, President Bush repeatedly signaled that he would carry out the executive will even in the face of laws to the contrary. Many political commentators noted Bush's apparent reluctance to employ his veto power (the president vetoed only one congressional act in his first seven years in office). But instead of vetoing legislation, Bush found he could sign it into law and simply refuse to carry out those provisions that—under his expansive view of executive power—he considered unconstitutional.

A typical example comes from the USA PATRIOT Improvement and Reauthorization Act of 2005. Various sections, but especially number 119, call for congressional oversight of the implementation of the PATRIOT Act and establish deadlines for the administration to produce reports for Congress regarding the searches and seizures carried out under its authority.[14] In his signing statement, Bush explained that with regard to "furnishing information to entities outside the executive branch" (that's a reference to Congress, by the way, in case that flattering description was unclear), he would interpret the pertinent sections in light of "the President's constitutional authority to supervise the unitary executive branch and to withhold information the disclosure of which could impair foreign relations, national security, the deliberative processes of the Executive, or the performance of the Executive's constitutional duties."[15]

The McCain Amendment to the 2006 defense appropriations bill prohibited the use of "cruel, inhuman, or degrading treatment or punishment of persons under custody or control of the United States government." According to the president's signing statement, "The executive branch shall construe Title X in Division A of the Act, relating to detainees, in a manner consistent with the constitutional authority of the President to supervise the unitary executive branch and as Commander in Chief and consistent with the constitutional limitations on the judicial power."[16] In normal English, that means the president is reserving the right to behave in a manner exactly opposite to what the act authorizes. If he thinks using torture is necessary, he will go ahead and use it regardless of what Congress has said or the courts may say. Bush took that position in spite of the clear words of the Constitution, whose Article I, Section 8 confers upon Congress the exclusive power to "make Rules concerning Captures on Land and Water."

Another example involves Colombia, whose government was to receive economic but not military assistance from Washington in its campaign against rebels. Section 502(c) of the Intelligence Authorization Act of 2005 declares: "No United States Armed Forces personnel or United States civilian contractor employed by the United States armed forces may participate in any combat operation in connection with assistance [to the government of Colombia] made available under this section, except for the purpose of acting in self-defense or during the course of search-and-rescue operations for United States citizens."[17] As we have seen, the Bush administration (like many a Republican and Democratic administration before it) tendentiously interpreted the Constitution's Commander in Chief Clause to mean that Congress has little to no power to restrict the president's use of the armed forces. The president's signing statement therefore declared: "The executive branch shall construe the restrictions in that section [502] as advisory in nature." Those restrictions can have no binding force on the president, who must exercise his "constitutional authority as Commander in Chief."[18]

The Ronald W. Reagan National Defense Authorization Act for Fiscal Year 2005 set forth a series of rules regarding the operation of military prisons and the training of prison guards. The signing statement made clear that the president believed he could ignore all of those. The act also established the post of special inspector general for Iraq reconstruction. The signing statement ordered the person occupying this new post to refrain from investigating any matter involving intelligence or national security, or indeed any crime that the Pentagon would prefer to investigate.[19]

The importance of signing statements has sometimes been downplayed on the grounds that they have no legal standing, strictly speaking. But consider that Supreme Court justices have indeed begun to refer to presidential signing statements in support of their decisions. In July 2006 the Supreme Court ruled on the question of Guantánamo Bay military trials, with the majority arguing that the restrictive Detainee Treatment Act (DTA) of December 2005 had no effect on pending cases and applied only to those that might arise in the future. The dissent, written by Justice Antonin Scalia and joined by Justices Samuel Alito and Clarence Thomas, argued that the majority had not treated the legislative history of the act in its fullness which included the president's signing statement of December 30, 2005. Scalia wrote, "Of course in its discussion of legislative history the court wholly ignores the president's signing statement, which explicitly set forth his understanding that the DTA [stripped the court of] jurisdiction over pending cases."[20]

More important, we have good reason to believe that these statements mean what they say, and reflect the executive's genuine intention to disregard parts of the law or interpret them in a manner different from the congressional intent. In June 2007, the United States Government Accountability Office (GAO) issued a report, undertaken at the behest of Senator Robert Byrd and Representative John Conyers (chairmen of the committees on appropriations and the judiciary, respectively), following up on a number of the president's signing statements to see if the provisions to which they objected were in fact being enforced. The GAO looked into only a tiny fraction—just 19—of the 160 provisions the president had singled out in his signing statements over the course of eleven appropriations bills during fiscal 2006. The GAO found that in six of those instances the law was not being executed as written, while in three other cases the laws had yet to go into effect (because the legislation could be triggered only if some prior event occurred). In other words, the Bush administration had failed to enforce the law in well over a third of the cases investigated.

The GAO stopped short of attributing these failures to a deliberate presidential design to skirt the law: "Although we found the agencies did not execute the provisions as enacted, we cannot conclude that agency noncompliance was the result of the President's signing statements."[21] But George Washington University Law School's Jonathan Turley was less restrained, telling a television audience: "Congress writes the law. He [the president] can veto it, but he can't rewrite it. And when you look at these laws, that's what he's doing. Notably, many of these laws that he has refused to comply with involve sharing information with Congress, which is a long-standing problem with this president. He has, perhaps, the most contempt of any modern president for the separation of powers, and specifically the powers of the legislative branch."[22]

Even Republicans could be found expressing unease at the Bush administration's unheralded expansion of executive power. "There's a very clear pattern of aggressively asserting executive power," warned Chuck Hagel, Republican senator from Nebraska, "and the Congress has essentially been complicit in letting him do it. The key is that Bush has a Republican Congress; of course if it was a Clinton presidency we'd be holding hearings."[23] Lindsey Graham, Republican senator from South Carolina, was likewise concerned. "If you take this to its logical conclusion, because during war the Commander in Chief has an obligation to protect us, any statute on the books could be summarily waived."[24] Bruce Fein, who served as deputy attorney general to President Ronald Reagan, told the Senate Judiciary Committee in June 2006 that signing statements, which "have multiplied logarithmically under President George W. Bush, flout the Constitution's checks and balances and separation of powers. They usurp legislative prerogatives and evade accountability."[25] Conservative activist Grover Norquist cautioned, "If you interpret the Constitution's saying that the president is commander in chief to mean that the president can do anything he wants and ignore the laws you don't have a constitution: you have a king."[26]

Sometimes, as a strategic means of getting presidential approval for legislation, Congress deliberately inserts provisions the president likes alongside ones he dislikes. That is a fact of life with which the president has to contend. "No Founding Father uttered a single syllable insinuating that such a wrenching political choice amounted to duress or coercion which should be counteracted with presidential power to refuse to enforce the parts of the bill he had signed into [law] but which he disliked," Bruce Fein testified in 2006. After proposing various means to confront the problems posed by signing statements, Fein concluded that "Congress should contemplate impeachment for signing statements that systematically flout the separation of powers and legislative prerogatives. The epitome of an impeachable offense, as Alexander Hamilton amplified in the (*Federalist Papers*), is a political crime against the Constitution."[27]

It has been suggested, in Bush's defense, that these criticisms are all very impractical. After all, the kinds of bills that make their way to the president's desk in our day contain a great many provisions, and we cannot expect the president to veto an entire bill on the basis of one or two objections he may have. The American Bar Association's Task Force on Presidential Signing Statements and the Separation of Powers Doctrine anticipated this objection in its report: "The Founding Fathers contemplated bills with both attractive and unattractive features packaged together with unrelated provisions, including appropriations riders. The President nonetheless was expected to veto even 'urgent' bills that he believed were unconstitutional in part and, if the urgency were genuine, Congress could either delete the offending provisions or override the President."[28]

New York University law professor David Golove thinks the problem with all this is that Bush found an unreasonable number of statutes to be unconstitutional, and that that could mean the president rejected much of the accumulated constitutional law of recent decades. "Where you have a president who is willing to declare vast quantities of the legislation that is passed during his term unconstitutional, it implies that he also thinks a very significant amount of the other laws that were already on the books before he became president are also unconstitutional."[29]

But that is not the point at all. Most of the legislation passed during the Bush administration was certainly unconstitutional by the standards we employ in this book—that is, by the standards of the Constitution itself—and there is nothing outrageous in declaring it so. If anything, we need much more of that. And of course the president has every right to speak and act upon the unconstitutionality of legislation: Thomas Jefferson's theory of concurrent review held that all three branches of government were duty-bound to consider a bill's constitutionality. But the time for pointing out constitutional defects in proposed legislation is *before* the legislation reaches the president's desk, or while drafting a veto message.

Moreover, what should really concern us is the administration's philosophy of the executive branch, whose powers it considered so compendiously broad that it blanched at legislative restrictions that Congress in fact had every right to impose and traditionally has imposed. Richard Nixon once said, with regard to the national security authority of the president, "Well, when the President does it, that means it is not illegal."[30] If there is any difference between that view and the position of the Bush White House, it is not obvious what it could be.

What Are We "Conserving"?

Despite the immense authority that the Bush administration assigned itself through presidential signing statements, most Americans remained altogether unaware of what was happening. The media would cover the ceremony surrounding the signing of an important bill— the smiles, the handshakes, the troop of Girl Scouts. Meanwhile, the signing statement—which would not be read aloud at the signing— would be ignored altogether and wind up sitting unread in the *Federal Register*. Even if someone did track it down, the statement typically would be written in a technical style, making reference to minute details and subsections that required substantial knowledge of the law itself to understand.[31]

"One of the defining principles of the Bush administration has been a belief in unfettered executive power," wrote Jeffrey Rosen in the *New Republic* in 2006. "Indeed, President Bush has taken the principle to such unprecedented extremes that an ironic reversal has taken place: A conservative ideology that had always been devoted to limiting government power has been transformed into the largest expansion of executive power since FDR."[32] Rosen is correct, of course. Conservatives did not always support the strong executive that they accuse people of being "liberals" for opposing now.[33] To the contrary, genuine conservatism—that is, the strain that young conservatives are deliberately kept in the dark about—was traditionally wary of executive power. The Robert Taft wing of the Republican Party—1940s and 1950s conservatives—had an abiding distrust of presidential claims to inherent or emergency powers.

For all intents and purposes, that tradition is long gone, though it can be found lingering here and there among a small minority of principled opponents of the conservatism of recent years. If conservatives cannot bring themselves to oppose such deformations of the constitutional separation of powers, it may be worth asking what exactly it is they think they are conserving.

Conclusion

Can Anything Be Done?

THE CONSTITUTION IS dead.

That blunt but unavoidable truth should be clear by now. The examples from the past century of American constitutional history cited in this book reveal how the federal government's actions often bear no resemblance to what the Constitution's ratifiers intended, and in fact run directly counter to the plain text of the Constitution.

It should be noted that to the "dirty dozen" examples included here, we could have added many others. There is, for instance, the Supreme Court's highly controversial 1973 decision legalizing abortion in *Roe v. Wade*, every aspect of which was faulty—the constitutional arguments, the biological arguments, and the historical arguments—as even many proponents of abortion rights acknowledge. (For instance, legal scholar John Ely, writing in the *Yale Law Journal*, condemned the *Roe* decision "because it is bad constitutional law, or rather because it is *not* constitutional law and gives almost no sense of an obligation to try to be.")[1] There is also President Bill Clinton's bombing of Serbia in 1999, which struck a new low in presidential contempt for the Constitution because it directly defied a House vote refusing to endorse that bombing. Constitutional scholar

David Gray Adler called it "one of the most flagrant acts of usurpation of the war power in the history of the Republic."[2]

So if the Constitution is dead, how can we revive it? How can we reclaim the limited, republican government that the Constitution lays out and that prevailed for much of America's history?

Books such as this one typically end with a rousing call to action, a four-point plan to get the country back on track.

But what if *there is no solution*? What if the experiment with a written federal constitution has proven to be a failure?

What's Left of the Constitution

Nineteenth-century constitutional commentator Lysander Spooner once said that he believed "that by false interpretations, and naked usurpations, the government has been made in practice a very widely, and almost wholly, different thing from what the Constitution itself purports to authorize." At the same time, he could not exonerate the Constitution, for it "has either authorized such a government as we have had, or has been powerless to prevent it. In either case, it is unfit to exist."

As Spooner's statement assumes, the idea behind written constitutions was that a set of fixed, known rules—written rules—should bind government and limit its power over the population. If people decided that their government needed more power than they had given it, they could amend their constitution to give it more. But who was to interpret those rules and hand down authoritative rulings as to what they allowed and prohibited? According to the understanding of these matters advocated by federal officials, it was to be the very same federal government that was supposed to be bound by the Constitution in the first place.

Thomas Jefferson deserves respect for recognizing this problem. He knew that if the federal government had a monopoly on constitutional interpretation, it would naturally read the Constitution in its own favor, always announcing that it had discovered in the text yet more power that it could exercise. He insisted that the states, twelve of whose delegates had drafted the Constitution, and all of which by 1790 had ratified it, were entitled to make ultimate constitutional determinations, because the only alternative was a central government monopoly that in the end would swallow up the states.

For nearly three-quarters of a century, the Left, meaning mainly but not solely the Democratic Party, has concocted arguments for the Constitution's essential meaninglessness, for the federal government's ability to do things the Constitution previously had been understood as banning. In some sense, in George W. Bush's administration the Left has gotten what it deserved, as the defanged Constitution they themselves have encouraged has proven to be no obstacle to even the most constitutionally outlandish initiatives of the Left's opponents. In matters of war, foreign affairs, and civil liberties, excellent and crushing constitutional arguments are available to critics of recent developments, since the Constitution's original intent is so clearly at odds with current practice. Yet who can take seriously the arguments of Bush administration critics from the Brennan Center or the *Nation* magazine? They have pulled the very rug out from under themselves. Their sudden interest in obedience to the Constitution rings hollow.

We hasten to note that this is not fundamentally a Left-Right issue (although the traditional Right would have opposed all of the offenses against the Constitution that we document in this book). As the great Virginian John Taylor of Caroline noted, the problem is not the character of members of one party or the other, one section of the country or the other, but the effect of power on the human ego, regardless of party or section. People in power exercise all the power they can get, even after they have howled in the wilderness against legislating judges, imperial presidents, and the death of states' rights. That is why Taylor's friend Jefferson believed the Constitution must act as a set of chains to bind down the federal government.

The federal government, of course, has long since busted out of those chains. But the history reviewed in this book raises an important question, not only about the United States Constitution but also about *any* written constitution: in the end, are these constitutions just another doomed attempt to limit something that cannot be limited?

It is perhaps jarring to consider the possibility that constitutions are destined to fail. After all, we are indoctrinated from early childhood with the idea that the Constitution is the font of our liberties—even though Americans were free before it was written. And it is to the U.S. Constitution that every government official still swears his fidelity. But when we look beyond the grand rhetoric to the actual record, we must confront a troubling conclusion: once an institution obtains supreme force, it is probably utopian to expect its powers to remain limited over time—especially when the one thing doing the limiting is a document that is interpreted and enforced by the very institution it is supposed to restrain.

So what, then, is left of the Constitution? To be sure, our federal government has perverted beyond recognition the system that the Founding Fathers created. The chief restraint on government officials is merely their sense of what they can get away with. Nonetheless, the Constitution can still serve a purpose, as it remains a useful bludgeon to employ against government power grabs. By calling attention to what the Constitution really says, we can alert the people to just how consistently and dramatically their fundamental law has been betrayed. What they do with that knowledge is up to the American people themselves to decide.

Appendix

The Constitution of the United States

Preamble

We the People of the United States, in Order to form a more perfect Union, establish Justice, insure domestic Tranquility, provide for the common defence, promote the general Welfare, and secure the Blessings of Liberty to ourselves and our Posterity, do ordain and establish this Constitution for the United States of America.

Article I.

SECTION 1.

All legislative Powers herein granted shall be vested in a Congress of the United States, which shall consist of a Senate and House of Representatives.

SECTION 2.

The House of Representatives shall be composed of Members chosen every second Year by the People of the several States, and the Electors in each State shall have the Qualifications requisite for Electors of the most numerous Branch of the State Legislature.

No Person shall be a Representative who shall not have attained to the Age of twenty five Years, and been seven Years a Citizen of the United States, and who shall not, when elected, be an Inhabitant of that State in which he shall be chosen.

Representatives and direct Taxes shall be apportioned among the several States which may be included within this Union, according to their respective Numbers, which shall be determined by adding to the whole Number of free Persons, including those bound to Service for a Term of Years, and excluding Indians not taxed, three fifths of all other Persons. The actual Enumeration shall be made within three Years after the first Meeting of the Congress of the United States, and within every subsequent Term of ten Years, in such Manner as they shall by Law direct. The Number of Representatives shall not exceed one for every thirty Thousand, but each State shall have at Least one Representative; and until such enumeration shall be made, the State of New Hampshire shall be entitled to chuse three, Massachusetts eight, Rhode-Island and Providence Plantations one, Connecticut five, New-York six, New Jersey four, Pennsylvania eight, Delaware one, Maryland six, Virginia ten, North Carolina five, South Carolina five, and Georgia three.

When vacancies happen in the Representation from any State, the Executive Authority thereof shall issue Writs of Election to fill such Vacancies.

The House of Representatives shall chuse their Speaker and other Officers; and shall have the sole Power of Impeachment.

SECTION 3.

The Senate of the United States shall be composed of two Senators from each State, chosen by the Legislature thereof for six Years; and each Senator shall have one Vote.

Immediately after they shall be assembled in Consequence of the first Election, they shall be divided as equally as may be into three Classes. The Seats of the Senators of the first Class shall be vacated at the Expiration of the second Year, of the second Class at the Expiration of the fourth Year, and of the third Class at the Expiration of the sixth Year, so that one third may be chosen every second Year; and if Vacancies happen by Resignation, or otherwise, during the Recess of the Legislature of any State, the Executive thereof may make temporary Appointments until the next Meeting of the Legislature, which shall then fill such Vacancies.

No Person shall be a Senator who shall not have attained to the Age of thirty Years, and been nine Years a Citizen of the United States, and who shall not, when elected, be an Inhabitant of that State for which he shall be chosen.

The Vice President of the United States shall be President of the Senate, but shall have no Vote, unless they be equally divided.

The Senate shall chuse their other Officers, and also a President pro tempore, in the Absence of the Vice President, or when he shall exercise the Office of President of the United States.

The Senate shall have the sole Power to try all Impeachments. When sitting for that Purpose, they shall be on Oath or Affirmation. When the President of the United States is tried, the Chief Justice shall preside: And no Person shall be convicted without the Concurrence of two thirds of the Members present.

Judgment in Cases of Impeachment shall not extend further than to removal from Office, and disqualification to hold and enjoy any Office of honor, Trust or Profit under the United States: but the Party convicted shall nevertheless be liable and subject to Indictment, Trial, Judgment and Punishment, according to Law.

Section 4.

The Times, Places and Manner of holding Elections for Senators and Representatives, shall be prescribed in each State by the Legislature thereof; but the Congress may at any time by Law make or alter such Regulations, except as to the Places of chusing Senators.

The Congress shall assemble at least once in every Year, and such Meeting shall be on the first Monday in December, unless they shall by Law appoint a different Day.

Section 5.

Each House shall be the Judge of the Elections, Returns and Qualifications of its own Members, and a Majority of each shall constitute a Quorum to do Business; but a smaller Number may adjourn from day to day, and may be authorized to compel the Attendance of absent Members, in such Manner, and under such Penalties as each House may provide.

Each House may determine the Rules of its Proceedings, punish its Members for disorderly Behaviour, and, with the Concurrence of two thirds, expel a Member.

Each House shall keep a Journal of its Proceedings, and from time to time publish the same, excepting such Parts as may in their Judgment require Secrecy; and the Yeas and Nays of the Members of either House on any question shall, at the Desire of one fifth of those Present, be entered on the Journal.

Neither House, during the Session of Congress, shall, without the Consent of the other, adjourn for more than three days, nor to any other Place than that in which the two Houses shall be sitting.

Section 6.

The Senators and Representatives shall receive a Compensation for their Services, to be ascertained by Law, and paid out of the Treasury of the United States. They shall in all Cases, except Treason, Felony and Breach of the Peace, be privileged from Arrest during their Attendance at the Session of their respective Houses, and in going to and returning from the same; and for any Speech or Debate in either House, they shall not be questioned in any other Place.

No Senator or Representative shall, during the Time for which he was elected, be appointed to any civil Office under the Authority of the United States, which shall have been created, or the Emoluments whereof shall have been encreased during such time; and no Person holding any Office under the United States, shall be a Member of either House during his Continuance in Office.

Section 7.

All Bills for raising Revenue shall originate in the House of Representatives; but the Senate may propose or concur with Amendments as on other Bills.

Every Bill which shall have passed the House of Representatives and the Senate, shall, before it become a Law, be presented to the President of the United States: If he approve he shall sign it, but if not he shall return it, with his Objections to that House in which it shall have originated, who shall enter the Objections at large on their Journal, and proceed to reconsider it. If after such Reconsideration two thirds of that House shall agree to pass the Bill, it shall be sent, together with the Objections, to the other House, by which it shall likewise be reconsidered, and if approved by two thirds of that House, it shall become a Law. But in all such Cases the Votes of both Houses shall be determined by yeas and Nays, and the Names of the Persons voting for and against the Bill shall be entered on the Journal of each House respectively. If any Bill shall not be returned by the President within ten Days (Sundays excepted) after it shall have been presented to him, the Same shall be a Law, in like Manner as if he had signed it, unless the Congress by their Adjournment prevent its Return, in which Case it shall not be a Law.

Every Order, Resolution, or Vote to which the Concurrence of the Senate and House of Representatives may be necessary (except on a question of Adjournment) shall be presented to the President of the United States; and before the Same shall take Effect, shall be approved by him, or being disapproved by him, shall be repassed by two thirds of the Senate and House of Representatives, according to the Rules and Limitations prescribed in the Case of a Bill.

SECTION 8.

The Congress shall have Power To lay and collect Taxes, Duties, Imposts and Excises, to pay the Debts and provide for the common Defence and general Welfare of the United States; but all Duties, Imposts and Excises shall be uniform throughout the United States;

To borrow Money on the credit of the United States;

To regulate Commerce with foreign Nations, and among the several States, and with the Indian Tribes;

To establish an uniform Rule of Naturalization, and uniform Laws on the subject of Bankruptcies throughout the United States;

To coin Money, regulate the Value thereof, and of foreign Coin, and fix the Standard of Weights and Measures;

To provide for the Punishment of counterfeiting the Securities and current Coin of the United States;

To establish Post Offices and post Roads;

To promote the Progress of Science and useful Arts, by securing for limited Times to Authors and Inventors the exclusive Right to their respective Writings and Discoveries;

To constitute Tribunals inferior to the supreme Court;

To define and punish Piracies and Felonies committed on the high Seas, and Offences against the Law of Nations;

To declare War, grant Letters of Marque and Reprisal, and make Rules concerning Captures on Land and Water;

To raise and support Armies, but no Appropriation of Money to that Use shall be for a longer Term than two Years;

To provide and maintain a Navy;

To make Rules for the Government and Regulation of the land and naval Forces;

To provide for calling forth the Militia to execute the Laws of the Union, suppress Insurrections and repel Invasions;

To provide for organizing, arming, and disciplining, the Militia, and for governing such Part of them as may be employed in the Service of the United States, reserving to the States respectively, the Appointment of the Officers, and the Authority of training the Militia according to the discipline prescribed by Congress;

To exercise exclusive Legislation in all Cases whatsoever, over such District (not exceeding ten Miles square) as may, by Cession of particular States, and the Acceptance of Congress, become the Seat of the Government of the United States, and to exercise like Authority over all Places purchased by the Consent of the Legislature of the State in which the Same shall be, for the Erection of Forts, Magazines, Arsenals, dock-Yards, and other needful Buildings;—And

To make all Laws which shall be necessary and proper for carrying into Execution the foregoing Powers, and all other Powers vested by this Constitution in the Government of the United States, or in any Department or Officer thereof.

Section 9.

The Migration or Importation of such Persons as any of the States now existing shall think proper to admit, shall not be prohibited by the Congress prior to the Year one thousand eight hundred and eight, but a Tax or duty may be imposed on such Importation, not exceeding ten dollars for each Person.

The Privilege of the Writ of Habeas Corpus shall not be suspended, unless when in Cases of Rebellion or Invasion the public Safety may require it.

No Bill of Attainder or ex post facto Law shall be passed.

No Capitation, or other direct, Tax shall be laid, unless in Proportion to the Census or enumeration herein before directed to be taken.

No Tax or Duty shall be laid on Articles exported from any State.

No Preference shall be given by any Regulation of Commerce or Revenue to the Ports of one State over those of another; nor shall Vessels bound to, or from, one State, be obliged to enter, clear, or pay Duties in another.

No Money shall be drawn from the Treasury, but in Consequence of Appropriations made by Law; and a regular Statement and Account of the Receipts and Expenditures of all public Money shall be published from time to time.

No Title of Nobility shall be granted by the United States: And no Person holding any Office of Profit or Trust under them, shall, without the Consent of the Congress, accept of any present, Emolument, Office, or Title, of any kind whatever, from any King, Prince, or foreign State.

Section 10.

No State shall enter into any Treaty, Alliance, or Confederation; grant Letters of Marque and Reprisal; coin Money; emit Bills of Credit; make any Thing but gold and silver Coin a Tender in Payment of Debts; pass any Bill of Attainder, ex post facto Law, or Law impairing the Obligation of Contracts, or grant any Title of Nobility.

No State shall, without the Consent of the Congress, lay any Imposts or Duties on Imports or Exports, except what may be absolutely necessary for executing its inspection Laws: and the net Produce of all Duties and

Imposts, laid by any State on Imports or Exports, shall be for the Use of the Treasury of the United States; and all such Laws shall be subject to the Revision and Controul of the Congress.

No State shall, without the Consent of Congress, lay any Duty of Tonnage, keep Troops, or Ships of War in time of Peace, enter into any Agreement or Compact with another State, or with a foreign Power, or engage in War, unless actually invaded, or in such imminent Danger as will not admit of delay.

Article II.

SECTION 1.

The executive Power shall be vested in a President of the United States of America. He shall hold his Office during the Term of four Years, and, together with the Vice President, chosen for the same Term, be elected, as follows:

Each State shall appoint, in such Manner as the Legislature thereof may direct, a Number of Electors, equal to the whole Number of Senators and Representatives to which the State may be entitled in the Congress: but no Senator or Representative, or Person holding an Office of Trust or Profit under the United States, shall be appointed an Elector.

The Electors shall meet in their respective States, and vote by Ballot for two Persons, of whom one at least shall not be an Inhabitant of the same State with themselves. And they shall make a List of all the Persons voted for, and of the Number of Votes for each; which List they shall sign and certify, and transmit sealed to the Seat of the Government of the United States, directed to the President of the Senate. The President of the Senate shall, in the Presence of the Senate and House of Representatives, open all the Certificates, and the Votes shall then be counted. The Person having the greatest Number of Votes shall be the President, if such Number be a Majority of the whole Number of Electors appointed; and if there be more than one who have such Majority, and have an equal Number of Votes, then the House of Representatives shall immediately chuse by Ballot one of them for President; and if no Person have a Majority, then from the five highest on the List the said House shall in like Manner chuse the President. But in chusing the President, the Votes shall be taken by States, the Representation from each State having one Vote; A quorum for this purpose shall consist of a Member or Members from two thirds of the States, and a Majority of all the States shall be necessary to a Choice. In every Case, after the Choice of the President, the Person having the greatest Number of Votes of the Electors shall be the Vice President. But if there should remain two or more who have equal Votes, the Senate shall chuse from them by Ballot the Vice President.

The Congress may determine the Time of chusing the Electors, and the Day on which they shall give their Votes; which Day shall be the same throughout the United States.

No Person except a natural born Citizen, or a Citizen of the United States, at the time of the Adoption of this Constitution, shall be eligible to the Office of President; neither shall any Person be eligible to that Office who shall not have attained to the Age of thirty five Years, and been fourteen Years a Resident within the United States.

In Case of the Removal of the President from Office, or of his Death, Resignation, or Inability to discharge the Powers and Duties of the said Office, the Same shall devolve on the Vice President, and the Congress may by Law provide for the Case of Removal, Death, Resignation or Inability, both of the President and Vice President, declaring what Officer shall then act as President, and such Officer shall act accordingly, until the Disability be removed, or a President shall be elected.

The President shall, at stated Times, receive for his Services, a Compensation, which shall neither be increased nor diminished during the Period for which he shall have been elected, and he shall not receive within that Period any other Emolument from the United States, or any of them.

Before he enter on the Execution of his Office, he shall take the following Oath or Affirmation: "I do solemnly swear (or affirm) that I will faithfully execute the Office of President of the United States, and will to the best of my Ability, preserve, protect and defend the Constitution of the United States."

SECTION 2.

The President shall be Commander in Chief of the Army and Navy of the United States, and of the Militia of the several States, when called into the actual Service of the United States; he may require the Opinion, in writing, of the principal Officer in each of the executive Departments, upon any Subject relating to the Duties of their respective Offices, and he shall have Power to grant Reprieves and Pardons for Offences against the United States, except in Cases of Impeachment.

He shall have Power, by and with the Advice and Consent of the Senate, to make Treaties, provided two thirds of the Senators present concur; and he shall nominate, and by and with the Advice and Consent of the Senate, shall appoint Ambassadors, other public Ministers and Consuls, Judges of the supreme Court, and all other Officers of the United States, whose Appointments are not herein otherwise provided for, and which shall be established by Law: but the Congress may by Law vest the Appointment of such inferior Officers, as they think proper, in the President alone, in the Courts of Law, or in the Heads of Departments.

The President shall have Power to fill up all Vacancies that may happen during the Recess of the Senate, by granting Commissions which shall expire at the End of their next Session.

Section 3.

He shall from time to time give to the Congress Information of the State of the Union, and recommend to their Consideration such Measures as he shall judge necessary and expedient; he may, on extraordinary Occasions, convene both Houses, or either of them, and in Case of Disagreement between them, with Respect to the Time of Adjournment, he may adjourn them to such Time as he shall think proper; he shall receive Ambassadors and other public Ministers; he shall take Care that the Laws be faithfully executed, and shall Commission all the Officers of the United States.

Section 4.

The President, Vice President and all civil Officers of the United States, shall be removed from Office on Impeachment for, and Conviction of, Treason, Bribery, or other high Crimes and Misdemeanors.

Article III.

Section 1.

The judicial Power of the United States shall be vested in one supreme Court, and in such inferior Courts as the Congress may from time to time ordain and establish. The Judges, both of the supreme and inferior Courts, shall hold their Offices during good Behaviour, and shall, at stated Times, receive for their Services a Compensation, which shall not be diminished during their Continuance in Office.

Section 2.

The judicial Power shall extend to all Cases, in Law and Equity, arising under this Constitution, the Laws of the United States, and Treaties made, or which shall be made, under their Authority;—to all Cases affecting Ambassadors, other public Ministers and Consuls;—to all Cases of admiralty and maritime Jurisdiction;—to Controversies to which the United States shall be a Party;—to Controversies between two or more States;—between a State and Citizens of another State;—between Citizens of different States;—between Citizens of the same State claiming Lands under Grants of different States, and between a State, or the Citizens thereof, and foreign States, Citizens or Subjects.

In all Cases affecting Ambassadors, other public Ministers and Consuls, and those in which a State shall be Party, the supreme Court shall have original Jurisdiction. In all the other Cases before mentioned, the supreme Court shall have appellate Jurisdiction, both as to Law and Fact, with such Exceptions, and under such Regulations as the Congress shall make.

The Trial of all Crimes, except in Cases of Impeachment, shall be by Jury; and such Trial shall be held in the State where the said Crimes shall have been committed; but when not committed within any State, the Trial shall be at such Place or Places as the Congress may by Law have directed.

Section 3.

Treason against the United States, shall consist only in levying War against them, or in adhering to their Enemies, giving them Aid and Comfort. No Person shall be convicted of Treason unless on the Testimony of two Witnesses to the same overt Act, or on Confession in open Court.

The Congress shall have Power to declare the Punishment of Treason, but no Attainder of Treason shall work Corruption of Blood, or Forfeiture except during the Life of the Person attainted.

Article IV.

Section 1.

Full Faith and Credit shall be given in each State to the public Acts, Records, and judicial Proceedings of every other State. And the Congress may by general Laws prescribe the Manner in which such Acts, Records and Proceedings shall be proved, and the Effect thereof.

Section 2.

The Citizens of each State shall be entitled to all Privileges and Immunities of Citizens in the several States.

A Person charged in any State with Treason, Felony, or other Crime, who shall flee from Justice, and be found in another State, shall on Demand of the executive Authority of the State from which he fled, be delivered up, to be removed to the State having Jurisdiction of the Crime.

No Person held to Service or Labour in one State, under the Laws thereof, escaping into another, shall, in Consequence of any Law or Regulation therein, be discharged from such Service or Labour, but shall be delivered up on Claim of the Party to whom such Service or Labour may be due.

Section 3.

New States may be admitted by the Congress into this Union; but no new State shall be formed or erected within the Jurisdiction of any other State; nor any State be formed by the Junction of two or more States, or Parts of States, without the Consent of the Legislatures of the States concerned as well as of the Congress.

The Congress shall have Power to dispose of and make all needful Rules and Regulations respecting the Territory or other Property belonging to the United States; and nothing in this Constitution shall be so construed as to Prejudice any Claims of the United States, or of any particular State.

Section 4.

The United States shall guarantee to every State in this Union a Republican Form of Government, and shall protect each of them against Invasion; and on Application of the Legislature, or of the Executive (when the Legislature cannot be convened), against domestic Violence.

Article V.

The Congress, whenever two thirds of both Houses shall deem it necessary, shall propose Amendments to this Constitution, or, on the Application of the Legislatures of two thirds of the several States, shall call a Convention for proposing Amendments, which, in either Case, shall be valid to all Intents and Purposes, as Part of this Constitution, when ratified by the Legislatures of three fourths of the several States, or by Conventions in three fourths thereof, as the one or the other Mode of Ratification may be proposed by the Congress; Provided that no Amendment which may be made prior to the Year One thousand eight hundred and eight shall in any Manner affect the first and fourth Clauses in the Ninth Section of the first Article; and that no State, without its Consent, shall be deprived of its equal Suffrage in the Senate.

Article VI.

All Debts contracted and Engagements entered into, before the Adoption of this Constitution, shall be as valid against the United States under this Constitution, as under the Confederation.

This Constitution, and the Laws of the United States which shall be made in Pursuance thereof; and all Treaties made, or which shall be made, under the Authority of the United States, shall be the supreme Law of the

Land; and the Judges in every State shall be bound thereby, any Thing in the Constitution or Laws of any State to the Contrary notwithstanding.

The Senators and Representatives before mentioned, and the Members of the several State Legislatures, and all executive and judicial Officers, both of the United States and of the several States, shall be bound by Oath or Affirmation, to support this Constitution; but no religious Test shall ever be required as a Qualification to any Office or public Trust under the United States.

Article VII.

The Ratification of the Conventions of nine States, shall be sufficient for the Establishment of this Constitution between the States so ratifying the Same.

Done in Convention by the Unanimous Consent of the States present the Seventeenth Day of September in the Year of our Lord one thousand seven hundred and Eighty seven and of the Independence of the United States of America the Twelfth. In Witness whereof We have hereunto subscribed our Names.

George Washington—President and deputy from Virginia
Delaware: George Read, Gunning Bedford Jr., John Dickinson,
*   Richard Bassett, Jacob Broom*
Maryland: James McHenry, Daniel of St Thomas Jenifer, Daniel Carroll
Virginia: John Blair, James Madison Jr.
North Carolina: William Blount, Richard Dobbs Spaight,
*   Hugh Williamson*
South Carolina: John Rutledge, Charles Cotesworth Pinckney,
*   Charles Pinckney, Pierce Butler*
Georgia: William Few, Abraham Baldwin
New Hampshire: John Langdon, Nicholas Gilman
Massachusetts: Nathaniel Gorham, Rufus King
Connecticut: William Samuel Johnson, Roger Sherman
New York: Alexander Hamilton
New Jersey: William Livingston, David Brearley, William Paterson,
*   Jonathan Dayton*
Pennsylvania: Benjamin Franklin, Thomas Mifflin, Robert Morris,
*   George Clymer, Thomas Fitzsimons, Jared Ingersoll, James Wilson,*
*   Gouverneur Morris*

Attest: William Jackson, Secretary

THE PREAMBLE TO THE BILL OF RIGHTS

Congress of the United States begun and held at the City of New-York, on Wednesday the fourth of March, one thousand seven hundred and eighty nine.

THE Conventions of a number of the States, having at the time of their adopting the Constitution, expressed a desire, in order to prevent misconstruction or abuse of its powers, that further declaratory and restrictive clauses should be added: And as extending the ground of public confidence in the Government, will best ensure the beneficent ends of its institution.

RESOLVED by the Senate and House of Representatives of the United States of America, in Congress assembled, two thirds of both Houses concurring, that the following Articles be proposed to the Legislatures of the several States, as amendments to the Constitution of the United States, all, or any of which Articles, when ratified by three fourths of the said Legislatures, to be valid to all intents and purposes, as part of the said Constitution; viz.

ARTICLES in addition to, and Amendment of the Constitution of the United States of America, proposed by Congress, and ratified by the Legislatures of the several States, pursuant to the fifth Article of the original Constitution.

Amendment I

Congress shall make no law respecting an establishment of religion, or prohibiting the free exercise thereof; or abridging the freedom of speech, or of the press; or the right of the people peaceably to assemble, and to petition the Government for a redress of grievances.

Amendment II

A well regulated Militia, being necessary to the security of a free State, the right of the people to keep and bear Arms, shall not be infringed.

Amendment III

No Soldier shall, in time of peace be quartered in any house, without the consent of the Owner, nor in time of war, but in a manner to be prescribed by law.

Amendment IV

The right of the people to be secure in their persons, houses, papers, and effects, against unreasonable searches and seizures, shall not be violated, and no Warrants shall issue, but upon probable cause, supported by Oath or affirmation, and particularly describing the place to be searched, and the persons or things to be seized.

Amendment V

No person shall be held to answer for a capital, or otherwise infamous crime, unless on a presentment or indictment of a Grand Jury, except in cases arising in the land or naval forces, or in the Militia, when in actual service in time of War or public danger; nor shall any person be subject for the same offence to be twice put in jeopardy of life or limb; nor shall be compelled in any criminal case to be a witness against himself, nor be deprived of life, liberty, or property, without due process of law; nor shall private property be taken for public use, without just compensation.

Amendment VI

In all criminal prosecutions, the accused shall enjoy the right to a speedy and public trial, by an impartial jury of the State and district wherein the crime shall have been committed, which district shall have been previously ascertained by law, and to be informed of the nature and cause of the accusation; to be confronted with the witnesses against him; to have compulsory process for obtaining witnesses in his favor, and to have the Assistance of Counsel for his defence.

Amendment VII

In Suits at common law, where the value in controversy shall exceed twenty dollars, the right of trial by jury shall be preserved, and no fact tried by a jury, shall be otherwise re-examined in any Court of the United States, than according to the rules of the common law.

Amendment VIII

Excessive bail shall not be required, nor excessive fines imposed, nor cruel and unusual punishments inflicted.

Amendment IX

The enumeration in the Constitution, of certain rights, shall not be construed to deny or disparage others retained by the people.

Amendment X

The powers not delegated to the United States by the Constitution, nor prohibited by it to the States, are reserved to the States respectively, or to the people.

Amendment XI

Passed by Congress March 4, 1794. Ratified February 7, 1795.
Note: Article III, section 2, of the Constitution was modified by amendment 11.
The Judicial power of the United States shall not be construed to extend to any suit in law or equity, commenced or prosecuted against one of the United States by Citizens of another State, or by Citizens or Subjects of any Foreign State.

Amendment XII

Passed by Congress December 9, 1803. Ratified June 15, 1804.
Note: A portion of Article II, section 1 of the Constitution was superseded
by the 12th amendment.
The Electors shall meet in their respective states and vote by ballot for President and Vice-President, one of whom, at least, shall not be an inhabitant of the same state with themselves; they shall name in their ballots the person voted for as President, and in distinct ballots the person voted for as Vice-President, and they shall make distinct lists of all persons voted for as President, and of all persons voted for as Vice-President, and of the number of votes for each, which lists they shall sign and certify, and transmit sealed to the seat of the government of the United States, directed to the President of the Senate;—the President of the Senate shall, in the presence of the Senate and House of Representatives, open all the certificates and the votes shall then be counted;—The person having the greatest number of votes for President, shall be the President, if such number be a majority of the whole number of Electors appointed; and if no person have such majority, then from the persons having the highest numbers not exceeding three on the list of those voted for as President, the House of Representatives shall choose immediately, by ballot, the President. But in choosing

the President, the votes shall be taken by states, the representation from each state having one vote; a quorum for this purpose shall consist of a member or members from two-thirds of the states, and a majority of all the states shall be necessary to a choice. [And if the House of Representatives shall not choose a President whenever the right of choice shall devolve upon them, before the fourth day of March next following, then the Vice-President shall act as President, as in case of the death or other constitutional disability of the President.]* The person having the greatest number of votes as Vice-President, shall be the Vice-President, if such number be a majority of the whole number of Electors appointed, and if no person have a majority, then from the two highest numbers on the list, the Senate shall choose the Vice-President; a quorum for the purpose shall consist of two-thirds of the whole number of Senators, and a majority of the whole number shall be necessary to a choice. But no person constitutionally ineligible to the office of President shall be eligible to that of Vice-President of the United States.

Amendment XIII

Passed by Congress January 31, 1865. Ratified December 6, 1865.
Note: A portion of Article IV, section 2, of the Constitution was superseded by the 13th amendment.

SECTION 1.

Neither slavery nor involuntary servitude, except as a punishment for crime whereof the party shall have been duly convicted, shall exist within the United States, or any place subject to their jurisdiction.

SECTION 2.

Congress shall have power to enforce this article by appropriate legislation.

---

* Superseded by Section 3 of the Twentieth Amendment.

Amendment XIV

Passed by Congress June 13, 1866. Ratified July 9, 1868.
Note: Article I, section 2, of the Constitution was modified by section 2
of the 14th amendment.

SECTION 1.

All persons born or naturalized in the United States, and subject to the jurisdiction thereof, are citizens of the United States and of the State wherein they reside. No State shall make or enforce any law which shall abridge the privileges or immunities of citizens of the United States; nor shall any State deprive any person of life, liberty, or property, without due process of law; nor deny to any person within its jurisdiction the equal protection of the laws.

SECTION 2.

Representatives shall be apportioned among the several States according to their respective numbers, counting the whole number of persons in each State, excluding Indians not taxed. But when the right to vote at any election for the choice of electors for President and Vice-President of the United States, Representatives in Congress, the Executive and Judicial officers of a State, or the members of the Legislature thereof, is denied to any of the male inhabitants of such State, being twenty-one years of age,* and citizens of the United States, or in any way abridged, except for participation in rebellion, or other crime, the basis of representation therein shall be reduced in the proportion which the number of such male citizens shall bear to the whole number of male citizens twenty-one years of age in such State.

SECTION 3.

No person shall be a Senator or Representative in Congress, or elector of President and Vice-President, or hold any office, civil or military, under the United States, or under any State, who, having previously taken an oath, as a member of Congress, or as an officer of the United States, or as a member of any State legislature, or as an executive or judicial officer of any State, to support the Constitution of the United States, shall have engaged in insurrection or rebellion against the same, or given aid or comfort to the enemies thereof. But Congress may by a vote of two-thirds of each House, remove such disability.

---

* Changed by Section 1 of the Twenty-sixth Amendment.

Section 4.

The validity of the public debt of the United States, authorized by law, including debts incurred for payment of pensions and bounties for services in suppressing insurrection or rebellion, shall not be questioned. But neither the United States nor any State shall assume or pay any debt or obligation incurred in aid of insurrection or rebellion against the United States, or any claim for the loss or emancipation of any slave; but all such debts, obligations and claims shall be held illegal and void.

Section 5.

The Congress shall have the power to enforce, by appropriate legislation, the provisions of this article.

Amendment XV

Passed by Congress February 26, 1869. Ratified February 3, 1870.

Section 1.

The right of citizens of the United States to vote shall not be denied or abridged by the United States or by any State on account of race, color, or previous condition of servitude—

Section 2.

The Congress shall have the power to enforce this article by appropriate legislation.

Amendment XVI

Passed by Congress July 2, 1909. Ratified February 3, 1913.
Note: Article I, section 9, of the Constitution was modified by amendment 16.
The Congress shall have power to lay and collect taxes on incomes, from whatever source derived, without apportionment among the several States, and without regard to any census or enumeration.

Amendment XVII

Passed by Congress May 13, 1912. Ratified April 8, 1913.
Note: Article I, section 3, of the Constitution was modified
by the 17th amendment.
The Senate of the United States shall be composed of two Senators from each State, elected by the people thereof, for six years; and each Senator shall have

one vote. The electors in each State shall have the qualifications requisite for electors of the most numerous branch of the State legislatures.

When vacancies happen in the representation of any State in the Senate, the executive authority of such State shall issue writs of election to fill such vacancies: Provided, That the legislature of any State may empower the executive thereof to make temporary appointments until the people fill the vacancies by election as the legislature may direct.

This amendment shall not be so construed as to affect the election or term of any Senator chosen before it becomes valid as part of the Constitution.

Amendment XVIII

Passed by Congress December 18, 1917. Ratified January 16, 1919. Repealed by amendment 21.

SECTION 1.

After one year from the ratification of this article the manufacture, sale, or transportation of intoxicating liquors within, the importation thereof into, or the exportation thereof from the United States and all territory subject to the jurisdiction thereof for beverage purposes is hereby prohibited.

SECTION 2.

The Congress and the several States shall have concurrent power to enforce this article by appropriate legislation.

SECTION 3.

This article shall be inoperative unless it shall have been ratified as an amendment to the Constitution by the legislatures of the several States, as provided in the Constitution, within seven years from the date of the submission hereof to the States by the Congress.

Amendment XIX

Passed by Congress June 4, 1919. Ratified August 18, 1920.

The right of citizens of the United States to vote shall not be denied or abridged by the United States or by any State on account of sex.

Congress shall have power to enforce this article by appropriate legislation.

Amendment XX

Passed by Congress March 2, 1932. Ratified January 23, 1933.
Note: Article I, section 4, of the Constitution was modified by section 2
of this amendment. In addition, a portion of the 12th amendment was
superseded by section 3.

SECTION 1.

The terms of the President and the Vice President shall end at noon on the 20th day of January, and the terms of Senators and Representatives at noon on the 3d day of January, of the years in which such terms would have ended if this article had not been ratified; and the terms of their successors shall then begin.

SECTION 2.

The Congress shall assemble at least once in every year, and such meeting shall begin at noon on the 3d day of January, unless they shall by law appoint a different day.

SECTION 3.

If, at the time fixed for the beginning of the term of the President, the President elect shall have died, the Vice President elect shall become President. If a President shall not have been chosen before the time fixed for the beginning of his term, or if the President elect shall have failed to qualify, then the Vice President elect shall act as President until a President shall have qualified; and the Congress may by law provide for the case wherein neither a President elect nor a Vice President shall have qualified, declaring who shall then act as President, or the manner in which one who is to act shall be selected, and such person shall act accordingly until a President or Vice President shall have qualified.

SECTION 4.

The Congress may by law provide for the case of the death of any of the persons from whom the House of Representatives may choose a President whenever the right of choice shall have devolved upon them, and for the case of the death of any of the persons from whom the Senate may choose a Vice President whenever the right of choice shall have devolved upon them.

SECTION 5.

Sections 1 and 2 shall take effect on the 15th day of October following the ratification of this article.

Section 6.

This article shall be inoperative unless it shall have been ratified as an amendment to the Constitution by the legislatures of three-fourths of the several States within seven years from the date of its submission.

Amendment XXI

Passed by Congress February 20, 1933. Ratified December 5, 1933.

Section 1.

The eighteenth article of amendment to the Constitution of the United States is hereby repealed.

Section 2.

The transportation or importation into any State, Territory, or Possession of the United States for delivery or use therein of intoxicating liquors, in violation of the laws thereof, is hereby prohibited.

Section 3.

This article shall be inoperative unless it shall have been ratified as an amendment to the Constitution by conventions in the several States, as provided in the Constitution, within seven years from the date of the submission hereof to the States by the Congress.

Amendment XXII

Passed by Congress March 21, 1947. Ratified February 27, 1951.

Section 1.

No person shall be elected to the office of the President more than twice, and no person who has held the office of President, or acted as President, for more than two years of a term to which some other person was elected President shall be elected to the office of President more than once. But this Article shall not apply to any person holding the office of President when this Article was proposed by Congress, and shall not prevent any person who may be holding the office of President, or acting as President, during the term within which this Article becomes operative from holding the office of President or acting as President during the remainder of such term.

Section 2.

This article shall be inoperative unless it shall have been ratified as an amendment to the Constitution by the legislatures of three-fourths of the several States within seven years from the date of its submission to the States by the Congress.

Amendment XXIII

Passed by Congress June 16, 1960. Ratified March 29, 1961.

Section 1.

The District constituting the seat of Government of the United States shall appoint in such manner as Congress may direct:

A number of electors of President and Vice President equal to the whole number of Senators and Representatives in Congress to which the District would be entitled if it were a State, but in no event more than the least populous State; they shall be in addition to those appointed by the States, but they shall be considered, for the purposes of the election of President and Vice President, to be electors appointed by a State; and they shall meet in the District and perform such duties as provided by the twelfth article of amendment.

Section 2.

The Congress shall have power to enforce this article by appropriate legislation.

Amendment XXIV

Passed by Congress August 27, 1962. Ratified January 23, 1964.

Section 1.

The right of citizens of the United States to vote in any primary or other election for President or Vice President, for electors for President or Vice President, or for Senator or Representative in Congress, shall not be denied or abridged by the United States or any State by reason of failure to pay poll tax or other tax.

Section 2.

The Congress shall have power to enforce this article by appropriate legislation.

Amendment XXV

Passed by Congress July 6, 1965. Ratified February 10, 1967.
Note: Article II, section 1, of the Constitution was affected by the 25th
amendment.

SECTION 1.

In case of the removal of the President from office or of his death or resignation, the Vice President shall become President.

SECTION 2.

Whenever there is a vacancy in the office of the Vice President, the President shall nominate a Vice President who shall take office upon confirmation by a majority vote of both Houses of Congress.

SECTION 3.

Whenever the President transmits to the President pro tempore of the Senate and the Speaker of the House of Representatives his written declaration that he is unable to discharge the powers and duties of his office, and until he transmits to them a written declaration to the contrary, such powers and duties shall be discharged by the Vice President as Acting President.

SECTION 4.

Whenever the Vice President and a majority of either the principal officers of the executive departments or of such other body as Congress may by law provide, transmit to the President pro tempore of the Senate and the Speaker of the House of Representatives their written declaration that the President is unable to discharge the powers and duties of his office, the Vice President shall immediately assume the powers and duties of the office as Acting President.

Thereafter, when the President transmits to the President pro tempore of the Senate and the Speaker of the House of Representatives his written declaration that no inability exists, he shall resume the powers and duties of his office unless the Vice President and a majority of either the principal officers of the executive department or of such other body as Congress may by law provide, transmit within four days to the President pro tempore of the Senate and the Speaker of the House of Representatives their written declaration that the President is unable to discharge the powers and duties of his office. Thereupon Congress shall decide the issue, assembling within forty-eight hours for that purpose if not in session. If the Congress, within twenty-one days after receipt of the latter written declaration, or, if Congress is not in session, within twenty-one days after Congress is required to assemble, determines by two-thirds vote of both Houses that the President is unable to discharge the powers and duties of his office, the Vice President shall continue to discharge the same as Acting President; otherwise, the President shall resume the powers and duties of his office.

Amendment XXVI

Passed by Congress March 23, 1971. Ratified July 1, 1971.
Note: Amendment 14, section 2, of the Constitution was modified by section 1 of the 26th amendment.

Section 1.

The right of citizens of the United States, who are eighteen years of age or older, to vote shall not be denied or abridged by the United States or by any State on account of age.

Section 2.

The Congress shall have power to enforce this article by appropriate legislation.

Amendment XXVII

Originally proposed Sept. 25, 1789. Ratified May 7, 1992.
No law, varying the compensation for the services of the Senators and Representatives, shall take effect, until an election of representatives shall have intervened.

Note: The transcription of the Constitution included here is made available by the National Archives. For more information, you can access the National Archives' website. See http://www .archives.gov/national-archives-experience/charters/constitution.html.

Notes

Introduction: The Constitution Is Dead

1. Jefferson gave this advice in the eighth Kentucky Resolution of 1798. William J. Watkins Jr., *Reclaiming the American Revolution: The Kentucky and Virginia Resolutions and Their Legacy* (New York: Palgrave Macmillan, 2004), 177.

Chapter 1: Congress Shall Make No Law (Unless It Really Wants To)

1. Thomas Fleming, *The Illusion of Victory: America in World War I* (New York: Basic Books, 2003), 252.

2. Ibid., 94.

3. Paul L. Murphy, *World War I and the Origin of Civil Liberties in the United States* (New York: W. W. Norton, 1979), 119.

4. H. C. Peterson and Gilbert C. Fite, *Opponents of War, 1917–1918* (Seattle: University of Washington Press, 1957), 20.

5. Murphy, *World War I and the Origin of Civil Liberties*, 118–19.

6. Ibid., 131.

7. Peterson and Fite, *Opponents of War*, 117; Murphy, *World War I and the Origin of Civil Liberties*, 128–31.

8. Peterson and Fite, *Opponents of War*, 144.

9. Jerold S. Auerbach, "Woodrow Wilson's 'Prediction' to Frank Cobb: Words Historians Should Doubt Ever Got Spoken," *Journal of American History* 54 (December 1967): 608–17; quotation on 610. Auerbach is here quoting other historians' assessments of the remarks and what the president's words reveal about his interior disposition.

10. Ibid., pp. 608–15. Auerbach advances a variety of points that converge in the conclusion that Wilson did not utter this statement. Wilson's April 2 meeting with Frank Cobb, who supposedly recorded Wilson's words, may never have taken place. The White House appointment book includes no reference to any such meeting. Wilson's full quotation, excerpted in the chapter, is also "so exact a statement of what actually transpired between 1917 and 1920 that one is almost forced to conclude that it was written after these years, not before." Moreover, the quotation comes to us not directly from Cobb, but from Cobb as related by John Heaton seven years after the fact. Heaton himself heard the statement recalled by Maxwell Anderson and Laurence Stallings. This is all very dubious for a statement that is three pages long. For the entirety of Auerbach's argument, see Auerbach, "Woodrow Wilson's 'Prediction,'" 608–17.

11. Peterson and Fite, *Opponents of War*, 95.

12. Ibid., 104.

13. Murphy, *World War I and the Origin of Civil Liberties*, 119 n. 131.

14. Peterson and Fite, *Opponents of War*, 219.

15. Geoffrey R. Stone, *Perilous Times: Free Speech in Wartime from the Sedition Act of 1798 to the War on Terrorism* (New York: W. W. Norton, 2005), 217.

16. Ibid., 161; Arnon Gutfeld, "Western Justice and the Rule of Law: Bourquin on Loyalty, the 'Red Scare,' and Indians," *Pacific Historical Review* 65 (February 1996): 88–89.

17. Stone, *Perilous Times*, 217. The first two quotations come from Joseph H. Beale Jr., writing in the *Harvard Law Review* in 1902, and the third from *Commonwealth v. Peaslee*, 177 Mass. 267, 272, 59 NE 55, 56 (1901).

18. Stone, *Perilous Times*, 171.

19. Richard Polenberg, *Fighting Faiths: The Abrams Case, the Supreme Court, and Free Speech* (New York: Viking, 1987), 214.

20. Ibid., 215.

21. *Schenck v. United States*, 249 U.S. 47, 52 (1919).

22. Polenberg, *Fighting Faiths*, 213.

23. Murray N. Rothbard, *The Ethics of Liberty* (Atlantic Highlands, N.J.: Humanities Press, 1982), ch. 15.

24. Ibid.

25. Paul Johnson, *Modern Times: The World from the Twenties to the Nineties* (New York: HarperCollins, 2001), 216.

26. Peterson and Fite, *Opponents of War*, 228.

27. Ibid., 230.

28. See Murphy, *World War I and the Origin of Civil Liberties*, 267.

29. *Abrams v. United States*, 250 U.S. 616, 630 (1919).

30. Raoul Berger, *The Fourteenth Amendment and the Bill of Rights* (Norman: University of Oklahoma Press, 1989), 6.

Chapter 2: Another "Great President" versus the Constitution

1. Maeva Marcus, *Truman and the Steel Seizure Case: The Limits of Presidential Power* (Durham, N.C.: Duke University Press, 1994), 62. Throughout the text Marcus uncritically accepts the claim that some wage increases can be inflationary.

2. Ibid., 84.

3. Thomas V. DiBacco, "'Draft the Strikers and Seize the Mills (1952)': The Business Reaction," *Duquesne Review* 13 (1968): 68, 69.

4. Quoted in Neal Devins and Louis Fisher, "The Steel Seizure Case: One of a Kind?" *Constitutional Commentary* 19 (spring 2002): 68.

5. John P. Roche, "Executive Power and Domestic Emergency: The Quest for Prerogative," *Western Political Quarterly* 5 (December 1952): 593.

6. Devins and Fisher, "The Steel Seizure Case: One of a Kind?" 67.

7. Marcus, *Truman and the Steel Seizure Case*, 6–7.

8. David Gray Adler, "The Steel Seizure Case and Inherent Presidential Power," *Constitutional Commentary* 19 (spring 2002): 158.

9. U.S. House, *The Steel Seizure Case*, H. Doc. 534, 82nd Cong., 2nd sess., 1952, 371.

10. Ibid., 362.

11. Ibid., 372.

12. Ibid., 377.

13. Marcus, *Truman and the Steel Seizure Case*, 125.

14. Adler, "Steel Seizure Case and Inherent Presidential Power," 160.

15. Ibid.

16. Peter S. Canellos, "The Truman Precedent for Bush's Eavesdropping," *Boston Globe*, December 20, 2005.

17. William H. Rehnquist, "Constitutional Law and Public Opinion," *Suffolk University Law Review* 20 (winter 1986): 759–60.

18. Ibid., 765.

19. U.S. House, *The Steel Seizure Case*, 428.

20. David McCullough, *Truman* (New York: Simon & Schuster, 1992), 900.

21. Ralph Raico, "Harry S. Truman: Advancing the Revolution," in *Reassessing the Presidency*, ed. John V. Denson (Auburn, Ala.: Ludwig von Mises Institute, 2001), 570–71.

22. Ibid., 571 n. 67.

23. Marcus, *Truman and the Steel Seizure Case*, 100.

24. Lucius Wilmerding Jr., "The President and the Law," *Political Science Quarterly* 67 (September 1952): 321–38; see also Adler, "Steel Seizure Case and Inherent Presidential Power."

25. Wilmerding, "The President and the Law," 330.

26. "President Truman and the Steel Seizure Case: A 50-Year Retrospective, Transcript of Proceedings," *Duquesne Law Review* 41 (summer 2003): 691.

27. William H. Rehnquist, *The Supreme Court* (New York: Knopf, 2004), 190.

28. Wilmerding, "The President and the Law," 330.

29. Marcus, *Truman and the Steel Seizure Case*, 176–77. Emphasis in original.

30. See especially Patricia L. Bellia, "Executive Power in Youngstown's Shadows," *Constitutional Commentary* 19 (spring 2002): 87–154, whose close analysis of the decision is among the best ever written.

31. *Youngstown Sheet & Tube Co. v. Sawyer*, 343 U.S. 579, 610–11, 613 (1952).

32. Marcus, *Truman and the Steel Seizure Case*, 172.

33. Mencken's "Constitution for the New Deal" appeared in the *American Mercury*, June 1937, 129–36.

34. Bellia, "Executive Power in Youngstown's Shadows," 103.

35. *Youngstown Sheet & Tube Co. v. Sawyer*, 343 U.S. 579, 635–38 (1952).

36. Bellia, "Executive Power in Youngstown's Shadows," 133–34.

37. Wilmerding, "The President and the Law," 331.

38. Bellia, "Executive Power in Youngstown's Shadows," 94.

39. Quoted in ibid., 106.

40. Historian Maeva Marcus makes a good case that the initial avalanche of newspaper editorials denouncing Truman's action was not necessarily a reflection of public opinion; public opinion on the seizure had been difficult to gauge before Baldridge went before Judge Pine. Marcus, *Truman and the Steel Seizure Case*, 91–92.

41. Rehnquist, "Constitutional Law and Public Opinion," 766–69.

42. "This ingenious sophistry," writes John Roche, "converts the Constitution into a platonic form which exists in its full development somewhere, but which is not fully apprehended by any given generation. As new problems create new constitutional needs, the Constitution is found by the philosopher-Justices to contain adequate instruments to deal with emergent requirements." Roche, "Executive Power and Domestic Emergency," 597.

43. See Robert Higgs, *Crisis and Leviathan: Critical Episodes in the*

Growth of American Government (New York: Oxford University Press, 1987), 181–84. Emphasis added.

44. *Home Building and Loan Association v. Blaisdell*, 290 U.S. 398, 483 (1934).

45. Higgs, *Crisis and Leviathan*, 246.

Chapter 3: The Third Rail of American Jurisprudence

1. Michael J. Klarman, *From Jim Crow to Civil Rights: The Supreme Court and the Struggle for Racial Equality* (New York: Oxford University Press, 2004), vii.

2. According to Lino Graglia, "it is politically disqualifying and socially unacceptable to disapprove of *Brown*." Lino A. Graglia, " 'Interpreting' the Constitution: Posner on Bork," 44 *Stanford Law Review* 1019, 1037 (1992), cited in Raoul Berger, *Government by Judiciary: The Transformation of the Fourteenth Amendment*, 146 n. 1. Judge Richard Posner, perhaps the leading contemporary American legal scholar, says, "No constitutional theory that implies that *Brown* . . . was decided incorrectly will receive a fair hearing nowadays, though on a consistent application of originalism it *was* decided incorrectly." Ibid., citing Richard A. Posner, "Bork and Beethoven," 42 *Stanford Law Review* 1365, 1374 (1990). Jack M. Balkin notes that "Herbert Wechsler of Columbia Law School famously argued in 1959 that he could not come up with a neutral principle to justify the result in the case." *What* Brown v. Board of Education *Should Have Said: The Nation's Top Legal Experts Rewrite America's Landmark Civil Rights Decision*, ed. Jack M. Balkin (New York: New York University Press, 2001), xi. See also Raoul Berger, *Government by Judiciary: The Transformation of the Fourteenth Amendment*, 2nd ed. (Indianapolis: Liberty Fund, 1997), 147 n. 5.

3. *Slaughter-House Cases*, 83 U.S. 36 (1873). See generally Ronald M. Labbé and Jonathan Lurie, *The Slaughterhouse Cases: Regulation, Reconstruction, and the Fourteenth Amendment* (Lawrence: University Press of Kansas, 2003).

4. The best examination of this matter—indeed, the finest work in the entire historiography of American law—is Raoul Berger, *Government by Judiciary: The Transformation of the Fourteenth Amendment*, 2nd ed. (Indianapolis: Liberty Fund, 1997).

5. Section 1 of the Fourteenth Amendment annulled the *Dred Scott* decision's citizenship component. It also said that states could not abridge the privileges or immunities of citizens of the United States. Its Due Process Clause enjoined states from depriving any person of life, liberty, or property

without due process of law. And its Equal Protection Clause prohibited states from denying anyone the equal protection of the laws. Section 2 of the amendment provided for reduction of states' congressional representation in proportion as they denied their populations the franchise. Section 5 provided that Congress could enforce these provisions.

6. Berger, *Government by Judiciary: The Transformation of the Fourteenth Amendment*, 153.

7. Richard Kluger, *Simple Justice: The History of* Brown v. Board of Education *and America's Struggle for Equality* (New York: Vintage Books, 1975), 635.

8. 163 U.S. 537.

9. Erwin Chemerinsky, *Constitutional Law: Principles and Policies*, 3rd ed. (New York: Aspen Publishers, 2006), 705.

10. Paul Craig Roberts and Lawrence M. Stratton, *The New Color Line: How Quotas and Privilege Destroy Democracy* (Washington, D.C.: Regnery Publishing, 1995), 39.

11. Berger, *Government by Judiciary: The Transformation of the Fourteenth Amendment*, 133.

12. Roberts and Stratton, *The New Color Line: How Quotas and Privilege Destroy Democracy*, 37–44.

13. Ibid., 40.

14. Kluger, *Simple Justice: The History of* Brown v. Board of Education *and America's Struggle for Equality*.

15. Ibid., 612.

16. Berger, *Government by Judiciary: The Transformation of the Fourteenth Amendment*, 143.

17. Ibid., 145.

18. Bernard Schwartz, *A History of the Supreme Court* (New York: Oxford University Press, 1993), 292–93.

19. Ibid., 294.

20. Roberts and Stratton, *The New Color Line: How Quotas and Privilege Destroy Democracy*, 44.

21. *Brown v. Board of Education*, 347 U.S. 483, 493–94.

22. Justice Robert Jackson, *Brown v. Allen*, 344 U.S. 443 (1953).

Chapter 4: Discriminating to End . . . Discrimination

1. 349 U.S. 294.

2. Paul Craig Roberts and Lawrence M. Stratton, *The New Color Line: How Quotas and Privilege Destroy Democracy* (Washington: Regnery Publishing, 1995), 58.

3. 391 U.S. 430.

4. Far the best discussion of the Supreme Court's absurd line of race-and-schools cases is Lino A. Graglia, *Disaster by Decree: The Supreme Court Decisions on Race and the Schools* (Ithaca, N.Y.: Cornell University Press, 1976). *Green* is the topic of ch. 5.

5. This description of the case's factual background is based on that provided by Chief Justice Warren E. Burger in his majority opinion for the Court in *Swann v. Charlotte-Mecklenburg Board of Education* (1971).

6. 402 U.S. 1.

7. Roberts and Stratton, *The New Color Line: How Quotas and Privilege Destroy Democracy*, 59.

8. Several other types of courts existed as well, and where a plaintiff filed his complaint depended on the type of violation he had suffered, the place he had suffered it, and the type of action he wanted the court to take in response. So, for example, if a sailor had been injured at sea, he would file his lawsuit in an admiralty court. If someone had a complaint based on church law or related to marriage and custody, he might file in an ecclesiastical court. A complaint arising in the army could be a matter for a court-martial.

9. Dennis J. Hutchinson, *Swann v. Charlotte-Mecklenburg*, in *The Oxford Companion to the Supreme Court of the United States* (New York: Oxford University Press, 1992), 849–50, at 850.

10. Graglia, *Disaster by Decree: The Supreme Court Decisions on Race and the Schools*, 119–20.

11. 413 U.S. 189.

12. This discussion is heavily indebted to Graglia, *Disaster by Decree: The Supreme Court Decisions on Race and the Schools*, ch. 9.

13. These facts are taken from ibid., 169–73.

14. Ibid., 201.

15. Among the great number of studies of busing are Elmer Ernstrom Jr., *Busing Not Integration Opposed* (Santa Ana, Calif.: Graphic Publishers, 1998); Ronald P. Formisano, *Boston Against Busing: Race, Class, and Ethnicity in the 1960s and 1970s*, 2nd ed. (Chapel Hill: University of North Carolina Press, 2004); and Daniel J. Monti, *A Semblance of Justice: St. Louis School Desegregation and Order in Urban America* (Columbia: University of Missouri Press, 1985).

Chapter 5: Roads to Nowhere

1. Gabriel Roth, "A Road Policy for the Future," *Regulation* (spring 2003): 54–59, 56–57.

2. Thomas Jefferson, Sixth State of the Union Address (1806), http://www.presidency.ucsb.edu/ws/index.php?pid=29448.

3. James Madison, Sixth Annual Address (1815), *The Mind of the Founder: Sources of the Political Thought of James Madison*, ed. Marvin Meyers (Hanover: University Press of New England, 1973), 298–306, 304–5.

4. Ibid., 305.

5. Madison's Bonus Bill Veto Message is found at ibid., 306–9.

6. See Kevin R. Gutzman, "Preserving the Patrimony: William Branch Giles and Virginia Versus the Federal Tariff," *Virginia Magazine of History and Biography* 104 (1996): 341–72.

7. Roth, "A Road Policy for the Future," 55.

8. Lee Mertz, "Origins of the Interstate," U.S. Department of Transportation, Federal Highway Administration, Part 1, 2 (www.fhwa.dot.gov/infrastructure/origin.htm).

9. Ibid.

10. Ibid., Part 4, 10.

11. Ibid.

12. Ibid., Part 4, 4.

13. Ibid., Part 4, 5.

14. Roth, "A Road Policy for the Future," 55.

15. The terms "emanations" and "penumbras" would later play a prominent role in the Supreme Court's decision in *Griswold v. Connecticut* (1965), which invented a right to privacy out of the "penumbras" supposedly issuing from the Bill of Rights.

16. Mertz, "Origins of the Interstate," Part 6, 11.

17. Ibid., Part 6, 16–17.

Chapter 6: The Great Gold Robbery of 1933

1. Jesús Huerta de Soto, *Money, Bank Credit, and Economic Cycles*, trans. Melanie Stroup (Auburn, Ala.: Ludwig von Mises Institute, 2006), ch. 1.

2. Jesús Huerta de Soto, "New Light on the Prehistory of the Theory of Banking and the School of Salamanca," *Review of Austrian Economics* 9, 2 (1996): 59–81; Thomas E. Woods Jr., *The Church and the Market: A Catholic Defense of the Free Economy* (Lanham, Md.: Lexington, 2005), 98–99.

3. Murray N. Rothbard, *The Panic of 1819: Reactions and Policies* (New York: Columbia University Press, 1962), ch. V.

4. *Markham v. Cabell*, 326 U.S. 414 (1945, Burton, J., concurring); Edwin Vieira Jr., *Pieces of Eight: The Monetary Powers and Disabilities of the United States Constitution*, 2nd rev. ed. (Fredericksburg, Va.: Sheridan Books, 2002), 2:876.

5. *Congressional Record*, 73rd Cong., 1st sess., March 9, 1933, 80.

6. Henry Mark Holzer, "How Americans Lost Their Right to Own Gold

and Became Criminals in the Process," *Brooklyn Law Review* 39 (1973), available online at users.rcn.com/mgfree/Economics/goldHistory.html.

7. Ibid.

8. *Congressional Record*, 73rd Cong., 1st sess., 2453.

9. Vieira, *Pieces of Eight*, 2:1207.

10. Benjamin M. Anderson, *Economics and the Public Welfare: A Financial and Economic History of the United States, 1914–1946*, 2nd rev. ed. (Indianapolis: Liberty Press, 1980), 317.

11. John T. Flynn, *The Roosevelt Myth*, 50th anniv. ed. (San Francisco: Fox and Wilkes, 1998), 53.

12. Garet Garrett, *The People's Pottage* (Caldwell, Id.: Caxton Printers, 1953), 40.

13. *Congressional Record*, 73rd Cong, 1st sess., 4904.

14. Vieira, *Pieces of Eight*, 2: 1005.

15. Ibid., 1:127.

16. Ibid., 1:128.

17. Ibid., 1:140.

18. Ibid., 1:134.

19. Ibid., 124. Today, even this modest power could no longer be plausibly exercised by government. Market forces alone would be quite competent to determine the proper ratio between gold and silver, and given our dramatic improvements in communication, such forces would be able to do so far more swiftly and reliably than a bureaucracy entrusted with the task.

20. For a full refutation of any eminent domain defense, should the government have tried to offer one, see Vieira, *Pieces of Eight*, 2:901–16.

21. Holzer, "How Americans Lost Their Right to Own Gold and Became Criminals in the Process."

22. See Murray N. Rothbard, *A History of Money and Banking in the United States: The Colonial Era to World War II* (Auburn, Ala.: Ludwig von Mises Institute, 2002), a collection of Rothbard's writings previously published in other outlets; Murray N. Rothbard, *What Has Government Done to Our Money?* 4th ed. (Auburn, Ala.: Ludwig von Mises Institute, 1990); and Murray N. Rothbard, *America's Great Depression*, 5th ed. (Auburn, Ala.: Ludwig von Mises Institute, 2000).

23. Joseph A. Schumpeter, *History of Economic Analysis* (New York: Oxford University Press, 1954), 405–6. Thanks to Mark Thornton for this reference.

Chapter 7: The Court's "Wall of Separation"

1. 370 U.S. 421.

2. 32 U.S. 243.

3. 14 U.S. 304.

4. 310 U.S. 296.

5. *Barron v. Baltimore*, 32 U.S. 243 (1833).

6. *Slaughter-House Cases*, 83 U.S. 36 (1873).

7. 198 U.S. 45.

8. The Court staked out its new non-role in the epochal cases of *West Coast Hotel Co. v. Parish* (1937), *Helvering v. Davis* (1937), *National Labor Relations Board v. Jones & Laughlin Steel Corporation* (1937), *United States v. Darby* (1941), and, most notably, *Wickard v. Filburn* (1942).

9. Footnote 4 of *U.S. v. Carolene Products Co.* (1938).

10. Raoul Berger, *The Fourteenth Amendment and the Bill of Rights* (Norman: University of Oklahoma Press, 1989), 8–9.

11. Thomas J. Curry, *The First Freedoms: Church and State in America to the Passage of the First Amendment* (New York: Oxford University Press, 1986), 29.

12. Ibid., ch. 1.

13. The following exchange from the August 15, 1789, "Congressional Register" is found in *Creating the Bill of Rights: The Documentary Record from the First Federal Congress*, eds. Helen E. Veit, Kenneth R. Bowling, and Charlene Bangs Bickford (Baltimore, Md.: Johns Hopkins University Press, 1991), 157–59.

14. The text of the amendment can be found in *Creating the Bill of Rights*, eds. Veit, Bowling, and Bickford, 181.

15. The following discussion relies heavily on Philip Hamburger's seminal *Separation of Church and State* (Cambridge, Mass.: Harvard University Press, 2002).

16. Ibid., 292.

17. Ibid., 296–97.

18. Ibid., 343.

19. Ibid., 372.

20. Ibid., 399.

21. Ibid., 407.

22. Ibid., 408 n. 44.

23. Ibid., 425–26.

24. Ibid., 426–27.

25. Ibid., 428–29.

26. Ibid., 430–31.

27. 333 U.S. 203.

28. 370 U.S. 421.

Chapter 8: The Power to Draft

1. John Heilprin, "Rep. Rangel Will Seek to Reinstate Draft," Associated Press, November 19, 2006.

2. Daniel Webster, House of Representatives, December 9, 1814, available at http://www.constitution.org/dwebster/conscription.htm.

3. Roger B. Taney, "Thoughts on the Conscription Law of the United States," *The Military Draft: Selected Readings on Conscription*, ed. Martin Anderson with Barbara Honegger (Stanford, Calif.: Hoover Institution Press, 1982), 207–18.

4. Kevin R. C. Gutzman, "Roger B. Taney," *The World of Frederick Douglass*, ed. Paul Finkelman (New York: Oxford University Press, 2006), 223–24.

5. Kevin R. C. Gutzman, "Edmund Randolph and Virginia Constitutionalism," *Review of Politics* 66 (2004), 469–97; Kevin R. C. Gutzman, *The Politically Incorrect Guide to the Constitution* (Washington, D.C.: Regnery Publishing, 2007).

6. Iver Bernstein, *The New York City Draft Riots: Their Significance for American Society and Politics in the Age of the Civil War* (New York: Oxford University Press, 1991).

7. 245 U.S. 366.

8. The full list of foreign countries whose drafts White cited included Argentina, the Austro-Hungarian Empire, the Belgian Empire, Brazil, the Bulgarian monarchy, Bolivia, Colombia, Chile, the Chinese Empire, the Danish monarchy, Ecuador, the French Empire, the Greek monarchy, the German Empire, Guatemala, Honduras, the Italian monarchy, the Japanese Empire, Mexico, the Yugoslav monarchy, the Dutch Empire, Nicaragua, the Norwegian monarchy, Peru, the Portuguese monarchy, the Rumanian monarchy, the Russian Empire, the Siamese monarchy, the Spanish Empire, Switzerland, El Salvador, the Ottoman Empire, Canada, and South Africa.

9. "Massachusetts Bill of Rights of 1780," *The Founders' Constitution*, eds. Philip B. Kurland and Ralph Lerner, http://press-pubs.uchicago.edu/founders.

10. Virginia Declaration of Rights of 1776, *The Founders' Constitution*, eds. Philip B. Kurland and Ralph Lerner, http://press-pubs.uchicago.edu/founders.

11. See Kevin R. C. Gutzman, *Virginia's American Revolution: From Dominion to Republic, 1776–1840* (Lanham, Md.: Lexington Books, 2007), ch. 3.

12. Kevin R. C. Gutzman, review of Daniel Farber, *Lincoln's Constitution*, in *Law and Politics Book Review* 14 (2004), www.bsos.umd.edu/gvpt/lpbr/

subpages/reviews/Farber104.htm; Kevin R. C. Gutzman, *The Politically In-correct Guide to the Constitution*, ch. 7.

13. Ron Paul, "Remembering Ronald Reagan," *Congressional Record,* June 9, 2004; available at http://www.house.gov/paul/press/press2004/pr061004.htm.

Chapter 9: Do Americans Have a Constitutional Duty to Suffer?

1. Lawrence O. Gostin, "Medical Marijuana, American Federalism, and the Supreme Court," *Journal of the American Medical Association* 294 (August 17, 2005): 842.

2. *NewsHour with Jim Lehrer*, PBS, November 29, 2004. This account of Diane Monson's experience relies on this interview transcript.

3. Ibid.

4. Carol Mithers, "Fighting for the Right to 'Miracle' Marijuana," *Los Angeles Times*, November 14, 2004.

5. The case was initially known as *Raich v. Ashcroft*.

6. Randy E. Barnett, "The Original Meaning of the Commerce Clause," *University of Chicago Law Review* 68 (winter 2001), online at www.bu.edu/rbarnett/Original.htm.

7. Ibid.

8. Ibid.

9. Raoul Berger, "Judicial Manipulation of the Commerce Clause," *Texas Law Review* 74 (March 1996): 704.

10. Ibid., 705.

11. Ibid., 707.

12. Thomas E. Woods Jr., *33 Questions About American History You're Not Supposed to Ask* (New York: Crown Forum, 2007), ch. 25.

13. Quoted in Jonathan H. Adler, "Is *Morrison* Dead? Assessing a Supreme Drug (Law) Overdose," *Lewis and Clark Law Review* 9 (winter 2005): 754 n. 16.

14. Barry Cushman, *Rethinking the New Deal Court: The Structure of a Constitutional Revolution* (New York: Oxford University Press, 1998), 218.

15. Louisiana allows the use of medical marijuana in very rare instances.

16. Brief of the States of Alabama, Louisiana, and Mississippi as Amici Curiae in Support of Respondents, *Ashcroft v. Raich*, October 13, 2004.

17. Adler, "Is *Morrison* Dead?" 764.

18. Glenn H. Reynolds and Brannon P. Denning, "What Hath *Raich* Wrought? Five Takes," *Lewis and Clark Law Review* 9 (winter 2005): 923.

19. Fred Gardner, writing for the left-wing CounterPunch website, called Thomas's dissent "eloquent." Fred Gardner, "The *Raich* Decision: All Power to the Federal Government," CounterPunch.org, June 14, 2005.

20. Adler, "Is *Morrison* Dead?" 765.

21. *Gonzales v. Raich*, 125 S. Ct. 2195, 2208 (2005).

22. Ibid., at 2219.

23. Ilya Somin, "*Gonzales v. Raich*: Federalism as a Casualty of the War on Drugs," *Cornell Journal of Law and Public Policy* 15 (summer 2006): 530–31.

24. Randy E. Barnett, "The Presumption of Liberty and the Public Interest: Medical Marijuana and Fundamental Rights," *Washington University Journal of Law and Policy* 22 (2006): 41.

25. *Washington v. Glucksberg*, 521 U.S. 720–21 (1997).

26. Randy E. Barnett, "Reefer Madness," *Wall Street Journal*, March 16, 2007, A13.

27. Barnett, "The Presumption of Liberty," 42.

28. *Raich v. Gonzales*, 9th Circuit (2007), 3039.

29. Ibid., at 3041.

30. Ibid., at 3048. Emphasis in original.

31. Ibid., at 3048–49.

32. Barnett, "Reefer Madness," A13.

33. In the 1990s, for example, the American public was led to believe that House Speaker Newt Gingrich and the Republican Congress were dramatically slashing Medicare at a time when the Republican budget was actually calling for an increase in Medicare spending. The hysteria was a reaction to the 1.5 percentage point difference between the Republican and Democratic budgets in the anticipated rate of growth of Medicare spending. By 2002 the difference between the Democratic and Republican budget allocations for Medicare would have amounted to a difference in premiums of $5 a month.

34. Adler, "Is *Morrison* Dead?" 759–60.

35. *United States v. Lopez*, 514 U.S. 561.

36. Adler, "Is *Morrison* Dead?" 755.

37. Robert J. Pushaw Jr., "The Medical Marijuana Case: A Commerce Clause Counter-Revolution?" *Lewis and Clark Law Review* 9 (winter 2005): 884.

38. Somin, "*Gonzales v. Raich*," 509.

39. Susan Okie, "Medical Marijuana and the Supreme Court," *New England Journal of Medicine* 353 (August 18, 2005): 651.

Chapter 10: From Chief Executive to Prince

1. For the best account of the changes detailed in this chapter, and of the mid-twentieth-century transformation of the federal Constitution generally,

see G. Edward White, *The Constitution and the New Deal* (Cambridge, Mass.: Harvard University Press, 2000).

2. 252 U.S. 416.

3. This description of *Missouri v. Holland*'s background is based on Ronald D. Rotunda, *Constitutional Law: Principles and Cases* (St. Paul, Minn.: West Publishing Company, 1987), 142.

4. Charles A. Lofgren, *Government from Reflection and Choice: Constitutional Essays on War, Foreign Relations, and Federalism* (New York: Oxford University Press, 1986), 118.

5. Ibid.

6. John Taylor of Caroline, *New Views of the Constitution of the United States*, ed. and introduced by Kevin R. C. Gutzman (Leesburg, Va.: Alethes Press, 2008); Kevin R. C. Gutzman, *Virginia's American Revolution: From Dominion to Republic, 1776–1840* (Lanham, Md.: Lexington Books, 2007); Kevin R. C. Gutzman, "Edmund Randolph and Virginia Constitutionalism," *Review of Politics* 66 (2004): 469–97.

7. 206 U.S. 46, 90. Cited in Lofgren, *Government from Reflection and Choice*, at 118.

8. Ibid., 118–19, including n. 14 at 119.

9. Ibid., 120–21.

10. Holmes here cites the Supreme Court's decision in *Andrews v. Andrews*, 188 U.S. 14, 33.

11. David P. Currie, *The Constitution in the Supreme Court: The Second Century, 1888–1986* (Chicago: University of Chicago Press, 1990), 100–101.

12. Note, "The Power to Make Treaties," *Columbia Law Review* 20 (1920): 692–95, at 695.

13. Note, "Treaty-Making Power as Support for Federal Legislation," 29 *Yale Law Journal* (1920): 445–49, at 449.

14. Note, "The Treaty Power and the Tenth Amendment," 68 *University of Pennsylvania Law Review and American Law Register* (1920), 160–64, at 163. Also see Note, "Constitutional Law: Encroachment by Treaty Upon the Reserved Powers of the States," 8 *California Law Review* (1920): 177–80.

15. Lofgren, *Government from Reflection and Choice*, 150.

16. Interestingly, a similar argument about the limitations of Parliament's power was offered by Richard Bland of Virginia against the notion of parliamentary sovereignty in the days before the American Revolution. See his 1766 pamphlet, *An Inquiry into the Rights of the British Colonies*.

17. Lofgren, *Government from Reflection and Choice*, 153–55.

18. 299 U.S. 304. The following description of the facts in the case relies on that of Justice George Sutherland for the Court majority and on Lofgren, *Government from Reflection and Choice*, 167–68.

19. 293 U.S. 388.

20. G. Edward White, *The Constitution and the New Deal*, 47–53.

21. George Sutherland, *Constitutional Power and World Affairs* (New York: Columbia University Press, 1919), 47.

22. K[evin] R. Constantine Gutzman, "Jefferson's Draft Declaration of Independence, Richard Bland, and the Revolutionary Legacy: Giving Credit Where Credit is Due," *Journal of the Historical Society* 1 (2001): 137–54.

23. See Gutzman, *Virginia's American Revolution: From Dominion to Republic, 1776–1840;* and David C. Hendrickson, *Peace Pact: The Lost World of the American Founding* (Lawrence: University Press of Kansas, 2003).

24. Gutzman, "Edmund Randolph and Virginia Constitutionalism"; Gutzman, *The Politically Incorrect Guide to the Constitution.*

25. George Sutherland, *Constitutional Power and World Affairs*, 48–49.

26. Edwin Borchard, "Confiscations: Extraterritorial and Domestic," 31 *American Journal of International Law* (1937): 675–81, 677.

27. Note, "Confiscations: Extraterritorial and Domestic," 31 *American Journal of International Law* (1937): 675–81, at 665–76.

28. On the ratification debate in Virginia, see Kevin R. C. Gutzman, *Virginia's American Revolution: From Dominion to Republic, 1776–1840*, ch. 3.

Chapter 11: The Phony Case for Presidential War Power

1. D. A. Jeremy Tilman, "The Foreign Affairs Power: Does the Constitution Matter?" *Temple Law Review* 80 (spring 2007): 254.

2. Ibid., 256.

3. Louis Fisher, *Presidential War Power* (Lawrence: University Press of Kansas, 1995), 88.

4. John C. Yoo, "The Continuation of Politics by Other Means: The Original Understanding of War Powers," *California Law Review* 84 (1996): 264–68, 197.

5. Louis Fisher, "Lost Constitutional Moorings: Recovering the War Power," *Indiana Law Journal* 81 (fall 2005): 1234–35.

6. Testimony of Mr. John Yoo, Deputy Assistant Attorney General, Office of Legal Counsel, U.S. Department of Justice, before the U.S. Senate Committee on the Judiciary, April 17, 2002.

7. Memorandum Opinion for the Deputy Counsel to the President, "The President's Constitutional Authority to Conduct Military Operations Against Terrorists and Nations Supporting Them," September 25, 2001.

8. Fisher, "Lost Constitutional Moorings," 1241.

9. Yoo, "Continuation of Politics by Other Means," 286 n. 547.

10. Michael D. Ramsey, "Text and History in the War Powers Debate: A Reply to Professor Yoo," *University of Chicago Law Review* 69 (fall 2002): 1704.

11. Ibid., 1692.

12. Michael D. Ramsey, "Textualism and War Powers," *University of Chicago Law Review* 69 (fall 2002): 1543–1638.

13. Ramsey, "Text and History in the War Powers Debate," 1693. Furthermore, twentieth-century examples of statutes that go into effect with a declaration of war do not shed light on the situation in the eighteenth century.

14. Ibid., 1712, 1713.

15. Ibid., 1711, 1713–14.

16. For a brief overview of this history, see Thomas E. Woods Jr., *33 Questions About American History You're Not Supposed to Ask* (New York: Crown Forum, 2007), 87–91; for a lengthier treatment, see Fisher, *Presidential War Power*.

17. *Bas v. Tingy*, 4 U.S. 37, 43. Emphasis added.

18. Congress later voted to indemnify the naval commander in the case.

19. Jules Lobel, "The Commander in Chief and the Courts," *Presidential Studies Quarterly* 37 (March 2007): 54–55.

20. Gordon Silverstein, "Constitutional Contortion? Making Unfettered War Powers Compatible with Limited Government," *Constitutional Commentary* 22 (2005): 107.

21. Draft Memorandum from John Yoo, Deputy Assistant Attorney General, and Robert J. Delahunty, Special Counsel, to William J. Haynes II, General Counsel, Department of Defense, Application of Treaties and Laws to al Qaeda and Taliban Detainees (January 9, 2002), 14–15.

22. David Gray Adler, "The Steel Seizure Case and Inherent Presidential Power," *Constitutional Commentary* 19 (spring 2002): 165–66; Curtis A. Bradley and Martin S. Flaherty, "Executive Power Essentialism and Foreign Affairs," *Michigan Law Review* 102 (February 2004): 554.

23. Bradley and Flaherty, "Executive Power Essentialism and Foreign Affairs," 555.

24. Ibid., 560–71.

25. Adler, "Steel Seizure Case and Presidential Power," 167.

26. See Bradley and Flaherty, "Executive Power Essentialism and Foreign Affairs," 560–626; quotation on 625–26.

27. Interview with John Yoo, *Frontline*, PBS, January 10, 2007, http://www.pbs.org/wgbh/pages/frontline/homefront/interviews/yoo.html (accessed October 8, 2007).

28. Meredith Hobbs, "Yoo: History Will Prove President Right," Law.com,

September 20, 2007, http://www.law.com/jsp/article.jsp?id=1190192571189 (accessed September 26, 2007).

29. This section is drawn from the Yoo interview cited in note 27.

30. Glenn Greenwald, *How Would a Patriot Act? Defending American Values from a President Run Amok* (San Francisco: Working Assets Publishing, 2006), 63.

31. Bruce Fein, "Presidential Authority to Gather Foreign Intelligence," *Presidential Studies Quarterly* 37 (March 2007): 24.

32. Paul Craig Roberts, "Crime Blotter: 1600 Pennsylvania Avenue," http://www.lewrockwell.com/roberts/roberts202.html.

33. Paul Craig Roberts, "A Gestapo Administration," http://www .lewrockwell.com/roberts/roberts138.html.

34. George F. Will, "No Checks, Many Imbalances," *Washington Post*, February 16, 2006, quoted in Greenwald, *How Would a Patriot Act?*, 74.

35. Fein, "Presidential Authority to Gather Foreign Intelligence," 25.

36. David Cole, "What Bush Wants to Hear," *New York Review of Books*, November 17, 2005; memo from Jay Bybee to Alberto Gonzales, "Re: Standards of Conduct for Interrogation under 18 U.S.C. §§ 2340–2340A," August 1, 2002.

37. James Bovard, "He Wrote the Book on Torture," *The American Conservative*, October 9, 2006; Nat Hentoff, "Don't Ask, Don't Tell," *Village Voice*, January 27, 2006.

38. This discussion of Commager and Schlesinger relies on Louis Fisher, "Invoking Inherent Powers: A Primer," *Presidential Studies Quarterly* 37 (March 2007): 9.

39. Quoted in Greenwald, *How Would a Patriot Act?*, 72–73.

Chapter 12: The President Enforces the Law . . . Right?

1. George Washington to Edmund Pendleton, September 23, 1793, in *The Writings of George Washington*, ed. Jared Sparks (New York: Harper and Brothers, 1847), X: 372.

2. The Constitution's so-called Presentment Clause (Article I, Section 7, Clauses 2 and 3) reads, in relevant part:

Every Bill which shall have passed the House of Representatives and the Senate, shall, before it become a Law, be presented to the President of the United States; If he approve he shall sign it, but if not he shall return it, with his Objections to that House in which it shall have originated, who shall enter the Objections at large on their Journal, and proceed to reconsider it. . . . If any Bill shall not be returned by the President within ten Days (Sundays excepted) after it shall have been presented to him, the Same shall be a Law, in like Manner as if he had signed it, unless the Congress by their Adjournment prevent its Return, in which Case it shall not be a Law.

Every Order, Resolution, or Vote to which the Concurrence of the Senate and House of Representatives may be necessary (except on a question of Adjournment) shall be presented to the President of the United States; and before the Same shall take Effect, shall be approved by him, or being disapproved by him, shall be repassed by two thirds of the Senate and House of Representatives, according to the Rules and Limitations prescribed in the Case of a Bill.

3. William J. Olson and Alan Woll, "Executive Orders and National Emergencies: How Presidents Have Come to 'Run the Country' by Usurping Legislative Power," Cato Institute Policy Analysis no. 358, October 28, 1999, 14.

4. Mark H. Leff, "The Politics of Sacrifice on the American Home Front in World War II," *Journal of American History* 77 (March 1991): 1299.

5. Forrest McDonald, *The American Presidency: An Intellectual History* (Lawrence.: University Press of Kansas, 1994), 390.

6. Olson and Woll, "Executive Orders and National Emergencies," 13.

7. Christopher S. Kelley, "A Comparative Look at the Constitutional Signing Statement: The Case of Bush and Clinton," paper presented at the annual meeting of the Midwest Political Science Association, April 3–6, 2003, 6; Christopher N. May, *Presidential Defiance of "Unconstitutional" Laws: Reviving the Royal Prerogative* (Westport, Conn.: Greenwood Press, 1998), 73.

8. May, *Presidential Defiance of "Unconstitutional" Laws*, 101.

9. Charlie Savage, "Scalia's Dissent Gives 'Signing Statements' More Heft," *Boston Globe*, July 15, 2006; Christopher Lee, "Alito Once Made Case for Presidential Power," *Washington Post*, January 2, 2006, A11.

10. American Bar Association, Task Force on Presidential Signing Statements and the Separation of Powers Doctrine, "Recommendation," 14; available at http://www.abanet.org/op/signingstatements/aba_final _signing_statements_recommendation-report_7-24-06.pdf.

11. Quoted in Marjorie Cohn, *Cowboy Republic* (Sausalito, Calif.: PoliPointPress, 2007), 105.

12. Phillip J. Cooper, "George W. Bush, Edgar Allan Poe, and the Use and Abuse of Presidential Signing Statements," *Presidential Studies Quarterly* 35 (September 2005): 516.

13. Ibid., 522.

14. USA PATRIOT Improvement and Reauthorization Act of 2005, H.R. 3199 (P.L. 109-177).

15. "President Signs Justice Approps Authorization Act," http://www .whitehouse.gov/news/releases/2002/11/20021104-3.html (accessed October 8, 2007).

16. President's Statement on Signing of H.R. 2863, the Department of Defense, Emergency Supplemental Appropriations to Address Hurricanes in the Gulf of Mexico, and Pandemic Influenza Act, 2006, http://www .whitehouse.gov/news/releases/2005/12/20051230-8.html (accessed October 8, 2007).

17. Intelligence Authorization Act of 2005, Sec. 502(c), H.R. 4548 (P.L. 108-487).

18. President's Statement on the Intelligence Authorization Act, 2005, http://www.whitehouse.gov/news/releases/2004/12/20041223-6.html (accessed October 8, 2007).

19. Charlie Savage, "Bush Challenges Hundreds of Laws," *Boston Globe*, April 30, 2006.

20. *Hamdan v. Rumsfeld*, 548 U.S. ___ (2006).

21. Gary L. Kepplinger, General Counsel, Government Accountability Office, to Robert C. Byrd and John Conyers Jr., June 18, 2007, 9.

22. *Countdown with Keith Olbermann*, MSNBC, June 19, 2007.

23. Elizabeth Drew, "Power Grab," *New York Review of Books*, June 22, 2006.

24. Andrew Sullivan, "We Don't Need a New King George," *Time*, January 19, 2006.

25. Statement of Bruce Fein Before the Senate Judiciary Committee Re: Presidential Signing Statements, June 27, 2006.

26. Drew, "Power Grab."

27. Statement of Bruce Fein Before the Senate Judiciary Committee Re: Presidential Signing Statements, June 27, 2006.

28. American Bar Association, Task Force on Presidential Signing Statements and the Separation of Powers Doctrine, "Recommendation," August 2006, 23.

29. Savage, "Bush Challenges Hundreds of Laws."

30. Gene Healy and Timothy Lynch, *Power Surge: The Constitutional Record of George W. Bush* (Washington, D.C.: Cato Institute, 2006), 8.

31. Drew, "Power Grab."

32. Jeffrey Rosen, "Power of One," *New Republic*, July 24, 2006.

33. For challenges to the idea that a strong executive is the logical conservative position, see Russell Kirk, *A Program for Conservatives* (Chicago:

Henry Regnery, 1954), 258; and Clyde Wilson, "The Jeffersonian Conservative Tradition," *Modern Age* 14 (winter 1969–70): 36–48.

Conclusion: Can Anything Be Done?

1. John Hart Ely, "The Wages of Crying Wolf: A Comment on *Roe v. Wade*," *Yale Law Journal* 82 (1973): 920–49.

2. David Gray Adler, "Clinton, the Constitution, and the War Power," in *The Presidency and the Law: The Clinton Legacy*, eds. David Gray Adler and Michael A. Genovese (Lawrence: University Press of Kansas, 2002), 19.

Acknowledgments

In 1988 William Eaton published *Who Killed the Constitution? The Judges v. the Law*, in which he examined the Supreme Court's subversion of the Constitution's checks and balances. Twenty years later, we thought it was time to ask the question again, and to answer that it is not just the judiciary but *every* branch of the federal government that has trampled on the Constitution.

We would like to thank Jed Donahue of Crown Forum for his commitment to this project and his usual attention to detail. We would also like to thank Andrew Stuart, our literary agent, for his unsung labors.

Tom thanks Heather for her unflagging support during yet another book project, as well as our three girls, Regina, Veronica, and Amy, who always greet me with their smiling faces at the end of my workday. I'd also like to thank Lew Rockwell and the Ludwig von Mises Institute for giving me such a stimulating environment in which to work.

Kevin thanks Lorie for her good humor in the face of her husband's odd hours, strange travel schedule, and arcane lecturettes in support of his writing and academic career. I couldn't do it without you, Doll! Thanks, too, to Trianna, Marika, and Cyril, who are growing into great young people before my eyes. Finally, thank you for everything to my parents, to whom this book is dedicated.

Index

About the Authors

THOMAS E. WOODS JR. (A.B., Harvard, 1994; M.A., Columbia, 1996; M.Phil., Columbia, 1997; Ph.D., Columbia, 2000) is senior fellow in American history at the Ludwig von Mises Institute. His seven other books include the *New York Times* bestseller *The Politically Incorrect Guide™ to American History, 33 Questions About American History You're Not Supposed to Ask*, and *The Church Confronts Modernity: Catholic Intellectuals and the Progressive Era*. Woods won first place in the 2006 Templeton Enterprise Awards for *The Church and the Market: A Catholic Defense of the Free Economy*. He is co-editor of *Exploring American History: From Colonial Times to 1877*, an eleven-volume encyclopedia. More information is available at his website, ThomasEWoods.com.

KEVIN R. C. GUTZMAN (M.P.Aff., Texas, 1990; J.D., Texas, 1990; M.A., Virginia, 1994; Ph.D., Virginia, 1999) is associate professor of American history at Western Connecticut State University. He is the author of the *New York Times* bestseller *The Politically Incorrect Guide™ to the Constitution, Virginia's American Revolution: From Dominion to Republic, 1776–1840*, and the essay "Lincoln as Jeffersonian: The Colonization Chimera," in *Lincoln Emancipated: The President and the Politics of Race*, edited by Brian Dirck. Gutzman is also the editor of John Taylor of Caroline's *Tyranny Unmasked* and *New Views of the Constitution of the United States of America*. He appeared as a featured expert in the documentary *John Marshall: Citizen, Statesman, Jurist*.